Mar Gallego

Passing Novels in the Harlem Renaissance

D0760354

FORECAAST

(Forum for European Contributions
to African American Studies)

Volume 8

LIT

Mar Gallego

Passing Novels
in the Harlem Renaissance

Identity Politics and Textual Strategies

LIT

Cover photograph: Antonio Arcos Toscano

Bibliographic information published by Die Deutsche Bibliothek
Die Deutsche Bibliothek lists this publication in the Deutsche
Nationalbibliografie; detailed bibligraphic data are available in the Internet
at http://dnb.ddb.de.

ISBN 3-8258-5842-1

© LIT VERLAG Münster – Hamburg – London   2003
Grevener Str./Fresnostr. 2   48159 Münster
Tel. 0251-23 50 91   Fax 0251-23 19 72
e-Mail: lit@lit-verlag.de   http://www.lit-verlag.de

Distributed in North America by:

Transaction Publishers
New Brunswick (U.S.A.) and London (U.K.)

Transaction Publishers   Tel.: (732) 445 - 2280
Rutgers University   Fax: (732) 445 - 3138
35 Berrue Circle   for orders (U. S. only):
Piscataway, NJ 08854   toll free (888) 999 - 6778

In loving memory of Joaquín Durán Cuello

Contents

ACKNOWLEDGMENTS

I would like to acknowledge my debts to the people who have helped in various ways to make this book a reality. I wish to thank professor Pilar Marín Madrazo, with whom the project started, for her guidance and support. My colleagues Pilar Cuder and Mª Carmen Fonseca who patiently read it all and asked pointed questions, which contributed greatly to further precision and clarity in my thinking and writing. My friend Deborah Annett, who revised the whole thing without complaints. My deep gratitude also to professors Maria Diedrich and Hanna Wallinger for their useful comments and suggestions, and very especially to professor Justine Tally, for her moral support and most helpful editing. My colleagues at other universities, Ana Mª Manzanas, Jesús Benito, Isabel Soto, and Silvia Castro, who believed in this project and encouraged me throughout the years. My other colleagues at the University of Huelva and the University of Seville, who were always supportive and cooperative. My students, who have always given me strength and hope, especially those from the doctoral courses for their enthusiastic responses to my research. I would also like to thank professor Henry Louis Gates for his advice, and Ken McClane, Harryette Mullen, and Madhu Dubey for helping me along the way. Special appreciation goes to the English Department at Northwestern University for their warm welcome during my 1995 stay, the "Real Colegio Complutense" for their financial support to use Harvard University facilities in the final stages of my research in 1999, and the "Junta de Andalucía" for partly financing the publication. Finally, I would like to particularly express my gratitude to my family and loyal friends for their loving care and enduring faith. Stefano Foti, Lorenzo Foti, Dolores Durán Sixto, Cristina Gallego Durán, Miguel Gallego Monjo, Carlos Gallego Durán, Mª José Berro Franconetti, Yolanda González Bernabé, Rosa Román Sandoval, Mª Carmen López García de Beas, Isabel Páez García, Ana Cruz Carrillo, Jose Antonio Romero Zambrano, Carmen Leuzzo, Carmen Saen de Casas—to all of you, with affection, this book.

*   *   *

Earlier versions of portions of chapters 1, 2, 3, and 4 appeared as "Double Consciousness or Sheer Multiplicity," *Proceedings of the 24th International Conference of AEDEAN*, eds. Ángel Mateos-Aparicio and Silvia Molina Plaza (Ciudad Real: Publicaciones de la Universidad de Castilla-La Mancha, 2001); "On Which Side? James Weldon Johnson's *Autobiography of an Ex–Colored Man," Revista de estudios norteamericanos* 8 (2001): 33-48; "Rewriting History: The Slave's Point of View in *The Life of Olaudah Equiano," Revista de estudios norteamericanos* 7 (2002): 141-51; "Writing as Self-Creation: *Narrative of the Life of Frederick Douglass," Atlantis* XVI (1994): 153-164; "Liminality as Paradigm: Charles Chesnutt's *The House Behind the Cedars," XVIII Congreso de AEDEAN* (Alcalá de Henares: Servicio de Publicaciones, 1994); "*Black No More* or the Satiric Debate," *New Voices from the Harlem Renaissance*, eds. Australia Tarver and Paula Barnes (Rutheford: Farleigh Dickinson Press, forthcoming); and "'Indefinite longings': la sexualidad femenina en *Quicksand* y *Passing* de Nella Larsen," *La mujer: del texto al contexto*, eds. Laura Alonso, Pilar Cuder, and Zenón Luis (Huelva: Servicio de Publicaciones, 1996).

Passing Novels in the Harlem Renaissance

A long-term desire to delve into the literary rendering of the concept of African American identity in one of the most prolific periods in African American history and culture, the so-called "Harlem Renaissance," was the prime motivation of the research that eventually came to fruition with the writing of this book. Early on I was intrigued and, I have to admit, deeply fascinated by the confirmation of an insistent yet paradoxical phenomenon during the heyday of the Renaissance movement: the proliferation of novels of "passing" which were conventionally dismissed as conservative, even reactionary, at a time reputed to be one of the most progressive milestones in the history of African Americans. The existence of these novels seemed out of kilter with respect to the widespread critical contention that black writers of the era were actively engaged in a process of redefinition and reconstruction of a sense of African American identity that could challenge and subvert previously received Eurocentric notions. The rediscovery of and claim for cultural continuity with their African heritage and the need to affirm a fulfilling individual and collective sense of self arguably collided with the tendency emanating from nineteenth-century "tragic mulatto" novels. These novels depicted "mulatto" or "passing" protagonists, inevitably and tragically wavering between two worlds and unable to come to terms with their multiethnic and multicultural allegiances. Thus, Renaissance writers who were interested in passing characters and plots during this period were subsequently neglected, pejoratively labeled as representatives of the "Old Guard" or the "Genteel Tradition."[1] Until quite recently, the critical consensus assumed that these authors had failed to articulate the birth of

---

[1] The former term was used by the critic Robert Bone to refer to this specific group of writers in *The Negro Novel in America* in 1958. The latter epithet was coined by George Santayana in his oft-quoted speech delivered in 1911 under the title "The Genteel Tradition in American Philosophy," in which he described the American tradition dating from the nineteenth century as the paramount of reason and decorum. Although neither of these two designations were intended to be necessarily pejorative, they were quickly identified with the most negative criticism of the literary production of the Harlem Renaissance.

an African American consciousness taking place during that era; hence, they were systematically stigmatized as accomplices of the dominant racist ideology, even branded as "traitors" to their race. The persistence of what Bone designated as a "fondness with the novel of passing" (98) at the height of the Harlem Renaissance therefore seemed (although contradictory) worth exploring.

Fortunately, current reassessments of the novels of passing written during the decade of the twenties indicate that such a negative view of these works and their authors is no longer operative. Indeed, some relatively recent attempts have been successful in restoring these novels and authors to their rightful place within the African American literary canon.[2] Nevertheless, to date not a single full-length study has provided a detailed account of the unique and significant contribution of these novels to the literary and intellectual debate of the Harlem Renaissance. This is especially true with respect to the search for a suitable definition of a concept of African American identity which could effectively counteract centuries of derogatory stereotypes and become a valid alternative to that imposed by the dominant ideology. In effect, a comparative analysis of these works promptly revealed the presence of a highly subversive component which turns them into useful tools for comprehending the nature of the phenomenon of passing in all its richness and complexity. This preliminary approach offered a fresher, broader perspective from which to investigate the quest for self-definition depicted by these writers, who have made use of the key notion of hybridity inherent in their passing characters as an effective means of examining notions of identity. While the choice of a selected and representative corpus of passing texts was no easy task, I finally decided on what seemed to be the most productive and best-known novels, including (in chronological order) James Weldon Johnson's *Autobiography of an Ex-Colored Man* (1912), Nella Larsen's *Quicksand* and *Passing* (1928 and 1929

---

[2] Note the contemporary interest in interracial literature exemplified by the various monographs that have been recently published related to the topic, among which are especially illuminating, *Passing and the Rise of the African American Novel* by Giulia Fabi (2001), *Neither White Nor Black Yet Both* by Werner Sollors (1997), and *Passing and the Fictions of Identity* edited by Elaine Ginsberg (1996). Many studies have been devoted to the Harlem Renaissance of the twentieth century, so I mention here only a few of the most significant: Australia Tarver and Paula Barnes, eds. *New Voices from the Harlem Renaissance* (forthcoming); Nathan Huggins, *Voices from the Harlem Renaissance* (1995); William Andrews, ed. *Classic Fiction of the Harlem Renaissance* (1994); Amritjit Singh et al, eds. *The Harlem Renaissance: Revaluations* (1989); Cary Wintz, *Black Culture and the Harlem Renaissance* (1988); Victor Kramer, ed. *The Harlem Renaissance Re-examined* (1987); Charles Scruggs, *The Sage in Harlem* (1984); Bruce Kellner, ed. *The Harlem Renaissance. A Historical Dictionary for the Era* (1984); David Lewis, ed. *When Harlem Was in Vogue* (1981); and Jewis Anderson, *This Was Harlem 1900-1950* (1981).

respectively), Jessie Fauset's *Plum Bun* (1928), and George Schuyler's *Black No More* (1931).

For such a varied, complex corpus, an eclectic theoretical framework has proved to be both appropriate and illuminating, beginning with an essential rereading of W. E. B. Du Bois' influential theory of "double consciousness" devised in *The Souls of Black Folk* (1903) and its recent critical interpretations that propound a reconfiguration of the notion of a black multilayered self. The Duboisian explanation provides an intentional experimental framework within which to test the conception of the protagonist of novels of passing as straddling two races, two cultures, two opposite life-styles and worldviews derived from the Western and African American perspectives. Taking Du Bois' formulation of the figure of the black person as the sublime model for a hyphenated dichotomy to its ultimate consequences, the figure of the "mulatto/a" was portrayed as the perfect embodiment of that dichotomy, a suitable scenario for enacting the racial, social, and cultural confrontations this figure undeniably suggests. The mulatto/a, then, was conceived as a convenient literary trope to study the effects of the pervading influence of the idea of double consciousness on the African American literary and cultural terrain of the twenties.

This initial critical stance has been modified and enhanced by an examination of Du Bois' emphasis on the idea of parody, which has led directly to Mikhail Bakhtin's theory of "heteroglossia" so pertinent to contemporary analyses of rhetoric, parody, and double narratives. As a result of the adoption of a multiple perspective, African American novels could be defined as products of double consciousness, a hybrid genre born out of the convergence of two traditions—Western and African—in order to reflect a genuinely distinct African American viewpoint. Within this context, passing novels act as the most valid written expression of double consciousness for two crucial reasons: thematically speaking, they are heirs to both literary traditions in the depiction of the passage from an African American to a white identity, which forms the core of these narratives. And more significantly, from a generic standpoint, by drawing on many other literary genres and modes belonging to the aforementioned traditions—from the autobiography to satire through romance, fairy tales, science fiction, etc.,—novels of passing also exhibit a twofold character in order to generate the anti-conventional critique intended by these authors. The idea of "generic passing"[3] is, then, evidenced as the suitable veneer adopted by these authors to tackle a very problematic topic, namely a rather unconventional critique of Eurocentric ideology and worldview from an African American standpoint.

As this project developed, it became clear that the gender perspective was definitively a factor to take into account. The examination of African American feminist ideas have proved instrumental in updating the ongoing debate on the novels of passing of the Harlem Renaissance. I have thus sought to address and incorporate not only issues of race, but also the fundamental notion of gender in the constitution of a female self evident in the texts written by women at that time. Indeed, the best-known female novels of passing of the period are included here—Nella Larsen's *Quicksand* and *Passing* and Jessie Fauset's *Plum Bun*—thanks to the pioneering work carried out by critics like Barbara Christian, Deborah McDowell, and many others. Their enlightening contributions certainly enabled a rediscovery of these texts and brought them to the forefront of critical attention and discussion. The study of the three novels, fostered by a profound renegotiation of gender roles mainly in the areas of sexuality, marriage, and motherhood, enhanced my growing perception of the mechanisms employed by the authors to subvert the *status quo*, this time with regard to both race and gender.

The adoption of the gender perspective has also shaped the structure of the present analysis, which is accordingly divided into two sections focused on male and female views to facilitate and foreground similarities and differences. Likewise, I have adopted a similar structure for all chapters except for the first one: after accounting for the conventionally negative reception befallen the author and his/her text(s), I set out to explore the diverse ways in which the specific writer deconstructed the corresponding previous tradition by paying special attention to the genres or modes in which he/she chose to undertake his/her racial, social, cultural and, when applicable, gender subversion and rewriting. The detailed analysis concludes in each case with a brief overview in which the fundamental parameters arising from the study are made explicit, especially concerning the rejection of the dominant ideological system and the alternatives prompted by the

---

[3] My notion of "generic passing" is quite similar to Donald Goellnicht's version in his article on *The Autobiography of an Ex-Colored Man*, in which his working premise is the statement that Johnson intentionally creates in his text a "generic passing" in order for his novel to pass as an authentic autobiography, parallel to the "genetic passing" of the protagonist (18). Although I will

author's work. The contribution to the development of what I call the "passing tradition or sub-genre" is also taken into consideration in the discussion as well as in the closing pages.

In the first chapter, "Du Bois, Bakhtin, and the Black Feminist Critics: The Challenge of Double Consciousness," I explicitly acknowledge my indebtedness to some of the theoretical insights which are central to the critical stance I have chosen. I reconsider the Duboisian definition of double consciousness, its origins and possible meanings within a twofold paradigm: on the one hand, the Western legacy, in which double consciousness is viewed as a valid alternative to pervasive racism; on the other, the African influence, which easily connects double consciousness to the spheres of rhetoric and parody, and thus to Bakhtin's theory of the dialogic. This twofold inheritance allows for an interpretation of passing novels that confers on them the double status of belonging to two opposing literary traditions. Their double character makes them an appropriate means in which to convey the important subversive component of each of the texts selected here. Finally, the theoretical framework is completed with references to current feminist readings that illuminate many characteristics and objectives of the texts written by women and analyzed in the last two chapters.

The remaining chapters are classified in two main sections—male and female perspectives—devoted to the specific analysis of the proposed texts. Chapter 2, entitled "Questioning Race and Identity: *The Autobiography of an Ex-Colored Man* by James Weldon Johnson," begins by justifying the presence of this 1912 work in a book allegedly on Harlem Renaissance narratives. The 1927 reprinting of this work together with its importance as a crucial pillar for the passing tradition are explained. But I focus my analysis on the intimate connection that bonds Johnson's novel to the autobiographical mode and the Duboisian code. In fact, Johnson's text is a pioneer study on hybridity that crosses boundaries and categories in an attempt to conceal its fictional character. Consciously hiding in the genre of autobiography, Johnson's novel revises and updates the rhetorical strategies implicit in autobiographical writing. Moreover, *The Autobiography* follows the same process of revision and adaptation of the Duboisian code, not only with regard to the concept of double consciousness, but also to another key notion very dear to Du Bois, the so-called "talented tenth."

---

deal with the novel later in detail, the notion of "generic passing" works as an underlying subtext for this entire study.

The third chapter, dealing with Schuyler's novel *Black No More,* signifies a step forward in the formulation of a theory applicable to passing from the male viewpoint. Schuyler's work can be regarded as the absolute exaltation of novels of passing, achieving a status similar to *Don Quixote* with respect to tales of chivalry. It both elevates and destroys the category of novels of passing, as it constitutes the best example of subversion and deconstruction taken to its apex. Schuyler benefits from using a double cover, in this case satire and science fiction. He manages to completely destabilize the main parameters of the passing narrative previously questioned by Johnson, in such a way that the massive passing of the entire African American community becomes a useful metaphor for the novel itself that "passes" for another passing novel but which is much more than that.

Chapter 4, "'Ain't I a Woman' and a Mother?: Sexuality and Motherhood in Nella Larsen's *Quicksand and Passing,*" inaugurates the section devoted to the female point of view. The covers deployed heretofore are multiplied as Larsen reflects on the problematic issues of African American female sexuality and motherhood. This multiple covering implies the subversion of the "tragic mulatto" tradition from which passing novels derive, as well as the sentimental narrative springing from—and typical of—a nineteenth-century literary production mainly intended for a female audience. The history of the representation of the two key concepts of sexuality and motherhood is added to these two literary codes, as it directly contributes to the perpetuation of some of the racist and sexist stereotypes Larsen's novels deconstruct, ranging from the prostitute to the genteel lady, from the "mammy" to the perfect middle-class mother.

The following chapter pays special attention to the idea of female fancy in Jessie Fauset's *Plum Bun.* It can, therefore, be regarded as a continuation of the previous chapter in some fundamental aspects: first, it also takes the passing tradition as a suitable starting point to highlight the process of subversion of mulattas' stereotypical images in *Plum Bun.* Second, Fauset also approaches the ever controversial question of African American female sexuality by means of a multiple cover. In this case, the cover is even more complex, because it comprises the compulsory reference to the sentimental narrative together with those of fairy tales and nursery rhymes. The adoption of such a copious covering allows for the disclosure and denunciation of the ideological framework that imprisons African American women and deprives them of the right to self-expression and self-definition. Thus, both Fauset and Larsen reclaim that right for their female protagonists who are suffocating under the double bind of racism and sexism.

In the last chapter I conclude the work with an attempt to furnish satisfactory answers to the multiple queries arising from this study on social, racial, cultural, and gender levels. In addition, the conclusion serves to condense the main contributions each of the works analyzed here add to our understanding of the literary expression of the passing phenomenon. I pinpoint the significant legacy these works transmit to later African American writing and, by extension, to the configuration of an African American literary canon by restoring these texts and their authors to their fully deserved places in it. It is interesting to note here that the two latest anthologies of African American literature, *The Norton Anthology of African American Literature* edited by Henry Louis Gates and Nellie Y. McKay (1997) and *Call and Response. The Riverside Anthology of African American Literary Tradition* edited by Patricia Liggins Hill (1998), reserve quite a different treatment and status to the authors chosen here. The former devotes a few pages to the four of them and presents extracts from their passing novels, except for Schuyler's *Black No More*, which is only mentioned "in passing." The case of the latter anthology is far more troublesome, since only James Weldon Johnson and Nella Larsen are actually anthologized, and Johnson mainly as a poet. I believe that neither Fauset's nor Schuyler's work should be overlooked, since their novels deserve our utmost interest and respect. It is my hope that this book contributes to significantly increasing the presence of these four authors in future anthologies and critical studies on the Harlem Renaissance era and on African American literature in general.

ONE

Du Bois, Bakhtin, and the Black Feminist Critics:
The Challenge of Double Consciousness

> The history of the American Negro is the history of this strife,—this longing to attain self-conscious manhood, to merge his double self into a better and truer self. In this merging he wishes neither of the older selves to be lost. He would not Africanize America, for America has too much to teach the world and Africa. He would not bleach his Negro soul in a flood of white Americanism, for he knows that Negro blood has a message for the world. He simply wishes to make it possible for a man to be both a Negro and an American, without being cursed and spit upon by his fellows, without having the doors of Opportunity closed roughly in his face.

> W. E. B. Du Bois
> *The Souls of Black Folk*

Although the concept of "double consciousness" delineated by W. E. B. Du Bois has been extraordinarily relevant to the African American cultural context from the time of its birth in *The Souls of Black Folk* (1903) to the present, it plays an *essential* role in the flourishing of the so-called Harlem Renaissance during the decade of the nineteen-twenties. Many critics have repeatedly highlighted the importance of this literary period in establishing the bases for subsequent African American literature and culture.[1] Among these, the notion of double consciousness occupies a central position; in fact, the dualism implicit in Du Bois' formulation is at the very root of the cultural and literary movement of the time and explains most of its main claims and controversies.

---

[1] The great number of studies bearing witness to such importance makes it impossible to offer here anything close to a comprehensive summary or overview. As an illustration, Angelyn Mitchell qualifies this period as "the inaugurating era of African American literary criticism" (2), and considers it crucial for the development of African American literary criticism.

ORIGINS AND MEANINGS OF THE CONCEPT OF DOUBLE CONSCIOUSNESS

The metaphorical and veiled character of the idea of double consciousness in its Duboisian version has prompted multiple and various interpretations of the concept. The variety and multiplicity when interpreting such a key notion in the African American cultural sphere is a direct result of the origin of the term itself, as it simultaneously partakes of two cultural legacies: an intellectual inheritance stemming from the dominant Western ideology[2] and the African heritage transmitted through the African American community. Thanks to its mixed parentage, the idea of double consciousness functions from the very beginning as a trope in and of itself, its very genesis determining the double essence that characterizes it. Both elements—white and black, Western and African—combine to create a complete whole, *sine qua non* it is impossible to understand African American literature and, more specifically, the literature produced by African Americans during the Harlem Renaissance.[3] Indeed, the implications that are derived from Du Bois' conception have not yet been fully explored in all their multi-layered plurality. The two cultural systems to which it adheres—Western and African—create a twofold set of possibilities within the discursive universe of the term, either as a valid alternative to racism, or as a parodic and rhetorical instrument to subvert the dominant racial and social order, even within literary texts.

*   *   *

---

[2] The denomination "Western" is privileged over white or Eurocentric as this part of the analysis centers on trends at work in European thought during the nineteenth century.

[3] In this sense of fusing both traditions—Western and African—the present project directly answers a call issued by Henry Louis Gates to the critics of African American literature in the early eighties, but which is as relevant now as it was then:

> This is the challenge of the critic of black literature in the 1980s: not to shy away from literary theory; rather, to translate it into the black idiom, *renaming* principles of criticism where appropriate, but especially *naming* indigenous black principles of criticism and applying these to explicate our own text. ("What's Love Got to Do with It?" 352; author's emphasis)

Throughout this chapter I merge both traditions with the aim of devising a theory applicable to the study of novels of passing during the nineteen-twenties.

The Western Legacy: An Alternative to Racism

Focusing on the first level, that of the Western heritage or the dominant cultural model, double consciousness is basically viewed as a valid alternative to racism. However, within this context Du Bois' theory offers two main definitions of the term that may at first seem contradictory and oppositional: a positive perspective condensed in the notion of the so-called "third self," and a negative view informing the duplicity inherent in what Du Bois himself names as "the life within the veil." To analyze the first connotations of the concept of "third self," three main spheres of significance need to be taken into account, namely the literary, medical, and psychological, the latter mainly represented by William James.[4] Thanks to Du Bois' ample intellectual formation, he was likely to have been well aware of the most relevant scientific and humanistic tendencies of his time, which would prove extremely valuable for his later work, especially for the conception and development of his theory of double consciousness.[5]

In literature, European romanticism and American transcendentalism converge in a definition of double consciousness as a state of continuous agitation originated by the dialectical conflict between two diametrically opposed forces inhabiting the same body: "the downward pull of life in society" and "the upward pull of communion with the divine" (Bruce 22). This definition leads to the division between "understanding" and "soul" ever present in transcendentalist literature, as epitomized by Emerson in "The Transcendentalist" (1842):

> The worst feature of this double consciousness is, that the two lives, of the understanding and of the soul, which we lead, really show very little relation to each other; never meet and measure each other: one prevails now, all buzz and din; and the other prevails then, all infinitude and paradise; and, with the progress of life, the two discover no greater disposition to reconcile themselves. (204)

---

[4] This part of the analysis is based on the illuminating article "W. E. B. DuBois and the Idea of Double Consciousness" by Dickson D. Bruce (1992), in which Bruce reveals some of the main sources for the idea of double consciousness.

[5] For a detailed account of Du Bois' formal education and his familiarity with the most important intellectual movements of his time, see *The Art and Imagination of W. E. B. DuBois* by Arnold Rampersad (1976), especially the chapter entitled "The Age of Miracles" (19-47) where Rampersad describes Du Bois' nine university years spent at Fisk, Harvard, and Berlin.

In this extract the dialectical tension between world and spirit appears as a constant in the lives of transcendentalists, who feel divided between two poles. The impossibility of reconciling both driving tendencies forms the basis for the transcendentalists' sense of self-divided identity. Despite this inner fracture, Emerson confers primacy to the soul when he affirms that "the thoughts which these few hermits [transcendentalists] strove to proclaim . . . shall abide in beauty and strength" (206), thus proclaiming the superiority of the life of the soul over that of the mind. The same dichotomy between the two opposite poles of world and spirit and the notion of a resulting internally fragmented self could then be easily equated to the vision of the African American individual's schismatic nature, identifying African spirituality with the notion of soul and American materialism with the negative effect of understanding. Thus, from this first connection, Du Bois invests his theory with a positive portrait of African spirituality, which is inherently superior to the materialistic attitude pervasive in American society.

In medical studies, Bruce dates the concept back to the early nineteenth-century cases of "split personality," in which patients assumed two different personalities with no apparent relation between them.[6] This concept was actually popularized by the incipient field of psychology in which it was used by doctors such as William James to diagnose cases of double personality. In fact, James specifically focuses on this idea in his work *Principles of Psychology* (1890) in describing some of his patients' symptoms. Although it is impossible to assure that Du Bois actually read James' work, it is not altogether improbable that he was familiar with it, since "of all his Harvard teachers, none influenced him more . . . than William James" (Rampersad 25).[7] For James, the state of double consciousness implied an opposition between two consciousnesses that shared the

---

[6] The best-known case was that of Mary Reynolds, who alternated personalities for fifteen or sixteen years until she adopted the second state permanently. Bruce refers the reader to two enlightening articles on this case: "A Double Consciousness, or a Duality in the Same Individual" by Samuel L. Mitchell and "Mary Reynolds: A Case of Double Consciousness" by William S. Plumer (30, note 9).

[7] Rampersad briefly mentions James' importance in Du Bois' intellectual formation (25-29). Du Bois himself talks about his relationship with James in his autobiography, portraying him as "a friend and guide to clear thinking," and identifying him as a crucial influence in his life who led him to abandon his philosophical studies in order to pursue history and social sciences (*Dusk of Dawn* 38-9). The debt that Du Bois owed to James has been the subject of controversy between two contrasting opinions: whereas some critics claim evidence for such a debt (Rampersad 73-4; Sollors, *Beyond Ethnicity* 249; Bruce 304; Sundquist, *To Wake* 571-2), David Lewis denies it (*Biography* 96). Ronald Judy summarizes this debate, while pointing out the dangers and inconsistencies of each side (278-9, note 27).

same body, but what most interested Du Bois in James' concept was the fact that both personalities were distinct and independently autonomous.[8] This equal status resulting from James' theory was very useful for Du Bois, since "double consciousness allowed for a sense of distinctiveness that really did entail equality, a sense of distinctiveness that did not imply inferiority" (Bruce 27). Thus, it facilitated the articulation of Du Bois' notion of the two consciousnesses as identical.

What is even more important is the prevalence of African spirituality over the materialism typical of white American society, coinciding with the transcendentalist vision of the term in which the soul prevails over understanding. Such a positive image proved highly instrumental for Du Bois because it gave him the opportunity of uniting both of them within a single "truer and better self" (*Souls* 3), basing his theory on James' concept of equivalence. That is, Du Bois makes conscious use of the psychological rhetoric of his time to shape a sort of myth whereby the combination of two identities in a single entity gives way to the creation of a third identity, better and more complete than the former ones.

In effect, a look back to the origins of double consciousness allows us to grasp Du Bois' attempt to appropriate and adapt the concept in order to devise a positive representation of African Americanness as the perfect union of the two identities in a so-called "third self," whose main attribute is its spirituality. Indeed, Andrew Angyal expands on this idea: "Rejecting the notion that his African-Americanness is somehow a problem for the African American, Du Bois argues that it is a unique gift, part of the racial heritage . . . of the African American *folk*—in the sense of indigenous people" (68; author's emphasis). Du Bois intends, then, to completely subvert the dominant racial system by a positive reassessment of what he considers to be an inherent characteristic of African Americans, their spirituality.

Hence, the emphasis on African American spirituality is the result of a double process of rejection and destabilization of the dominant racial code, precisely because it questions its essentialist racist bias. Consciously constructing it as a valid alternative to racism, Du Bois is able to promote a positive representation

---

[8] In his article "Genealogical Shifts in Du Bois's Discourse on Double Consciousness as the Sign of African American Difference" (1996), Bernard Bell cites a definition of the term by Oswald Kulpe which is strikingly similar to the one employed by James: "[a] general derangement of memory . . . characterized by the existence of a more or less complete separation of two aggregates of conscious processes, which alternate at certain intervals or can be called up in irregular sequence by favourable conditions" (90).

of African Americans that actually encompasses what he himself terms the "spiritual message" of the black race. The problem that emerges at this point is how to actually interpret this message, crucial to Du Bois' agenda but which he never clarifies. For example, before the publication of *Souls*, in a speech entitled "The Conservation of Races" delivered at the American Negro Academy on the occasion of its foundation, Du Bois claims that "some of the great races of today—particularly the Negro race—have not as yet given to civilization the full spiritual message which they are capable of giving" (9). However, in chapter one of *Souls*, "Of Our Spiritual Strivings," he infers that a measure of such a message can already be found in the contributions that African Americans have made to American culture:

> [T]here are no truer exponents of the pure human spirit of the Declaration of Independence than the American Negroes; there is no true American music but the wild sweet melodies of the Negro slave; the American fairy tales and folklore are Indian and African; and all in all, we black men seem the sole oasis of simple faith and reverence in a dusty desert of dollars and smartness. (8)

In the passage civil, cultural, and religious motifs are enumerated as part of that spiritual message so dear to Du Bois. In the first place, and very tellingly, Du Bois underlines the adherence to the spirit of the Declaration of Independence, and in consequence, to the genuinely American way of life. Such adherence can be certainly read as ambiguous, but nevertheless charged with meaning as it claims for African Americans their rightful place in America. Secondly, slave songs or spirituals and folklore are intentionally listed as the key points on which his defense of the cultural contribution of African Americans is grounded. Du Bois enhances this defense throughout *Souls,* but especially in the chapter devoted to spirituals that closes the book, "Of Sorrow Songs."[9] And lastly, he reiterates the dichotomy between African American religiosity and white materialism. In the end, what may be even more striking for the reader is the fact that Du Bois places himself in a

---

[9] The importance of this chapter and of the spiritual songs that head each chapter in *Souls* has been rightly interpreted as a conscious gesture on the part of Du Bois to revalue the African legacy that had been unjustly scorned by both white and black critics because of its connection to slavery. On the contrary, as Eric Sundquist suggests in *To Wake the Nation* (1993), these songs can act as support for an autonomous African American critical and interpretative apparatus, which is precisely what Sundquist undertakes in his work.

seemingly contradictory position, demanding African Americans' right to full American citizenship on the basis of their unique cultural contributions.

Therefore, the project of double consciousness enunciated by Du Bois as an alternative to the dominant racist canon draws from an amalgam of diverse fields with the objective of attesting to the great spiritual value of the African American community. According to Du Bois, this message actually foregrounds the cultural field as the most prolific terrain in which to demonstrate African American worth and to challenge the stereotypical, negative image imposed by the white world. Thus, Du Bois defines the role of any African American as "to be a co-worker in the kingdom of culture" (*Souls* 3). Du Bois envisions the cultural project as "a glorious crusade where I and my fellows were to match our mettle against white folk and show them what black folk could do" ("Concept of Race" 95). He signals here that the suitable scenario for enacting the demystification of racist stereotypes, and of claiming black people's right to parity in all senses, is cultural.

The plea for a spiritual message translated into cultural terms is thus underlined as the main contribution of African Americans to the dominant culture and proves to be a strategic move for calling into question the racial rhetoric of the pseudo-scientific thought of his time. Du Bois is subtly replacing the biological formulation of race with socio-cultural parameters, and thus problematizing the racist assumption of the supremacy of the white race. An overview of that racial rhetoric evidences an increasing number of supposedly scientific studies that allegedly attempt to uphold white supremacy on the grounds of the implied inferiority of other races, as exemplified by *The Passing of the Great Race* by Madison Grant (1916) and *The Rising Tide of Color* by Lohrop Stoddard (1920) (Gossett 389-98).[10] Displacing attention from the merely biological terrain to the

---

[10] As studies like those by Thomas Gossett (1963), Peter Rose (1968), Jan N. Pieterse (1992), and Kwame Anthony Appiah (1995) corroborate, the history of the idea of "race" has its origin in classical antiquity and in the Bible, but acquires more relevance in the sixteenth century with the trade of African slaves and the beginning of colonialism. As a biological concept, it is fixed in the eighteenth century with the different racial classifications elaborated by eminent anthropologists, among whom the best-known are François Bernier, Carl von Linne, Georges Buffon, and Johann Blumenbach. Greatly influential was the work of the latter who, although hesitant about his own conclusions, inaugurates the hierarchical division that elevates the Caucasian race to the top rank to the detriment of the other four—Mongolian, Ethiopian, American, and Malay. Blumenbach's classification promotes the so-called science of "craneology" or the study of the human brain as an instrument to classify different human species, which would lead, already well in the nineteenth century, to "scientific racism." To this pseudo-science the impact of philosophical racist thought from the eighteenth century onwards needs to be added, with crucial figures such as Hume, Kant, and Hegel who deny Africans the possibility of intellectual capacity, and as a consequence, of creating art and history (Gates, "Writing 'Race'" 9-11; Gates, *Figures* 17-21; Rose, *Subject* 19).

cultural, Du Bois also dismantles the racist barriers that associate biological traits with mental and behavioral features, acknowledging only the cultural standard as measure and emphasizing its viability for overturning racism.[11] This move allows him to open up new venues for conferring legitimacy to the important cultural task that the African American community might perform in American society.[12] The fact that Du Bois recurs to such varied, at times contradictory, sources—African spiritual roots, the pseudo-science of his time, and the utopian vision fostered by European romanticism and American transcendentalism—suggests that his intention is to take maximum advantage of the ambiguity the concept of double consciousness entails to counteract the negative effects of a restrictive racial categorization. It also propounds that the cultural terrain is ideal place for both Western and African traditions to coexist in complete harmony, as Du Bois himself asserts in the following oft-quoted passage:

> I sit with Shakespeare and he winces not. Across the color line I move arm in arm with Balzac and Dumas, where smiling men and welcoming women glide in gilded halls. From out the caves of evening that swing between the strong-limbed earth and the tracery of the stars, I summon Aristotle and Aurelius and what soul I will, and they come all graciously with no scorn nor condescension. (*Souls* 76)

The idyllic vision of the possibility of a pacific and harmonious coexistence in the cultural sphere is taken as reference to formulate the idea of double consciousness

---

Grant and Stoddard's texts are direct heirs to both currents, which converge in the racist attitudes that mark the period of the twenties, so they can be taken as good illustrations of what Gates terms "fictions of racial essence . . . sanctioned by science" ("'Talkin' that Talk" 403).

[11] In the second chapter of *Race and Ethnicity* (1986), John Rex specifies the relationship that racist ideology has established and popularized between biological traits—fundamentally physical and genetic ones—and mental or behavioral patterns. The influence of this pseudo-scientific and racist thought continued until the decade of the fifties and encouraged the so-called "UNESCO meetings" in 1950 and 1952, where biologicians and sociologists met and united to confirm definitively the falseness of such equation. The product of their investigation is known as "The UNESCO Statements on Race" (Montagu, Appendix A).

[12] Anthony Appiah devotes his article "The Uncompleted Argument: DuBois and the Illusion of Race" (1985) to the analysis of different writings by Du Bois in order to verify the way in which he rejects the pseudo-scientific rhetoric of his time and "assigns to race a moral and metaphorical significance different from that of his contemporaries" (29). Here Appiah comments on the importance of the socio-historical dimension transmitting the very metaphorical and moral significance to which Du Bois alludes. Although agreeing partly with Appiah's argument, the emphasis on the socio-historical component fails to acknowledge the cultural aspect as essential for a full understanding of the Duboisian theory, an aspect that constitutes the focus of my concerns.

as an inclusive racial theory, capable of merging both worlds—black and white—in an indissoluble whole, devoid of any kind of friction.

Despite the idealized perception of double consciousness and of the cultural realm as the unifying element between both races, Du Bois does not ignore the social reality of his time. On the contrary, he shows his keen awareness of the racist ideology that dominates white society and its hideous effects on African American mentality. As I indicated at the beginning of the chapter, the concept of double consciousness goes beyond a single definition and comprises a wide range of possibilities. Together with this first eminently positive and optimistic description of double consciousness, *Souls* presents another vision of the term, its direct negative counterpart, which exposes the undesirable consequences of double consciousness on the African American community. This basically means that Du Bois does not only desire to fashion a positive image of African Americanness, but that he also aspires to launching a profound attack on the very foundations of the racist society of his time, urging an open condemnation of all racist practices. Thus, the famous sentence, "the problem of the Twentieth Century is the problem of the color line" (*Souls* xxxi), encapsulates the second main objective of the analysis of double consciousness reflected in *Souls*: to reveal the life "within the veil," as Du Bois himself called the African American way of life.

The metaphor of the veil that Du Bois employs to contain that second sense of double consciousness originates in the allusion to Corinthians, "For now we see through a glass, darkly" (23:13-15), whose Paulinian echo constitutes "the most striking device in *Souls of Black Folk* . . . as the metaphor of black life in America" (Rampersad 79). In fact, the metaphor of the veil stands out as one of the most interesting allegories for black life, as phrased by Du Bois: "The Negro is a sort of seventh son, born with a veil, and gifted with second-sight in this American world,—a world which yields him no true self-consciousness, but only lets him see himself through the revelation of the other world" (*Souls* 3), whereby the veil represents "a figure of oppression" (Sundquist, *To Wake* 494), identified with "a social burden . . . a product of institutionalized racism" (Bell, "Genealogical Shifts" 95). Du Bois' usage of the term refers to the notion of identity that African Americans must confront, constantly labouring under the distorted and extremely stereotypical image that a racist society imposes on them. Du Bois is seriously concerned about the kind of influence such a negative image produces on individuals systematically excluded for racial reasons.

As an unwelcome by-product of the constant influence of a racist vision, Du Bois continues, the African American individual may come to *believe* that distorted image imposed upon him/her. This image involves a duplicity that obliges him/her to lead a sort of double life "with double thoughts, double duties, and double social classes" (*Souls* 142), which inevitably "must give rise to double words and double ideas, and tempt the mind to pretence or to revolt, to hypocrisy or to radicalism" (*Souls* 142). The latter nuances of double consciousness entail, then, a negative duplicity which affects each aspect of human existence—social, political, cultural, and personal—and gives rise to undesirable effects that Du Bois openly condemns. Du Bois had already strongly attacked this double life, warning of the dangers of such a duplicity: "This waste of double aims, this seeking to satisfy two unreconciled ideals . . . has sent them wooing false gods and invoking false means of salvation, and has even seemed about to make them ashamed of themselves" (*Souls* 4).

Moreover, Du Bois contends that the harmful effects of double consciousness also extend to those who apparently live "outside the veil," specifically white people, since "the primary aspect of the Veil seems to be the inability of most people on either side to see themselves clearly, whether they realize it or not" (Burke 91). Although whites do not experience racism in their own skin, what truly characterizes them is "a decided blindness—to the effects on others of the line drawn from their side; to the recurring effects on them caused by the complicity, whether active or passive" (Lemert 386). Racism then marks not only those who fall victim to its terrible intolerance, but also all those who collaborate somehow in the perpetuation of its value system. Their willing blindness is constitutive of a position that Lemert defines as an intrinsic feature of Western culture: "a structured inability to see those in the racially Other position" (387), which is at the heart of the dominant ideology Du Bois intends to unmask.[13]

This second vision of double consciousness as intrinsically negative and destructive both for the African American community and for whites dominates Du Bois' life and thought after the Harlem Renaissance, when his early ideas about fair competition crumble before the horror of the continuation of segregationist practices in the States:

---

[13] The theme of blindness on the part of white society and the consequent invisibility that African Americans have to face appear from the beginning of the African American literary tradition, culminating in *The Invisible Man* by Ralph Ellison (1947). In addition, as Lemert confirms, it

> I saw the race problem was not as I conceived, a matter of clear, fair competition, for which I was ready and eager. It was rather a matter of segregation, of hindrance and inhibitions, and my struggles against it and resentment at it began to have serious repercussions upon my inner life. ("Concept of Race" 95)

The disillusion that is distilled from these words denotes the inner fight that takes place in Du Bois between his realistic conception of the society of his time, and an early idealized notion of double consciousness as the final biracial and bicultural resolution to the problem of racism: "all these ideas must be melted and welded into one" (*Souls* 8). The latter option becomes, despite pervasive racism, the only way to foment the full development of the African American community.

*   *   *

The African Heritage and Bakhtin: Rhetoric, Parody, and Double Narratives

Turning now to the origins of the second cultural realm of double consciousness, the African legacy is firstly linked to the Yoruba tradition of Esu-Elegbara and its African American counterpart, the "Signifying Monkey," illustrated by Henry Louis Gates in his classic book *The Signifying Monkey* (1988). Apart from the epistemological significance that has been assigned to the term so far, double consciousness can become a powerful, productive, and effective rhetorical and parodic tool, as the significance of the concept continues to expand and take on new meanings and nuances which link it to its African ancestry.

A quick overview of some of the characteristics of the figure of Esu-Elegbara within the Yoruba tradition is sufficient to reveal the important connection between this figure and the Signifying Monkey: "individuality, satire, parody, irony, magic, indeterminacy, open-endedness, ambiguity, sexuality, chance, uncertainty, disruption and reconciliation, betrayal, closure and disclosure, encasement and rupture" (6). This list can be reduced to the two key ideas of multiplicity and plurality, since, Gates continues, "Esu possesses all of these

---

constitutes one of the main bases for contemporary African American criticism, with such interesting representatives as Morrison, West, Mudimbe, and many more (387).

characteristics, plus a plethora of others" (6), and personifies "the power of sheer plurality or multiplicity" (37) or the power that turns him into "the figure of indeterminacy" (37) *par excellence*. Moreover, these two principles of multiplicity and indeterminacy inform the description of Esu as "the dynamic of process, the dialectical element of the system" (38). Esu emerges thus as a result of the union of two primary elements and transforms itself into "the third principle" (38), which the critics Juana and Deoscoredes dos Santos astutely identify with the principle of criticism itself (qtd. in *Signifying Monkey* 38). In this sense, Esu can be easily connected to the idea of double consciousness, especially to the "third self" which is generated out of the dialectical struggle of two elements and their synthesis. It can be then asserted that Esu, together with the Signifying Monkey, could be constructed as the rhetorical counterpart of double consciousness in African American letters.

Following this correspondence, the analogy drawn between Esu and the Sygnifying Monkey is, first of all, of a rhetorical order since "the monkey is Esu, and both are doctors of interpretation" (20). This second figure partakes of many of Esu's features, but it is also different because "the Signifying Monkey exists not primarily as a character in a narrative but rather as a vehicle for narration itself" (52), that is, even more than Esu, the Signifying Monkey incarnates the rhetorical game typical of the African American community materialized in the process of "Signifying," characteristic of vernacular language.[14] The central problem is how to define that process of signification and the role that the Signifying Monkey plays in it, acknowledging the link between both and the concept of double consciousness. One of the best-known definitions of the two former ones was provided by Abrams in 1962: "The name 'Signifying Monkey' shows [the hero] to be a trickster, 'signifying' being the language of trickery, that set of words or gestures which arrives at 'direction through indirection'" (qtd. in *Signifying Monkey* 74).[15] The last

---

[14] As Sandra Adell observes, the usage on the part of Gates of the hermeneutic and rhetorical fields is quite confusing and tends to overlap on several occasions (52-55). For instance, Gates regards both figures—Esu and the Signifying Monkey—as "figures of the same order, the hermeneutical one" (20), whereas he constantly differentiates them on the grounds that "if Esu stands for discourse upon a text, then his Pan-African kinsman, the Signifying Monkey stands for the rhetorical strategies of which each literary text consists" (21). Although agreeing with Adell's distinction, the crucial value of Gates' contribution lies not in such a differentiation, but in the emphasis on the rhetorical strategies that both tropes, especially the Signifying Monkey, foreground.

[15] The figure of the trickster enjoys a long and sustained history within African American culture with ancient roots going back to African folklore, in which innumerable legends and stories of tricksters abound, as illustrated for example in those collected by Harold Scheub in his volume *The*

quote is also very significant, since it illuminates the common points that exist between the Signifying Monkey and the idea of double consciousness: the African American individual possessed of double consciousness, resembles a trickster, a liminal being wavering between two worlds. Drawing the parallelism between both tropes, it follows that the process of "signifying" is inherent in Duboisian double consciousness.

As the Signifying Monkey is decoded as "technique . . . the great signifier" (Gates, "Blackness of Blackness" 288) and his occupation of "signifying" as "to engage in certain rhetorical games" (*Signifying Monkey* 48), "signifying" itself is constructed as "the trope of tropes." Framed by its rhetorical status, signifying comprises other rhetorical tropes such as "metaphor, metonymy, synecdoque and irony . . . and also hyperbole, litotes and metalepsis" (52) and many others. The different explanations contribute to enhance the multiple and indeterminate character that the three terms share. This commonality enforces the possibility of "naming by indirection" mentioned above, which is elucidated by the critic Mitchell-Kernan as the fact that "the apparent significance of the message differs from its real significance" (qtd. in "Blackness of Blackness" 291), or in essence, saying one thing while intending to say something quite different. All this finally leads to a definition of "signifying" as a synonym of "figuration" transcribed as "the figurative difference between the literal and the metaphorical, between surface and latent meaning" (*Signifying Monkey* 82). John Sheeshy provides a very perceptive view of signification arguing that it "proceeds from the . . . assumption that meaning is not fixed, that all signs are constructions and are therefore susceptible to *reconstruction*" (404; author's emphasis), in which the inherently constructed and figurative nature of the process is put forcefully.

This parodic sense mainly consists of the repetition and inversion of previous models (*Signifying Monkey* 103-9) and is really what binds "signifying" to double consciousness: if the trickster makes use of "signifying" to parody the dominant

---

African Storyteller (65-122). This figure invariably outwits his/her opponent due to his/her cunning and his/her superior verbal qualities. Esu-Elegbara is just a version of such a figure in the Yoruba tradition (*Signifying Monkey* 4-5). Two important contributions to the study of the trickster within African and African American cultures respectively are *The Trickster in West Africa: A Study of Mythic Irony and Sacred Delight* by Robert Pelton (1980) and "Structural Analysis of the Afro-American Trickster Tale" by Jay Edwards included in *Black Literature & Literary Theory* (81-105). Within the Western tradition, the trickster finds its correlate in the "picaro," who also uses his rhetorical abilities to survive. Moreover, both figures occupy a marginal status with respect to the society of their time and position themselves as suitable social critics. A brief summary of the picaro can be found in *Figures in Black* by Gates (81-2).

racial and social order, the idea of double consciousness can be also acknowledged as a parody of that value system. The interpretation of "signifying" and double consciousness as parody serves as the main argument for a great part of the present analysis, in which the texts under study consistently show a parodic intention with respect to previous models by means of a systematic repetition with one or more significant variations.[16] Even more, both elements embody the same kind of parody, that of a "dissemblance" similar to jazz variations, and roughly correspond to Mikhail Bakhtin's definition of the term. Bakhtin's analysis proves very useful at this point indeed, since his two notions of "parody" and "hidden polemic" enlarge the scope of Gates' study. Bakhtin's premise brings to the forefront two features characteristic of these notions: that they are verbal devices and that their discourse "maintains a double focus, aimed at the referential object of speech, as in ordinary discourse, and simultaneously at a second context of discourse, a second speech act by another addresser" ("Discourse Tipology" 285). In this first description many crucial ingredients of the Bakhtinian model are already present: his interest in the verbal nature of discourse and the vision of this discourse as a twofold universe. In fact, this double component is what integrates "doubly oriented discourse" or his well-known concept of "double-voiced discourse," of which the two notions of "parody" and "hidden polemic" are good examples. In the Bakhtinian model his theories of language and the novel are patterned on this concept.

In the first theory concerning language and the linguistic plane, Bakhtin affirms that double voice belongs to the level of the utterance: "Within a single utterance there may occur two intentions, two voices" ("Discourse Tipology" 289). However, Bakhtin incorporates the idea of two voices within one single utterance to a wider context dominated by the so-called "heteroglossia" which he renders as follows:

> The base condition governing the operation of meaning in any utterance. It is that which insures the primacy of context over text. At any given time, in any given place, there will be a set of conditions—social, historical, meterological, physiological—that will insure that a word

---

[16] A very similar definition of the concept of parody is suggested by Linda Hutcheon in her compelling study entitled *A Theory of Parody* (1985), in which she describes it as "repetition with difference," identifying that difference as "critical distance . . . implied between the backgrounded text being parodied and the new incorporating work" (32). For Hutcheon, "parody is," appropriating Golopentia-Eretescu's terminology, "a bitextual synthesis" (33) that insists more on difference than on similarity between the two texts.

uttered in that place and at that time will have a meaning different than it
would have under any other conditions. (Bakhtin, "Discourse in the
Novel" 428)

Michael Holquist expands this definition of heteroglossia arguing that "all
utterances are heteroglot in that they are shaped by forces whose particularity and
variety are practically beyond systematization" (*Dialogism* 70). Therefore,
heteroglossia is found at the core of each expression or statement, which is
basically composed by its "social context," understanding it in its widest possible
sense as the amalgam of conditions that have a considerable influence on the
meaning assigned to an utterance at any given moment.[17]

Bakhtin goes on to denounce the fact that the social and multiple aspect of
discourse has been practically ignored and proclaims its central role, since
"language is heteroglot from top to bottom" ("Discourse in the Novel" 291). This
characteristic of language is precisely the main focus of his article "Discourse in the
Novel," in which he unveils the way the different forces shaping the socio-
ideological background coexist and interact as part of the process that he termed
"dialogization."[18] This process affects and yields meaning to both language in
general and novelistic prose in particular, moving from the level of the word to that
of the whole novelistic utterance. Any word, according to the Bakhtinian model,
lives "on the boundary between its own context and another, alien, context" (284),
wherein, Bakhtin continues,

---

[17] Bakhtin's stress on the social context is partly responsible for his rupture with Formalist
aesthetics, since his work can be said to embody the transition between Russian formalism and
pragmatics on the one hand (Aullón de Aro 196; Dentith 37), and between Russian formalism and
Marxist literary theory on the other (Selden 25-31; Dentith 9).

[18] The process of dialogization is essential to a clear comprehension of Bakhtinian language and
novel theories, whose parallelism Dentith accounts for as follows:

> There comes a moment when the recognition of a fact about language—that an
> utterance only acquires meaning in relation to the utterance of an other—takes on the
> status of a moral command: all utterances ought to anticipate the word of the other. In
> an analogous way, Bakhtin's recognition that in Dostoevsky's novels the words of the
> characters are highly dialogized . . . leads him to insist that the whole novel ought
> therefore to be dialogic. (46)

Due to the importance of this conceptualization, Bakhtin's theory is known as "dialogism," despite
the fact that Bakhtin never used the term, as Holquist dutifully reminds readers (*Dialogism* 15).
Although the present analysis is restricted to the linguistic and novelistic dimensions of his theory,
Bakhtin's dialogism covers a wider spectrum. It is an epistemological theory of Neokantesian
order, where the consciousness of the self fuses with "otherness" in a symbiotic relation between
them, reminiscent of Duboisian double consciousness. For a closer and more complete study of
Bakhtin's theory and its manifold implications, see *Dialogism* by Holquist (1990) and *Bakhtinian
Thought* by Simon Dentith (1995).

The word in language is *half someone else's*. It becomes "one's own" only when the speaker populates it with his own intention, his own accent, when he appropriates the word, adapting it to his own semantic and expressive intention. Prior to this moment of appropriation, the word does not exist in a neutral and impersonal language . . . but rather it exists in other people's mouths, in other people's contexts, serving other people's intentions: it is from there that one must take the word, and make it one's own. (293-4; my emphasis)

Thus the way in which dialogization is inherent in words can be verified, since any word emerges out of the dialogue between two contexts, two voices, that of the "I" and that of the "other."[19] In the same way, "language . . . lies on the borderline between oneself and the other" (293) and must take into account both elements in a continuous and uninterrupted dialogue. The novel becomes the dialogic genre *par excellence*, essentially polyphonic. Embedded with "a plurality of independent and unmerged voices and consciousnesses, a genuine polyphony of fully valid voices" (Bakhtin, *Problems* 6), the marked dialogic character is "one of the most fundamental aspects of prose style" (284).

Within the dialogized or polyphonic novel, the two tropes of parody and hidden polemic occupy center stage, as they present two concrete materializations of dialogic energy. In fact, more than establishing a dialogue, both tropes convey an opposition between the two voices that constitute them. Both parody and hidden polemic foreground a contrast between the author's intention and the other's intention, so they are inherently double-voiced. The main difference between them consists of different degrees: in parody the voices are "antagonistically opposed" ("Discourse Tipology" 293); whereas in hidden polemic one of these voices seems to be absent, erased but nevertheless juxtaposed provoking a reaction "which determines the author's speech" ("Discourse Tipology" 295). As Bakhtin himself indicates, both concepts can merge and overlap. So the present analysis groups

---

[19] The latter term comes from the Russian "Nu˘zoj" and implies the other with respect to the speaking subject or "svoj." In English the term can be translated as "alien," "other," "another," "someone else's," but all of these possiblities connote alterity in relation to the speaker. Holquist defines it as follows: "In Bakhtin's system, we are all Nu˘zoj to one another by definition: each of us has his or her own [svoj] language, point of view, conceptual system that to all others is Nu˘zoj. Being Nu˘zoj makes dialogue possible" (*Dialogic Imagination* 423), so both elements—speaker and other—are vital to establishing a dialogue.

them under the broad category of "parody," in which the two voices, present or not, constantly collide and generate a conflict that profoundly affects the nature of the work.[20]

After analyzing the basic meanings that the African legacy and Bakhtinian theory contribute to the key concepts of parody and double voice, there should be a clearer understanding of the relationship between them and the idea of double consciousness. But a last meaning of double consciousness needs to be added, which projects itself onto the idea of "biculturalism" that Dale Peterson defines as "the double-tongued speech of African-Americans" ("Notes" 243). This results from the verbal and written transcription of the double life imposed by racist society, the "double words" that Du Bois alludes to in his famous passage of *Souls* already quoted here.[21] The literary effect of double consciousness manifests itself in the inclusion of certain techniques that tend to stress the bivocality present in any African American novel. This bivocality is the sublime expression of double

---

[20] This Bakhtinian concept of parody recalls the well-known "call/response process" devised by Robert Stepto in *From Behind the Veil* (1979), whereby texts respond to previous ones that represent the tradition or the established canon (xvi-xvii). That is to say, African American texts constantly signify or revise previous ones. The difference between Stepto's model and Bakhtin's parody is the absence of conflict and antagonism in the former. Another concept that is systematically associated, and in many cases identified or even confused, with parody is "intertextuality." In her excellent study on parody Hutcheon alerts repeatedly of the danger of reducing parodic nuances to mere intertextuality. She concludes her pragmatic approach by locating the difference between both notions in the producer's intention and in the receptor's semiotic competence (37).

[21] Although Dale Peterson approaches the theme of Duboisian biculturalism through a comparison with Dostoevsky in "Notes from the Underworld: Dostoevsky, DuBois, and the Discovery of Ethnic Soul" (1994), the roots of this comparison are to be traced in the close relationship that many critics have perceived between Duboisian double consciousness theory and Bakhtinian double voice (see below). Despite the usefulness of the Duboisian-Bakhtinian paradigm that has been advocated up to now, several opinions have been raised objecting to it, mainly on the basis of a partial application of the Bakhtinian theory. A good example of such objections is another article by Dale Peterson, in which the author analyzes the interest of African American literary criticism in Bakhtin, noticing that "there has been a rather selective hearing of Bakhtin's available words, a hearing that has been particularly sensitive to the empowering and emancipatory implications of the Russian's polyphonic discourse analysis" ("Response and Call" 766), and which, as a consequence, has avoided other more problematic aspects of Bakhtinian theory difficult to adapt to the Duboisian vision. Like Peterson, Dorothy Hale in "Bakhtin in African American Literary Theory" (1994) reckons this adaptation questionable on the grounds of a basic mistake which consists of holding the key terms of "consciousness" and "voice" as interchangeable. That mistake, according to Hale, entails more disadvantages than advantages, as it empties the content of African American identity, transforming it into "the subaltern language of empty self-expression" (464). Counteracting all these oppositions, I have tried to articulate the perfect adaptability of two of Bakhtin's essential notions—parody and double voice—as adequate instruments for interpreting African American literature, and especially, novels of passing.

consciousness and evolves into what critics have termed a "double narrative,"[22] or double-voiced narrative, where many elements constantly signal the presence of unresolved tensions throughout the text.

In *The Afro-American Novel and Its Tradition* (1987) Bernard Bell grounds the intimate relationship between double consciousness and African American novels and their subsequent double nature. He affirms that African American novels are fit instruments to provide an outlet of expression for double consciousness:

> From its inception . . . the Afro-American novel has been concerned with illuminating the meaning of the black American experience and the complex double-consciousness, socialized ambivalence, and double vision which is the special burden and blessing of Afro-American identity. (35)

The adaptability of African American novels to the purposes and scope of double consciousness leads Bell to proclaim them the sublime examples of double narratives, particularly because they constitute a "hybrid narrative whose distinctive tradition and vitality are derived basically from the sedimented indigenous roots of black American folklore and literary genres of the Western world" (xii). Gates alludes to the same ideas of Bakhtinian double voice and parody insisting on the fact that "the 'heritage' of each black text written in a Western language . . . is a double heritage, two-toned, as it were" ("Criticism in de Jungle" 123). The parodic imposition of both voices—African and Western—allows for a vision of these narratives as the privileged locus and sublime representation of the theories of both Duboisian double consciousness and Bakhtinian double-voicedness.

The double character that can be detected in any African American novel becomes more self-evident and easily traceable in the case of the corpus of texts that constitute the focus of the present analysis: the novels of passing written by James W. Johnson, George Schuyler, Nella Larsen, and Jessie Fauset. These novels are revealed to be authentic double or multiple narratives, thanks to the incorporation and integration of diverse and divergent voices arising from the two

---

[22] In his doctoral dissertation entitled "Rhetoric versus Eloquence in the Afro-American Double Narrative: Perspectives on Audience, Ambivalence and Ambiguity" (1985), Myles R. Hurd seems to have used this term for the first time to designate the structural problems that emerge out of the

traditions to which they belong. The relationship established among these voices is fundamentally parodic and discloses a marked antagonism. The authors especially exploit the Western tradition in order to revise previous texts, genres or modes by means of a systematic inversion or variation of their paradigms and postulates. The main aim of the parodic revision is to subvert the standard modes of representation of African American identity and to create alternative models. Finally, that conscious subversion is directly linked to the "passing" motif itself, since its themes serve as covers or masks to elaborate a "generic" passing that informs and pervades the texts under analysis.[23] While all the selected novels seem to tackle the issue of racial passing by focusing on characters who cross the so-called "color line" into the white race; in fact, the authors use this argument as a pretext to investigate questions pertaining to the racial as well as the social, cultural, and literary spheres. By laying bare the parodic subversion underlying these novels, I will attempt to demonstrate that these novels about "passing" function essentially as parodies of their own tradition.

DOUBLE CONSCIOUSNESS AND FEMINISM

Despite the fact that the concept of double consciousness and the bivocality inherent in African American novels form an adequate critical support widely used by currently eminent specialists in African American literature,[24] there are many opposing views that regard double consciousness as a divisive means that does not

---

bivocality omnipresent in African American texts. The term employed herein starts with Hurd's conception, but privileges its expansion to the wider context of Bakhtinian poliphony.

[23] The perspective of "generic passing" is also enhanced by the ideas of double voice and parody which fit extremely well into the pattern, as will be shown in the analysis of each of the selected novels.

[24] The suitability of the application of double consciousness as paradigm for the study and investigation of African American literature and novels in particular has been justly and repeatedly acknowledged by many critics. For instance, Darlene Hine declares that "Du Bois's analysis dominated black thought for most of the twentieth century" (338). Beside those cited above, it is worth mentioning several other critics that make use of the Duboisian design such as Robert Stepto in *From Behind the Veil* (1979), James B. Stewart in "Psychic Duality of Afro-Americans in the Novels of W. E. B. DuBois" (1983), Michael Cooke in *Afro-American Literature in the Twentieth Century* (1984), Houston A. Baker in *Blues, Ideology, and Afro-American Literature* (1984), William E. Cain in "New Directions in Afro-American Literary Criticism: *The Signifying Monkey*" (1990), and William Lyne in "The Signifying Modernist: Ralph Ellison and the Limits of Double Consciouness" (1992).

contribute at all to the development of the genre.[25] Nevertheless, the Duboisian
model has become particularly useful for the purposes of feminist criticism, as the
proliferation of feminist analyses patterned on double consciousness demonstrate.[26]
The intimate relationship between Duboisian and feminist discourses merge in the
notion of "divided identity" coined by Mary Helen Washington (*Black-Eyed Susans*
22). This divided identity can be articulated as a survival strategy adopted by
women who develop a keen understanding of two opposing definitions of their
sense of self: one imposed by the male world and their own. The sense of double
identity or feminine double consciousness is more significant in the case of African
American women, who are interpreted within the parameters of both their gender
and their race as double negation with respect to the dominant paradigm of white
maleness. A good expression which summarizes this notion is Michelle Wallace's
concept of African American women as "the 'other' of the 'other'" ("Variations"
53). This double dichotomy constitutes the basis for African American feminist
criticism from its beginning, as Quandra Prettyman Stadler states: "black women
live with a double consciousness and sing a dual song—of gender and of race"
(241). It is thus impossible to separate racial from gender discourses, and viceversa,
as Barbara Smith also confirms: "sexual politics are as real in black women's lives
as racial politics" ("Toward a Black Feminist Criticism" 33). Hence, she propounds
her famous notion of "simultaneity of oppressions" (*Home Girls* xxxiii) as a
suitable framework for criticisms. Deborah King would later rephrase it as
"multiple jeopardy" (294), stressing the interlocking nature of all the factors of

---

[25] Among the most recent disparaging critics who absolutely refuse Duboisian dualism, Stanley
Crouch is a good case in point. He defines it as "an aching split . . . alienation between national
and racial identity, casting them as 'warring ideals'" (83-4). Kristin Hunter Lattany coincides with
Crouch in a negative conception of double consciousness: "to me, DuBois's double consciousness
implies duality, an unhealthy state for the individual and for the group. As Lincoln said: 'A house
divided against itself cannot stand'" (168), and C. Eric Lincoln agrees too, going beyond rejection
when he denounces that such internal division brings along self-hatred: "The 'lure and loathing,' a
romantic euphemism for black self-hatred, is the extrapolation of the Duboisian dubiety that
allegedly commits the African American to unending irresolution and self-flagellation in the
fruitless effort to fully realize the 'American' component of his being" (196).
[26] For instance, Elaine Showalter insists on the crucial role of this model when she argues: "For
those of us who work within 'oppositional' or cultural criticisms—black, socialist, feminist, or
gay—questions of the critic's double consciousness, double audience and double role come with
the territory and arise every day" ("A Criticism of Our Own" 348-9). Barbara Johnson reiterates
this affirmation when she observes: "if the woman's voice, to be authentic, must incorporate and
articulate division and self-difference, so, too, has Afro-American literature always had to assume
its double-voicedness" (qtd. in Tally 22). Others will be cited in the text.

oppressions—race, gender, class, nationality, religion, etc.,—that black women are subject to.[27]

From this quick overview a remarkable connection can be firmly established between female divided identity and Duboisian double consciousness, even to the point that the former could be redefined as "double double consciousness."[28] At this point it seems relevant to examine Du Bois' conception of African American women, which may throw light on the close link between race and gender and therefore justify the inclusion of feminist criticism in this chapter. In his writings specifically about the women of his race, Du Bois seems ever ready to give them credit and importance: "The uplift of women is, next to the problem of the color line and the peace movement, our greatest modern cause" ("Damnation" 574). This passage is quite telling, since Du Bois himself places emphasis on the idea that both discourses—racial and sexual—interrelate and intersect, both are rated almost equally on his political agenda. Du Bois had previously proclaimed the existence of such interconnection on several occasions, demanding sexual equality as well as racial equality.

His article "Awake America" (1917) provides a good example when he mentions "to stop disfranchisement for race and sex" (379) as one of the basic demands for his political program. The need to fight against discrimination on any grounds—either racial or sexual—sets the mood for most of his political and social campaigns, and seems to be at the core of his attack on discriminatory practices. He is well aware that such practices attempt to gain legitimacy by hoisting the supposed inferiority of both groups—blacks and women—as their flag. His absolute rebuke is articulated in clear terms: "The statement that woman is weaker than man is sheer rot: It is the same kind of thing that we hear about 'darker races' and 'lower classes'" ("Woman Suffrage" 378). Here Du Bois rejects the alleged inferiority of African Americans and women, equating it to the unacceptability of social discrimination based on class. Thus, gender equality cannot be depicted as a

---

[27] For analyses of concepts of double, triple, and multiple jeopardy, see Frances Beale's "Double Jeopardy: To Be Black and Female" (1970), Angela Davis' *Women, Race, and Class* (1981), bell hooks' *Ain't I a Woman* (1981), Patricia Hill Collins' "The Social Construction of Black Feminist Thought" (1989), Deborah K. King's "Multiple Jeopardy, Multiple Consciousness: The Context of a Black Feminist Ideology" (1988), and Andrée McLaughin's "Black Women, Identity, and the Quest for Humanhood and Wholeness: Wild Women in the Whirlwind" (1990).

[28] In her dissertation entitled "African-American Modernism in the Novels of Jessie Fauset and Nella Larsen" (1992), Mary Hairston McManus employs this term taken from a poem by Ken McManus (17).

minor issue within the Duboisian code, but, on the contrary, acquires great relevance.

Du Bois' involvement in gender issues has prompted many critics to qualify him as the first African American feminist intellectual, above all for his forceful defense of women's right to vote in "Woman Suffrage" (1915).[29] But he is especially sympathetic to the plea of African American women, since for him they play a fundamental role in the progress of the race—"[I]t is the five million women of my race who really count" ("Damnation" 573)—and, in general, in the contemporary world—"[T]he actual work of the world today depends more largely upon women than upon men" ("Woman Suffrage" 378). Starting from the crucial role of women, Du Bois in "The Damnation of Women" (1920) traces the origins of history to acknowledge black women, and concretely "the primal black All-Mother of men" (565) as the source for the birth of Western civilization. In this way, Du Bois accomplishes a twofold goal: on the one hand, he pays homage to the figure of that "first woman" and to all her descendants and, on the other, he manages to forge a harsh critique of the unjust treatment they have been subjected to on the part of the white patriarchal system, which "wills to worship womankind," but which purposely "forgets its darker sisters" (565). Bearing in mind all the injustice that African American women have suffered, Du Bois claims equal rights for all women without any racial distinction. He also contests the contradictory images that patriarchy itself imposes: "it [the world] wavers between the prostitute and the nun" (565). He explains that such a dichotomy cannot be operative any more, because it does not take into account the reality of contemporary women who are economically and intellectually independent, and consequently, cannot easily adapt to preestablished patterns or roles. In this sense, Du Bois seems to anticipate many of the concerns of the present study, particularly the revision and reshaping of sexist and racist stereotypes. A new conception of womanhood emerges from Du

---

[29] Two critics who have endorsed Du Bois for his pro-feminist attitude and his defense of the crucial role of African American women in the economic and cultural development of their community are Nellie Y. McKay in "The Souls of Black Women Folk in the Writings of W. E. B. DuBois" (1990) and Cheryl Towsend Gilkes in "The Margin as the Center of a Theory of History" (1996). Angela Davis also supports this view in *Women, Race & Class* (1981), regarding him as "the leading male advocate of woman suffrage in the twentieth century" (145). Other critics, though, question his alleged feminism especially because of the ambiguous relationship that Du Bois maintained with declared feminists of his time like Anna Julia Cooper and Ida B. Wells Barnett. See "The Profeminist Politics of W. E. B. Du Bois with Respect to Anna Julia Cooper and Ida B. Wells Barnett" by Joy James (1996) or "'The Five Million Women of My Race': Negotiations of Gender in W. E. B. Du Bois and Anna Julia Cooper" by Hanna Wallinger (1999). I would like to thank Hanna Wallinger for sending me a copy of her article.

Bois' redefinition, embodied in the figure of the "free woman" of his time with power of decision over her own life and body.

Within this new Duboisian conception of women, the idea of "double double consciousness" preserves its original strength, and contributes significantly to a new feminine discourse. African American women occupy a unique position in the crossroads of race and gender issues, as described by Barbara Christian: "The development of Afro-American women's fiction is . . . a mirror image of the intensity of the relationship between sexism and racism in this country" ("Trajectories" 234). Therefore, African American feminist criticism should investigate the manifold implications of such a difficult but productive position. Reflecting on its problematic nature, Valerie Smith notes that "[b]lack feminist literary theory proceeds from the assumption that black women experience a unique form of oppression . . . because they are victims at once of sexism, racism, and by extension classism" ("Black Feminist Theory" 47). Hence, the Duboisian vision of women as the centre of society is directly addressed in the interest of feminist criticism to affirm the exclusive and singular character of African American women's experience. An obvious consequence that derives from this affirmation is a claim for their own space, wherein to express the way in which both spheres—racial and sexual—interact with each other and engender a new discourse, African American feminist discourse.

Among the many specialists that have discussed the relationship that links the idea of double consciousness to the revision of the role of African American women and their discourse, two have made important contributions and should be briefly acknowledged: Mae Gwendolyn Henderson in "Speaking in Tongues: Dialogics, Dialectics, and the Black Woman Writer's Literary Tradition" (1990), and Michael Awkward with his introduction to *Inspiriting Influences: Tradition, Revision and Afro-American Women's Novels* (1989). Both critics clearly adhere to Du Bois and Bakhtin's theories and their application to feminist criticism. Certain commonalities articulate the link between these two theories and feminist objectives, as their starting point or premise is a dialogical conception of discourse easily detected in the heteroglossia that characterizes feminist discourse. Such heteroglossia is the product of an internal dichotomy inherent in feminist discourse, in which the patriarchal discourse and the African American female tradition are constantly invoked. The result of this disparity is a "simultaneity of discourse" that marks African American feminist discourse.

In Henderson's analysis, such a simultaneity of discourse leads to the emphasis on the "interlocutory, or dialogic character" of African American women's writings, which she defines as follows: "[n]ot only a relationship with the 'other(s),' but an internal dialogue with the plural aspects of self that constitute the matrix of black female subjectivity" (118). Henderson here calls up the two Bakhtinian poles of social linkage with the "Other"—in this case the "Other" with respect to the speaker would comprise white men, African American men, and white women—and of unity with the internal "Other" where the multiple aspects of the African American female self are integrated. Out of these two poles, external and internal, two important phenomena emerge, which Henderson identifies with "glossolalia" and "heteroglossia" or "speaking in tongues," respectively (114-5). The most interesting phenomenon is undoubtedly the second one, not only because it basically coincides with the Bakhtinian term, but especially because it can be used as a trope for the multiple voices or languages that arise from the multiple selves. It enables "multivocality" (136) to take place in texts written by African American women writers.

Advocating a multivocal depiction, Henderson explores the way in which such polyphony is articulated. There are two main objectives common to those texts: "[t]he self-inscription of black womanhood, and the establishment of a dialogue of discourses with the other/s" (131). To achieve these two aims their authors employ two main strategies: either "disruption"—subverting texts produced by other/s—or "revision"—rewriting texts to fit their needs. These two strategies or tools directly recall the concept of parody already mentioned here, which mainly consists of the employment of a polyphonic discourse that deconstructs other voices by means of revision and variation. It is precisely the latter concept of variation that Michelle Wallace highlights in "variations on negation" ("Variations" 62), in which she suggests that to invert the rejection that African American women have faced at all levels—racial, social, and sexual—proves instrumental in reformulating their role especially within the social and cultural realms.

All these ideas seem to drive at a conception of African American feminist discourse as basically involved in the subversion, inversion or variation of other discourses that marginalize African American women. If African American discourse in general has been stigmatized and erased from dominant discourse, the case of the female voice has been even more poignant. Therefore, Henderson conceives African American feminist discourse in a wider sense as a suitable tool to focus on the social relationships with the other/s, particularly on the strategies deployed by Sherley Anne Williams and Toni Morrison "to make visible the invisible." According to Henderson, both authors are intent on giving voice back to African American women by breaking the silence that has been imposed on them.[30]

In the same way, Awkward devotes his introduction to articulating "a heretofore repressed and silenced black female's story and voice" (1), taking as reference the Bakhtinian vision and transforming it into what he terms "denigration":

> By *denigration*, I mean here precisely those appropriative acts by Afro-Americans which have successfully transformed, by the addition of black expressive cultural features, Western cultural and expressive systems to the extent that they reflect, in black "mouths" and "contexts," what we might call (in Bakhtinian terms) Afro-American "intention" and "accent." (9; author's emphasis)

The concept of denigration is thus quite similar to the other two mentioned above, "variations on negation" by Wallace and "disruption/revision" by Henderson. Such a fact cannot be merely coincidental and leads to the same conclusion: all these critics aim at the subversion and deconstruction of the Eurocentric canon and the creation of a unique space for African American women's self-expression and self-definition.

Both Henderson and Awkward are also interested in the dialogic nature of the relation with other African American women's voices. Barbara Smith refers to this idea in her groundbreaking 1977 essay when she holds that "a black feminist critic . . . would also work from the assumption that black women writers constitute an identifiable literary tradition" ("Toward a Black Feminist Criticism" 36).[31]

---

[30] The rupture with the imposed silence and the desire to make African American women visible and present can be acknowledged as one of the main concerns behind a great part of African American feminist criticism. Some pioneering examples are "Toward a Black Feminist Criticism" by Barbara Smith (1977), "New Directions for Black Feminist Criticism" by Deborah McDowell (1980), "Visibility and Difference: Black Women in History and Literature—Pieces of a Paper and Some Ruminations" by Quandra Prettyman Stadler (1980), *Black Women Novelists: The Development of a Tradition 1892-1976* (1980) and *Black Feminist Criticism: Perspectives on Black Women Writers* by Barbara Christian (1985), to name a few.

[31] The acknowledgment of an African American female tradition has been and still is one of the main objectives of African American feminist criticism. In her interesting overview of the history of this movement, Valerie Smith identifies this thrust as the first period or "archaelogical work" ("Black Feminist Theory" 46), whereby there was an intense search and reedition of previous texts written by African American women that had been practically relegated to oblivion. Several critics and writers have devoted themselves to this difficult task, as Alice Walker and her recovery of

According to Awkward, the relationship that can be verified between the different generations of African American women writers is mainly conciliatory and cohesive: "[t]he textual affinities between black women's works generally exist . . . as a function of black women writers' conscious acts of refiguration and revision of the earlier canonical texts" (4). Contrary to what happens in the dominant canon, each of these writers feels intimately connected to the previous ones.

Moreover, Awkward continues, this link is mainly cooperative opposing the mechanisms employed to generate the male canon. In the latter, the influence of some authors over the rest is to be understood mainly in terms of competitiviness, as Gates and Stepto's theories prove (6-7). On the other hand, in the case of women writers this influence becomes "an occasion for cooperative textual interactions with maternal figures" (7). According to Awkward's depiction, there is, then, a radical differentiation in the creation of both canons.[32] However, the model devised by Awkward suggests a problematic fusion of the white male canon and the African American male canon in their opposition to the African American female tradition. The perspective I have adopted in this analysis seeks to determine the differences among the three traditions and studies, first, the distinction between dominant canon and African American female canon and, then, between the African American female and male canons. The main reason for this choice resides in the transcendence of the notions of canon and canon formation for African American feminist critics who have traditionally withstood them, as Barbara Christian clearly puts it: "[c]anon formation has become one of the thorny dilemmas for the black feminist critic" ("But What Do We Think" 70). Such a dilemma is indeed multiple since it derives from two main causes: on the one hand, from the anxiety provoked by the discovery that "we may be imitating the very structure that shut our

---

Zora Neale Hurston and her works recounted in *In Search for Our Mothers' Garden* (1984), Deborah McDowell and her edition in Beacon Press of *Quicksand* and *Passing* by Nella Larsen (1986), Mary Helen Washington and her three anthologies *Black-Eyed Susans* (1975), *Midnight Birds* (1980) and *Invented Lives* (1987), and Henry Louis Gates in his editing of *The Schomburg Library of Nineteenth-Century Women Writers*.

[32] Awkward is not the first one to pinpoint this distinction when fashioning the canon in the two traditions—female and male—nor the only one who purposely employs Harold Bloom's theory to support his thesis. In fact, Awkward alludes to the main source for his work, namely Sandra Gilbert and Susan Gubar's pioneering study *The Madwoman in the Attic* (1979). As Elaine Showalter notes, Gilbert and Gubar's text is essential to the development of the gynocritic approach ("gynocritics") within African American feminist criticism that "derived much of its strength from its self-reflexive properties as a double-voiced mode of women's writing" ("A Criticism of Our Own" 364). To understand the important role played by this critical tendency and its reconstruction of the African American female tradition, see "Feminist Criticism in the Wilderness" also by Showalter (1981).

literatures out in the first place" ("But What Do We Think" 70), which has led to an enormous resistance to theorization on the part of African American feminist critics; and on the other, from their awareness of the impossibility of ever achieving a clear-cut separation between the different canons as there are always shifts and drains.

With respect to the dominant canon, the great majority of African American critics and writers have adopted very skeptical attitudes about what they regard as a kind of extension of the colonial structure to the sphere of criticism. Instead they have advocated "a counter-tradition" in Hortense Spillers' words ("Cross-Currents" 251):

> Reading against the canon, intruding into it a configuration of symbolic values with which critics and audiences must contend, the work of black women's writing community not only redefines tradition, but also disarms it by suggesting that the term itself is a critical fable intended to encode and circumscribe an inner and licit circle of empowered texts. (251)

The above extract seems to condense many African American feminist claims. It calls for a subversion of the dominant canon, while it deconstructs the notion of canon itself by means of the emphasis on two main ideas, specifically the arbitrariness to which canon formation responds and the subtle connection between it and the social section that is in power, in this case whites. Hence, the relationship between the white canon and African American feminist critics becomes an extremely difficult and almost unsolvable problem, constituting up to very recently a source for controversy among specialists in African American literature.[33]

---

[33] Indeed, the relationship with the dominant theoretical canon is found at the root of a great part of the debates that have taken place among African American critics. The best-known and oft-quoted example was the dispute among Henry Louis Gates, Joyce A. Joyce, and Houston A. Baker in *New Literary History* (1987). Again the present analysis tries to develop Gates' observations up to a certain point:

> By learning to read a black text within a black formal cultural matrix, and explicating it with the principles at work in *both* the Euro-American and Afro-American traditions, I believe that we critics can produce richer structures of meaning than are possible otherwise. ("'What's Love Got to Do with It?'" 352; author's emphasis)

The resistance to theorization has been one of the main characteristics of African American feminist criticism up to quite recently. Nevertheless, the latest tendency within this criticism is not to resist it, but to question any received notions. An illustration of this position is provided by Deborah McDowell who, analyzing the dichotomy theory/practice in 1995, concludes: "when the writings of black women and other critics of color are excluded from the category of theory, it

As far as the correlation between African American male and female criticism is concerned, it has not been particularly harmonious either. In fact, certain male critics have been accused of being as sexist as their white counterparts, imitating the way in which the latter ignore or devalue any text written by women.[34] The verification of sexist practices on the part of some male critics has led many women to endorse a complete separation between both spheres, advocated by Mary Helen Washington as early as 1980:

> Black women are searching for a specific language, specific symbols, specific images with which to record their lives, and, even though they could claim a rightful place in the Afro-American tradition and the feminist tradition of women writers, it is also clear that, for purposes of liberation, black women writers will first insist on their own name, their own space. (*Midnight Birds* 36)

Following Washington's lead, most of the contributions by African American feminist critics have been restricted to the female field, leaving aside male writers. This analysis, however, responds to Deborah McDowell who in 1980, while valuing the need for a particular attention to African American women writers, insisted on the fact that "[t]he countless thematic, stylistic, and imagistic parallels between Black male and female writers must be examined" ("New Directions" 196). Thus, I agree with the suggestion that "we should, rather, salvage what we find useful in past methodologies, reject what we do not, and, where necessary, move toward 'inventing new methods of analysis'" (193). Citing Kolodny, she shapes the main contours or guidelines to employ theory: to make use of what is useful from previous methodologies, either coming from the dominant canon or the African American one, and to reject any sexist or racist innuendo.

---

must be partly because theory has been reduced to a very particular practice" ("Transferences" 169).

[34] McDowell also exemplifies this kind of accusation in naming Stepto, Bone, and Littlejohn as examples of "phallic criticism," appropriating the term coined by Mary Ellman ("New Directions" 187), and well explained by Annis Pratt in "The New Feminist Criticisms" (1972). McDowell also recounts the several controversies that have taken place between male and female critics, mainly evolving around the use of markedly sexist arguments on the part of male critics in "Boundaries: Or Distant Relations and Close Kin" (56-59). Also in "Reading Family Matters" (1989) she describes each controversy, concluding that the debate is really about "an unacknowledged jostling for space in the literary marketplace" (83).

Hence, the methodological approach adopted here for the analyses of selected novels of passing is basically in the application of the theories of Du Bois and Bakhtin—mainly double consciousness, parody, and double voicedness, enhanced by insights drawn from African American feminist criticism. Within this theoretical framework an intermediary path has been negotiated among the different canons in order to analyze the five passing novels under study—two by men and three by women—and to account for the gender specificity especially found in the latter. In the ensuing chapters I will employ these basic guidelines in order to uncover and underline the multiple possibilities and levels of significance that each of the selected texts may invoke. This sense of multiplicity will then highlight the great multivocality that distinguishes these texts and gives way to their manifold interpretations, one of which is the present book.

SECTION I

Male

Perspectives

Two

Questioning Race and Identity: **The Autobiography of an Ex-Colored Man** *by James Weldon Johnson*

My old man's a white old man
And my old mother's black.
If ever I cursed my white old man
I take my curses back.

If ever I cursed my black old mother
And wished she were in hell,
I'm sorry for that evil wish
And now I wish her well.

My old man died in a fine big house
My ma died in a shack.
I wonder where I'm gonna die,
Being neither white nor black?

Langston Hughes
"Cross"

As a direct precursor to the passing novels of the decade of the twenties, *The Autobiography of an Ex-Colored Man* by James Weldon Johnson anticipates many of the central motifs and themes that concern Harlem intellectuals, mainly the reinterpretation of the key concepts of race and identity through a revision and updating of the autobiographical and Duboisian legacies. Johnson's work thus inaugurates a model for depicting the mulatto condition, a crucial contribution to the Harlem cultural renaissance in general, and to the later development of the sub-genre of the novel of passing particularly, by creating patterns that become consolidated in the subsequent literary production.

Published anonymously for the first time in 1912, *The Autobiography* is, above all, the work that most explicitly links the theme of passing in the decade before the twenties with the African American literary tradition stemming from the eighteenth and nineteenth centuries. Within this tradition the novel maintains a clear connection with two modes already established in the African American canon: on the one hand, the autobiographical tendency from the previous century heralded by slave narratives,[1] and on the other, the exploitation of the popular "tragic mulatto" figure reinterpreted in Johnson's protagonist, who becomes the epitome of the passing character *par excellence*. Especially with respect to the second tradition, Johnson's debt to Du Bois needs to be acknowledged, as Johnson employs Du Bois' ideas as a springboard for the further development of his own personal vision. The notion of double consciousness acquires a very relevant role in the novel as the basis for questioning received notions of race and identity. In the project of deconstruction undertaken by Johnson, the ambiguity that pervades the text thanks to the inclusion of the Duboisian ideology of the so-called "talented tenth" destabilizes the very foundations of the passing novel and reveals a rich substratum of markedly ironic overtones.

The kind of interrelation existing between all the previous texts and Johnson's novel is eminently parodic, as Johnson's main aim is to dismantle them through an intentional reworking of their structuring devices. The following study of the parodic pattern is composed of three main parts: first, a discussion of the productive relationship between Johnson's novel and the autobiography; second, an examination of the tragic mulatto tradition with the aid of Duboisian theory, thereby linking *The Autobiography* to Du Bois' *Souls of Black Folk*; and, third, a comparison between Johnson's novel and the previous tradition in order to define and delimit some of the key notions that *The Autobiography* lends to subsequent literary creation and, specifically, to the novels of passing written in the following decade.

---

[1] This tendency originates in the slave narratives that were first printed around 1760 and continues until the early twentieth century, works regarded as classic in African American literature evidence such as *Up From Slavery* by Booker T. Washington (1901) and *The Souls of Black Folk* by W. E. B. Du Bois (1903). Some important critical contributions are Stephen Butterfield and William L. Andrews in their respective books *Black Autobiography in America* (1974) and *To Tell a Free Story: The First Century of Afro-American Autobiography, 1760-1865* (1986).

Autobiographical Convention and Johnson's Work

The circumstances that surrounded the anonymous publication of *The Autobiography of an Ex-Colored Man* in 1912 and its reprinting in 1927 during the climatic period of the Harlem Renaissance can clarify, to a certain extent, the author's main motivation for writing the novel. He himself explains:

> When the book was published . . . most of the reviewers accepted it as a *human document*. This was a tribute to the writing, for I had done the book with the intention of its being so taken. But perhaps, it would have been more farsighted had I originally affixed my name to it as a frank piece of fiction. But I did get a certain pleasure out of anonymity, that no acknowledged book could have given me. (*Along the Way* 238; my emphasis)

Johnson again confirms his intention in a letter to George Towns, in which he states that "[w]hen the author is known, and known to be one who could not be the main character of the story, the book will fall flat" (qtd. in Levy 126). In the passage the author justifies anonymity as a means of causing a greater impact on the audience, who he supposes would be more receptive to his novel if they associated it with the popular autobiographical convention.[2] Johnson's statements seem to indicate that his decision to publish *The Autobiography* anonymously hinged simply on the question of credibility, as his readers were mostly white and probably familiar with the African American autobiographical mode of slave narratives.

The reasons invoked by Johnson constitute what Sollors calls "the fiction of authenticity" (*Neither White* 265) and provide a glimpse into the personal interest that may have motivated the author: he did not want his work rejected and trivialised as another piece of fiction, devoid of moral and social significance. Eugenia Collier bears witness to the success of Johnson's enterprise citing two representative examples: *The New York Times*, that claims "[the book] . . . does make an astute, dispassionate study of the race problem in the United States from the standpoint of a man who lived on both sides of it," confirming the reception of the text as social document; and an editorial by Jessie Fauset, who insists even

---

[2] Samira Kawash also studies the importance of the autobiographical tradition in Johnson's novel and its implications for identity formation (1996).

more on the question of veracity, portraying the novel as "the epitome of the race situation" (365). Thus, from the very beginning, Johnson's novel is valued solely on the basis of its content of racial and social denunciation.

The question of fiction/reality should have been reconsidered with the later edition of the work by Knopf in 1927, precisely during the zenith of the Harlem Renaissance, when the author is explicitly acknowledged. However, the second reprinting responds to two essential objectives: first, the reappraisal of the text as a direct antecedent of the cultural renaissance that was flourishing in Harlem at the time; and second, the corroboration of its categorization as a communal story, as the introduction by Van Vechten clearly indicates: "It reads like a composite autobiography of the Negro race in the United States in modern times . . . an invaluable sourcebook for the study of Negro psychology" (vi-vii). Van Vechten accepts the classification of the text as a document of psychological and sociological import, and not for what it actually was, a work of fiction. In spite of the acknowledgment of the author, and the consequent disclosure of the work as fiction, the strong conviction of the reality of its racial and social portrait prevailed for some time, until certain critics fortunately adopted an ironic approach which opened the way for an analysis of the subversive content of the work and its multiple levels of significance.[3]

Although more recent critics have questioned the importance of irony as key to the novel,[4] these earlier readings have, in fact, been quite fruitful and accordingly represent the starting point for the present chapter, before moving on to a parodic rather than an ironic approach to Johnson's text.[5] One key question that this critical stance highlights has to do with the motivations that led Johnson to "disguise" his narrative as part of the previous tradition. The reasons enunciated by critics are manifold and of a very diverse order. Charles Scruggs, for instance, alleges that the

---

[3] Picking up on Robert Bone's suggestions in *The Negro Novel in America* (1958), Robert Fleming initiated this trend in his well-known article "Irony as a Key to Johnson's *The Autobiography of an Ex-Colored Man*" (1971). The ironic mode has been explored by numerous critics such as Eugenia Collier (1971), Marvin Garrett (1971), Stephen M. Ross (1974), Joseph Skerrett (1980) or Roxanna Pisiak (1993). The most recent work in this vein belongs to Neil Brooks (1995), and Donald Goellnicht (1996).

[4] For example, Faulkner declared in 1985: "A key moment . . . in the history of criticism of the novel ought to have been a 1971 article by Robert Fleming which argues forcefully that Johnson was consistently ironic . . . Yet somehow Fleming's analysis has never caught hold" ("James Weldon Johnson" 147). Other critics before Faulkner rejected the ironic approach and proposed instead a direct relation between narrator and author: Hugh Gloster (1939), David Littlejohn (1969), Sterling Brown (1937), Nathan Huggins (1971), and Eugene Levy (1973).

[5] Giulia Fabi has convincingly argued for a parodic reading of the novel too, mainly focusing on the nineteenth-century novelistic tradition (2001).

anonymous publication of *The Autobiography* was "symbolic of the uncertainties of the times" ("H. L. Mencken and James Weldon Johnson" 191) and notes that, at the time, African American texts were not well received. Despite Scruggs' opinion, I wish to argue an interpretation of the anonymous publication of the text as a strategic move on Johnson's part: hiding behind the conventions of autobiography enables Johnson to develop more progressive and, therefore, more controversial ideas. As Roxanna Pisiak has well said, "it may be that the text was too subversive to be presented as fiction" (93). This blurring of the line between reality and fiction, leads Goellnicht to support the idea of subversion—"The deception was, then, clearly deliberate" (18), basing his judgment on an analysis of what he calls the "generic passing" manifest in the novel.[6] Goellnicht's idea of "generic passing," however, needs to be expanded to include other traditions latent in the text, namely the convention of the "tragic mulatto," Duboisian theory, and the sentimental novel of the nineteenth century. In sum, Johnson's novel "passes" for autobiography in order to revise and update all these traditions in an attempt to deconstruct the functioning parameters of the representation of both race and identity imposed by the dominant culture.

From the very beginning African American autobiography suffers from "an obsession with self-authentication" (Yarborough 111) and conceives the author as basically a "truth-teller" (Andrews, *To Tell* 1). This concern with credibility obviously arises with the publication of the first autobiographies which needed to establish a dialogue with the white world, a world that had silenced black voices and denied their humanity.[7] The autobiography becomes "a mediative instrument" (Andrews, "First Century" 22) between the African American author and his/her white readership, especially in the case of slave narratives.[8] To press the cause of abolition, these narratives need to persuade their white audience of two crucial ideas: of the actual identity of the author and of his/her "literacy" which signifies

---

[6] I have already mentioned Goellnicht's thesis in the introduction, in which he equates the "genetic passing" of the protagonist of *The Autobiography* to the "generic passing" that Johnson intentionally inserts in the narration (18).

[7] In chapter four of *Figures in Black* Gates provides an excellent overview of the trascendence of that lack of voice, which presupposes lack of consciousness and history according to the racist discourse of the time, elaborated by influential philosophers like Hegel and Diderot. He astutely describes the African American absence as "to figure like a nigger," which actually means "not to figure at all" (*Figures* 117).

[8] I only refer to slave narratives from the abolitionist period, since, as William Andrews has convincingly argued in "The Representation of Slavery and the Rise of Afro-American Literary Realism, 1865-1920" (1993), slave narratives written after the civil war imply deep changes and revision of the established patterns.

the right to their own voice.[9] The ability to read and write grants them access to the human race, and simultaneously unmasks the injustice of a slave system which relegates them to a subhuman condition.

Writing, then, represents the best way to forge a sense of self-identity that effectively counteracts contemporary racist theories of inferiority: "The slave, by definition, possessed at most a liminal status within the human community. To read and to write was to transgress this nebulous realm of liminality" (Gates, *Signifying Monkey 128)*. The only possibility for slave narrators to demonstrate both their existence and their literate skills was by means of language, or as Gates puts it, "slaves could inscribe their selves only in language" (*Figures* 105). The importance of language, mainly written language, is thus inherently inscribed in these narratives; in consequence, they evidence a marked awareness of the linguistic devices or rhetorical conventions deployed by the narrator to present a "truth" or "reality" credible for white readers.[10]

To look at these rhetorical devices in slave narratives and their influence on Johnson's work, two crucial narratives are instrumental: *The Life of Olaudah Equiano* published in 1789[11] and *Narrative of the Life of Frederick Douglass* printed in 1845.[12] In these two works a change in the model of representation of African American identity is effected by means of the evolution of the discursive universe employed by the authors. This evolution is revised and enhanced by Johnson in his novel, such that the similarities among the three narratives are striking, ranging from the treatment of the same themes to the choice of equivalent rhetorical and literary tropes.

---

[9] William Andrews accounts for both objectives, present in any slave narrative:
> (1) that the slave was, as the inscription of a famous antislavery medallion put it, "a man and a brother" to whites, especially to the white reader of slave narratives; and (2) that the black narrator was, despite all prejudice and propaganda, a truth-teller, a reliable transcriber of the experience and character of black folk. (*To Tell* 1)

[10] Andrews corroborates this rhetorical interest when he notes: "In the first 100 years of its existence, Afro-American autobiography was a genre chiefly distinguished by its rhetorical aims" (*To Tell* 1). He stresses his point further when he states that "autobiography answered a felt need for a rhetorical mode that would conduct the battle against racism and slavery on grounds other than those already occupied by pro- and antislavery polemics" (5).

[11] Despite the opinion of some critics who have reasoned that Equiano's narrative does not belong to the African American canon (Equiano wrote it addressing the British parliament and he did not remain long on American soil [see Andrews, *To Tell* 56-7]), Equiano's rightful place within this canon is attested by the rhetorical strategies that his narrative shares with African American slave accounts in general and with Douglass' in particular.

[12] The relationship between Johnson and Douglass' narratives has been previously studied by Stepto, *From Behind the Veil* (chapter four) and Lucinda Mackethan in "*Black Boy* and *Ex-Colored Man*: Version and Inversion of the Slave Narrators' Quest for Voice" (1988).

Among the themes common to the three works, the first one is undoubtedly the narrators' position within the social and racial system. Both Equiano and Douglass acknowledge their position of outsiders at the beginning of their respective narrations. Equiano repeatedly foregrounds it by presenting himself as "Gustavus Vassa, The African" (cover page) or by announcing his narrative as "the production of an unlettered African" (3). In Douglass' case, the recognition of his marginality is portrayed in a more subtle way. In the first place, the title closes with his introduction as "an American slave" (cover page), which obviously delineates the differences with that of Equiano: he admits his slave condition but chooses to emphasize his adherence to American society. He insists on this sense of belonging in the first sentence that opens the narrative: "I was born in Tuckahoe, near Hillsborough, and about twelve miles from Easton, in Talbot county, Maryland" (255). It is not until a few sentences later that the clearest indication of his marginal position is given: "I have no accurate knowledge of my age, never having seen any authentic record containing it" (255). The lack of knowledge is essential for the narrator, because it makes him immediately aware of the gap between himself and white children. At that early point of his life he pretends not to comprehend the reason why such an unjust gap exists: "I could not tell why I ought to be deprived of the same knowledge" (255). The lack of information and documentation proves, in Gates' words, "his . . . status as a piece of property" (*Figures* 100), symbolizing his marginal status with respect to white society.[13]

Also from the very outset, both authors emphasize their effort to write their narratives and "write themselves" within the dominant white discourse, attempting to turn their absence into presence. The writing of both narratives is the surest way to attain their objectives, and they underline it in their common subtitle: "written by himself." Moreover, Douglass affirms it openly in a very revealing passage in which Mr. Auld, his master at the time, forbids his wife to teach him to read: "It was a new and special revelation . . . From that moment, I understood the pathway from slavery to freedom" (275). This oft-quoted extract summarizes Douglass' understanding of the importance of writing and reading as his certificate for humanity, and consequently, for his right to freedom and inclusion in American society. The passage from slavery to freedom is equated, then, to the journey the narrator undertakes from oral to written culture.

---

[13] His marginal categorization becomes much more explicit when the narrator reveals, that, besides being a slave, he is also a mulatto with a black mother and a white father (255). This actually means that his position is doubly liminal.

With obvious added nuances, the case of the narrator in *The Autobiography* is quite similar: he also places himself in a liminal position with respect to white society. His marginality is ennunciated in the very title of the work, underlining his anonymity. Indeed, his anonymity is maintained thoughout the novel suggesting a clear correlation between Johnson's desire to publish his work anonymously and the choice of a nameless narrator. The lack of definition is already indicated, as in Douglass' narrative, in the opening pages when the narrator asserts: "I shall not mention the name of the town, because there are people still living there who could be connected with this narrative" (2). The need to keep his birthplace secret is, according to the narrator, dictated by his special circumstances, as he has crossed over the color line and is now a respectable "white" business man, or as he calls himself "an ex-colored man."[14] However, his namelessness seems to hint at a lack of definition that equates him to the condition of slaves who possess neither voice nor sense of identity. Johnson's narrator also attempts to write his narrative in order to "write himself" into legitimacy within a white society.

The devices that the three narrators employ to represent a liminal identity through writing vary significantly, ranging from Equiano's marked self-consciousness to the refined description that Johnson offers in his novel. This wide range of possibilities indicates a sophisticated evolution in the autobiography that can be traced from its origins to Johnson's narrative. Robert Stepto's distinction between "integrated narrative" and "generic narrative" facilitates a useful comparison of Equiano and Douglass, respectively (16-26).[15]

Equiano's narrative illustrates the model of "integrated narrative" as it integrates several voices within its structure. These voices can be divided into two main subgroups: on the one hand, the different authenticating documents that are defined as conventional, such as the inclusion of the photograph, a preface, legal documents, letters written by others—usually white people—and by himself, etc.; on the other hand, the coexistence of two voices in the narrative itself aptly described by Gates in his introduction as "the simple wonder with which the young

---

[14] According to Robert Fleming, the fact of passing is the literal reason for the nameless protagonist, but he also adds: "[T]he main character is nameless in a figurative sense because he is the bastard son of a wealthy white Southerner and a mulatto servant" ("Contemporary Themes" 120). In this sense, the protagonist approaches Douglass' liminal status by being mulatto as well. I seek to uncover other motivations for the pervasive presence of namelessness in the text.

[15] In chapter one of *From Behind the Veil* Stepto classifies slave narratives into three main types; however, the first, or "eclectic narrative," does not correspond to any of the narratives chosen for this study (3-6).

Equiano approached the New World of his captors, and the more sophisticated vision, captured in a more eloquently articulated voice, of the author's narrative 'present'" (xiv). This differentiation of voices demonstrates that Equiano is a writer well aware of the use of the literary conventions necessary to authenticate his narrative and, consequently, his portrait of the slave system. The technique is also used in Johnson's text, in which at least two voices can be distinguished, as I will explain below.

The attacks Equiano is subjected to are the clearest testimony of the kind of recurrent doubts which any author of a slave narrative was bound to face. There are two main accusations, namely the falsehood of his account based on the improbability of his existence, and the refusal to acknowledge his literacy. The recriminations are acknowledged in the text as follows: "They tried to asperse his character, by representing him as an impostor; and to invalidate his testimony, by accusing him of wilful falsehoods" (5); and also: "[I]t is not improbable that some English writer has assisted him in the compilement, or at least, the correction of his book, for it is sufficiently well-written" (8). To counter these charges Equiano makes use of the conventions of authentication at hand, which means that he must share control of the narration. The fact that these accusations are reflected in the preface itself is very significant in this kind of "integrated narrative," because it gives primacy to the editor over the author, defining Equiano's narrative in much the same way as Gates defines that of Solomon Northurp: "an integrated narrative unsure of itself" (11).

On the other hand, Douglass' narrative is a good example of "generic narrative"; that is, the integration of the different voices is ultimately dominated by that of the narrator who becomes the nucleus of the narrative. Although at first Douglass seems to fall back on the same conventional ways of authenticating his narrative, specifically in the preface and letters, "they remain segregated outside the tale in the all-important sense that they yield Douglass sufficient narrative and rhetorical space in which to render personal history in-and-as-literary form" (Stepto 20). The rhetorical space alloted to Douglass allows for a deeper investigation into the narrator's personality and into the control he exerts over his autobiography. Perhaps the most explicit example of such control is the scene in which Douglass is about to recount his escape from slavery and openly admits his willingness to keep silent about certain aspects: "But before narrating any of the peculiar circumstances, I deem it proper to make it known my intention not to state all the facts connected with the transaction" (315). In the passage the similarity between

Douglass and Johnson is strikingly evident, both narrators are depicted in absolute command over their narratives, as opposed to Equiano's shared control. Another common trait is the fact that both Douglass and Johnson superimpose two voices in their narration, obvious in this extract from Douglass: "I did not, when a slave, understand the deep meaning of those rude and apparently incoherent songs. I was myself within the circle . . . The mere recurrence to those songs, even now, afflicts me" (263). The slave Douglass and the author as free man intertwine continuously in the narrative, establishing an internal and constant dialogue that pervades the whole book.

Thanks to the number of features that are present in both Douglass' and Johnson's narratives, Stepto ventures to apply the same label to the two of them. However, there is a crucial variation consisting of a clear-cut differentiation between the narrators. According to Stepto, Johnson uses a narrator who is unable "to create and assume a heroic or communal voice" (97). This characteristic of Johnson's text has stirred up a great deal of controversy. A number of critics have rejected the type of character chosen by Johnson as being inadequate to undertake the sociological exploration repeatedly instrumentalized to present the narrative. According to this critical perspective, the "ex-colored man" does not retell an autobiography with heroic overtones in order to prove the humanity and intellectual worth of his race. On the contrary, his is basically a confession of a contrite nature about a marginal and therefore irrelevant life. A critic representative of this line is Eugene Levy in his book *James Weldon Johnson. Black Leader, Black Voice* (1973), who discredits Johnson's character as selfish: "Johnson makes clear that the key to his hero's suffering and thus to his tragedy lies in his selfishness" (141). Here again is an example of the way in which a partial vision of the heroic narrator of slave narratives is conjured as the standard from which African American autobiographies are to be measured and judged.

This distinction between Douglass' and Johnson's narrators is verified only at a superficial level, because both of them actually make use of very similar rhetorical strategies to "write themselves" in the text.[16] In *The Autobiography* Johnson employs the same techniques found in Douglass to effectuate this work of

---

[16] My interpretation contradicts the opinion of many critics about Johnson's work. Apart from the critics already mentioned such as Stepto and Levy, Lucinda Mackethan also holds Johnson's work as "an inversion of the slave narrative" (141) because the protagonist expresses "an inversion of the Slave Narrator's quest for voice" (123). On the contrary, the importance given by Johnson to the rhetorical tools of the text suggests that same quest for voice. Perhaps *The Autobiography* is an inversion of slave narratives, but for different reasons from those proposed by Mackethan.

self-inscription: duality of voices, control over the narrative, and fictionalization of the narrative "I," together with the use of rhetoric as a mask to disguise the true motivation behind the text.

With regard to the first strategy, at least two voices can be distinguished in *The Autobiography*: the more subjective one employed by the narrator to confess all the details of his personal life, and the objective one, which attempts to discuss the social and racial scene of his time. In the former, the intimate voice of the narrator allegedly uses the so-called "confessional technique" present from the beginning of the novel:[17] "I know that in writing the following pages I am divulging the great secret of my life, the secret which I have guarded far more carefully than any of my earthly possessions" (1), i.e., his "passing" into the white race. This personalized voice intermingles with another one charged with objectivity whose function is to dissect the social and racial framework, located for example, in the narrator's description of three distinct classes in the African American community (55-59). This kind of sociological study justifies statements like that in the preface: "Not before has a composite and proportionate presentation of the entire race, embracing all of its various groups and elements, showing their relations with each other and to the whites, been made" (xxxiii). The two voices thus constantly intertwine and intermingle in the text.

The bivocality of *The Autobiography* has never been acknowledged; critical interest has consistently focused on the more "intimate" voice, deeming it uniquely indicative of the author's intention. Pursuing Levy's thesis, many critics have instrumentalized the subjective voice to the point of drawing a dividing line between the previous autobiographical tradition and Johnson's novel. William L. Andrews illustrates this critical tendency in the introduction to his study, even as he argues for the validity of Johnson's text: "Before *The Autobiography of an Ex-Colored Man,* the African American narrative tradition, in both fiction and autobiography, had been devoted much more to public affairs than to personal self-investigation" ("Introduction" xvii).[18] In contrast, the analysis of Johnson's novel

---

[17] According to William Andrews in his introduction to the 1990 edition, Johnson's work should be ascribed to the confessional mode. Andrews' argument is based on the fact that Johnson introduces this mode in the African American canon and he names figures like San Augustine and Rousseau among his most illustrious predecessors (xvii). Although it is true that Johnson employs some of the conventions typical of confessional literature, I consider the autobiographical tradition much more significant for the study of the novel.

[18] Even Robert Fleming in his 1971 article, in which he postulates an ironic reading of the protagonist's character and inaugurates a fresh perception of the work, only perceives one subjective voice in the text. "*The Autobiography* is not so much a panoramic novel presenting race

from the perspective enriched by the duality of voices confirms the coexistence of both trends in the text: sociological reality *and* psychological investigation. This bivocality implies, then, a revision and subversion of traditional slave narratives by means of an innovative narrator. Endowed with an ambiguous nature, he must deal with external and internal conflicts which give way to a profound questioning of a definition of identity based on problematic issues such as race, class, and strictly personal considerations. Obviously, understanding this complex narrator is no easy task, and many have labeled him an "alienated modern hero" (Berzon 151). So I would like to contend with other critics that the narrator chosen by Johnson confers modernity to the novel, prompting later writers to regard *The Autobiography* as a very contemporary novel.[19]

The second feature that singles out Johnson's text is the narrator's control over the narrative. As mentioned above, the choice to keep silent over certain circumstances is an example of such control, but it is not the only one. In fact, one of the distinctive traits of *The Autobiography* is the careful selection of events that the narrator chooses to relate devoting ample narrative space to the first years of his life as an African American and a very brief final chapter to his "passing." He justifies that decision in the following terms: "I have now reached that part of my narrative where I must be brief and touch only on important facts; therefore the reader must make up his mind to pardon skips and jumps and meager details" (140). Here Johnson echoes Douglass and the shallow narration about his escape, insisting on his absolute command over the events described. Moreover, the incomplete narration of his life as a white man, thereby assigning less importance to that period of his existence, pursues yet another objective: the narrator wishes to stigmatize it as "a mess of pottage" compared to the "birthright" that would be rightfully his if he continued to be African American. Johnson, therefore, employs this rhetorical strategy to transform his text into a direct critique of passing but maintains, at the same time, a perfect equilibrium as a narrator. These considerations render inappropriate Fleming's perception of Johnson's narrator as limited because he is unable to actually comprehend what his words clearly reveal, or Brooks' conclusion that the modernist narrator in Johnson is "unable to achieve any modernist closure"

---

relations throughout America as it is a deeply ironic character study of a marginal man who narrates the story of his own life without fully realizing the significance of what he tells his readers" (83).

[19] To cite an instance, Andrews insists on the fact that one of the most attractive traits of the novel lies in the idea that it "invokes . . . the human drama of modernity in late nineteenth—and early twentieth-century America" ("Introduction" xix).

(21). Although it is true that the narrator does not achieve any kind of resolution at the end of the novel, this lack is rhetorically planned in advance. Johnson intentionally revives the slave narrative tradition, in order to prove the impossibility of closure for the phenomenon of passing.

Yet another dimension needs to be incorporated to the study of the three works: the fictionalization of the "I" of the narrator and the use of rhetoric as a mask to disguise the true motivation behind the text. The process of fictionalization of the narrative "I" is very often associated in slave narratives with the devices of authentication as explained above. For slave narrators to "tell the truth" and construct their "true" selves, they need to have recourse to other rhetorical tropes. As Richard Yarborough cautions, "Ironically, in their attempts to tell their true stories in autobiographical form, black authors frequently utilized strategies drawn from fiction—especially the sentimental romance—to appeal more effectively to the emotions of the readers" (112). The irony evidently resides in the imperious need to use fiction as a means to persuade the white readership of the veracity of their accounts. Yarborough here cites one of the main fictional influences on these works—the sentimental romance or novel—to which two others should be added: the adventure novel and the picaresque tradition.

The influence of the sentimental novel, so popular at the time,[20] is quite apparent in both texts, especially as to the emotional appeal to an overwhelmingly white audience. In Equiano's case, this strategy is a constitutive ingredient of the narrative right from its dedication, in which the author issues a call for Christian piety: "[T]he chief design . . . is to excite in your august assemblies a sense of compassion for the miseries which the Slave Trade has entailed on my unfortunate countrymen" (3). To attain his purpose, Equiano reiterates the tragic component over and over again throughout the narrative recounting episodes in which suffering and pain achieve maximum degree, as in the separation from his family: "I cried and grieved continually; and for several days I did not eat any thing but what they forced into my mouth" (26; sic), or the cruel and inhuman treatment to which the slaves were submitted on the ship that took them to slavery: "the shrieks of the women, and the groans of the dying, rendered it a scene of horror almost inconceivable" (35). Equiano does not let one occasion slip by without clearly expressing the cruelty of the white people toward the slaves or the enormous

---

[20] I will provide a more detailed description of sentimental novels as well as an analysis of its impact on African American literature in chapter four.

differences between the life of slaves and that of his readers, male or female, as in this telling passage: "O, you happy free women, contrast *your* New Year's day with that of the poor bond-woman!" (350; author's emphasis). In this way, Equiano tries to impose his perception of the brutality and agony inherent in slavery to promote abolition.

The same kind of appeal to sentimentality shapes the structure of Douglass' text. Gates draws a complete picture of the more recurrent features in stemming from the sentimental convention traceablen in Douglass' narrative: "[f]lorid asides, stilted rhetoric, severe piety, melodramatic conversation, destruction of the family unit, violation of womanhood, abuse of innocence, punishment of assertion, and the rags-to-riches story" (*Figures* 82). Some of these listed items are exemplified in the dramatic description that Douglass offers of the conditions under which he is forced to live as a "field hand," for him the lowest and most degraded point of his experiences as a slave: "I was broken in body, soul and spirit . . . The dark night of slavery closed in upon me; and behold a man transformed into a brute!" (293). Douglass' statement is quite significant, as it entails a profound inversion of the racist assumption about the animality characteristic of African Americans: it is only under the evil effects of slavery that the African slave is turned into a beast. Many other instances could be recalled here, but it is important to note that all these recourses to emotional scenes seek to attract the attention and empathy of the white readers and inspire them to join in the abolitionist cause.

In addition to the sentimental tradition, both narratives use other sources to seduce the reader and to promote their abolitionist goals, namely the adventure novel and the picaresque mode. The two authors deploy these two traditions, revising their conventions and adapting them to the exigencies of the abolitionist code, above all concerning the model of the ideal protagonist. The tradition of the adventure novel is consciously employed by the narrators to present a heroic vision of the protagonist, while the picaresque tradition stresses the character's marginal and parodic subtext.

Equiano inverts the role of the protagonist as a conventional hero by explicitly rejecting it: "I own I offer here the history of neither a saint, a hero, nor a tyrant" (11). Despite his blunt denial, his self-portrait is sprinkled with heroic overtones on many occasions throughout the narration. For instance, there is an episode in which everybody is about to drown due to the captain's neglect, and many lives are finally saved thanks to Equiano's efforts: "[T]here were only four people that would work with me at the oars . . . But had we not worked in this manner, I really believe the people could not have been saved" (111). The resistance to suffering and misery that the narrator constantly exhibits as a slave, and later as a free man, also enhances a heroic vision of the protagonist. The fact that he insists over and over again on his antiheroic behavior is forced by the narrator's need to undercut the natural drive to heroism derived from the adventure novel. As a slave, he must humble himself in front of his white audience to further his abolitionist intentions. The inversion of the conventional model of the adventure novel emerges, then, as another way of authenticating his narrative for the benefit of white readers.

The same dichotomy between the acceptance and rejection of the protagonist as a hero is verified in Douglass' case. On the one hand, the narrative itself is patterned as a heroic narration in which the character takes the initiative to escape and gain freedom. Douglass' words articulate his intention to survive his degraded status as a slave: "You have seen how a man was made a slave; you shall see how a slave was made a man" (129). Douglass is here echoing the heroic code typical of the adventure novel, whereby the protagonist is transformed into a hero when he is able to overcome all the obstacles in his way to achieve maturity, both as a hero and as a man. Moreover, the focus of attention on the slave's sense of masculinity directly opposes the racist ideology which emasculates African American men by featuring them as children.[21] According to McDowell, this focus explains the reason why Douglass "is so pivotal, so mythological a figure" ("In the First Place" 40): he appropriates the dominant cultural norms of masculinity, thus refuting the prohibition of racist society.

Furthermore, both narratives also make use of the picaresque tradition[22] as a source of inspiration, another means for an abolitionist end. In his study of Douglass' narrative Gates mentions this tradition and its main characteristics, among which the marginal position of "outsider" of both—the picaro and the slave—is worth analyzing. Both of them understand their liminal status in a very

---

[21] The rendering of the slave as a child and the master as his/her father is a typical trait of the slave system. Pieterse dates those images back to the middle of the nineteenth century mainly encouraged by missionary and colonialist propaganda, in which portraits of African children abound (71, 88-9). These images are even more charged for Douglass due to the fact that he is actually his own master's son, so he must liberate himself from a double burden to be considered an adult.

[22] Coming from Spanish sixteenth-century literature, the earliest instance of the English picaresque novel is *The Unfortunate Traveller* by Thomas Nashe (1594), although its influence can be felt up to the present century with works such as *The Adventures of Augie March* by Saul Bellow (1953). I have already commented on the intimate relation that links the picaro to the African American figure of the trickster in chapter one.

specific way: "Both the picaro and the slave, as outsiders, comment on, if not parody, collective social institutions" (*Figures* 82). Their situation closely recalls the traditional figure of the African American trickster who also parodies society. Both Douglass' and Equiano's narrators act as instruments to comment on and criticize the racial and social order imposed by the ideology of slavery. In the end, behind the appearance of an account of the slave's experiences which captures his white readership's utmost attention, both authors launch an attack on the dominant system that perpetuates slavery and the hypocritical attitude that allows for its continuation. The narration itself becomes a mask in order to question the dominant value system and to attempt its total subversion.

A patent example of the kind of critique devised by both authors is the episode in which Equiano directly addresses a Christian society which tolerates the practice of raping African American women: "it was almost a constant practice with our clerks, and other whites, to commit violent depredations on the chastity of the female slaves . . . I have known our mates commit these acts most shamefully, to the disgrace not of christians only, but of men" (74). The message cannot be more self-evident: a system that consents such atrocities cannot be sustained by a Christian membership. Likewise, Douglass denounces the way in which the slave system metamorphoses a man into a beast (as pointed out above). He demonstrates with a long series of examples that this brutality is not isolated and that the degrading effects of the system affect everyone equally, men and women, slaves and masters, as the illustrative example of Mrs. Auld shows: "Slavery proved as injurious to her as it did to me. When I went there, she was a pious, warm, and tender-hearted woman . . . Slavery soon proved its ability to divest her of these heavenly qualities" (277). The hideous transformation of his mistress is another reflection of the power of the slave system to manipulate and destroy human beings, reducing them to a subhuman condition.

Therefore, the employment of strategies belonging to these three traditions of fiction—sentimental, adventure, and picaresque—serves to achieve two basic objectives: to create a common discursive universe with the white readership through dialogue and identification which would encourage them to accept the narrated events as truthful and, in consequence, to formulate parameters for questioning and criticizing the slave system in order to invert the dominant cultural paradigm. The subversive intention hiding behind the apparent complicity of slave narrators with their white audiences is an important part of the legacy that the autobiographical tradition would transmit to Johnson's work. Indeed, it can be asserted that *The Autobiography* is not diametrically opposed to this tradition, but on the contrary, takes many components from it, especially the construction and fictionalization of the narrative "I."

While Douglass and Equiano's narratives take advantage of rhetorical recourses stemming from other literary traditions such as the sentimental romance, the adventure novel or the picaresque tale, Johnson also exploits those same sources thanks to his indebtedness to the autobiographical tradition. The fact that Johnson makes his narrative "pass" as an autobiography turns it into a model of the "deconstructive acts," which, according to Andrews, "prepare the discursive ground once again for a new assay on the basis of which a usable truth could be constructed" ("Representation" 89). Johnson then has recourse to the autobiographical heritage of slave narratives and, through them, to the three previously mentioned traditions in order to take advantage of the rich potential that fictionalization can yield. the position of slave narratives between fiction and reality points the way to the possibility of Johnson's anonymous narrator "writing" himself into the text. In addition to the autobiographical tradition, the narrator also exploits another tradition to complete his task: the influence of Duboisian double consciousness through Du Bois' main work, *The Souls of Black Folk*.

<hr />

THE AUTOBIOGRAPHY: REVISION OF THE DUBOISIAN CODE OF DOUBLE CONSCIOUSNESS AND BICULTURALISM

By means of the conscious reworking of Du Bois' key concepts of double consciousness and the "talented tenth" within a parodic paradigm, Johnson questions and deconstructs notions of race and identity, while conversely exploring the social component of the work. The result of this process of deconstruction forms the basis for the legacy that *The Autobiography* lends to future writers: a new conception of the novel of passing, which constitutes a profound reflection on previous works of the African American literary tradition.

The influence of Duboisian thought is evident throughout *The Autobiography*. In the introduction Andrews names Du Bois, together with Alexander Crummel, as the theorists whose ideas marked Johnson's literary and intellectual development most profoundly (xviii). Especially noticeable is the influence of Du Bois' fundamental work *The Souls of Black Folk*, as Johnson himself declares: "I was deeply moved and influenced by the book" (*Along the Way* 203). The critic Houston Baker describes the relation between both works quite accurately: "*The Autobiography of an Ex-Colored Man* is a fictional rendering of *The Souls of Black Folk*" (*Singers* 22), adding that, "informing both *The Autobiography of an Ex-Colored Man* and *Invisible Man* are the cultured stance and carefully delineated 'double consciousness' found in W. E. B. Du Bois's *The Souls of Black Folk*" (30). Hence, there is an unquestionable nexus between both texts, especially thanks to the idea of double consciousness which functions as an essential guideline for their structure. Stepto also notices this dependence: "That Johnson is struggling with the example of *The Souls* while composing *The Autobiography* is . . . manifest almost to the point of embarrassment" (99), and he cites a passage of the preface of Johnson's book, of which an extract should suffice: "[I]t is as though a veil had been drawn aside: the reader is given a view of the inner life of the Negro in America, is initiated into the freemasonry, as it were, of the race" (xxxiv). The passage echoes the metaphor of the veil so dear to Duboisian cosmology (*Souls* 3) and unquestionably demonstrates Johnson's indebtedness to Du Bois.[23]

Johnson himself emphasizes the affinity between the two texts right from the beginning of the novel, making his preface practically coincide with the image of the veil which symbolizes the idea of double consciousness postulated by Du Bois. Johnson places this almost literal coincidence intentionally at the outset of the narrative in order to call attention to the existence of that relationship. But what is really interesting is the fact that their similarity implies once more a dimension of revision which is inherent in the practice of parody. That is to say, although Johnson seemingly repeats some of the concepts already present in Du Bois' work, his imitation is always accompanied with variations, as in a jazz composition. The archetypical example is located in the oft-quoted description of the idea of double conciousness itself that Johnson elaborates upon:

> And this is the dwarfing, warping, distorting influence which operates
> upon each and every colored man in the United States. He is forced to
> take his outlook on all things, not from the viewpoint of a citizen, or a

---

[23] A perceptive discussion of the similarities between both works is Kenneth Warren's "Troubled Black Humanity in *The Souls of Black Folk* and *The Autobiography of an Ex-Colored Man*" (1995).

man, or even a human being, but from the viewpoint of a colored man. It is wonderful to me that the race has progressed so broadly as it has, since most of its thought and all of its activity must run through the narrow neck of this one funnel. (14)

Although there exist clear allusions to the Duboisian text, the subtle but significant divergences from it indicate the presence of a revisionist intention on Johnson's part.

One of the most noticeable differences is related to the dichotomy that the author establishes between the categories "man, or even a human being" and "colored man," where the latter category is defined by opposition as the negative side of the pair. While Du Bois makes use of a twofold metaphor in his desire to integrate the white and black identities in a conciliatory union or "third self," Johnson is posing the question of double consciousness as a clash wherein only one identity is possible with the total exclusion of the other. The contrast between the categories aforementioned makes clear that, because of social pressure, only one identity can prevail in the end, as the resolution of the novel shows. Consequently, the protagonist will change racial identity throughout the work alternating between the two possibilities, only to end up permanently assuming the white one. Johnson regards the idea of double consciousness in the same individual as impracticable, considering the rigid social categorization. Thus he deconstructs the traditional vision of the mulatto as a tragic being divided between two warring identities by propounding a third category which is as inclusive as it is impossible.

Moreover, the effect that belonging to the second category creates is connected in the passage with a highly negative "dwarfing, warping, distorting influence." The harmful effect of double consciousness is even more stressed when interpreted as the negation of humanity, as Maurice O'Sullivan's words document: "Johnson found such doubleness fundamentally destructive and belittling, even to the point where he makes his narrator belittle his own destruction" (61). Indeed, one plausible interpretation of the text describes the development of the narrator's life as a failed attempt to lead an existence in accordance with the parameters of double consciousness, as if Johnson had wanted to give shape to a living embodiment of the third self in the figure of the protagonist.

Another crucial idea in the excerpt above is precisely the kind of approach adopted throughout the narration that can be defined as a combination between objectivity and subjectivity, a result of the bivocality pervasive in the work as explained above. Contrary to the narrator of *Souls,* who always acknowledges his racial allegiance, the narrator chosen by Johnson distances himself from the African American community: "Sometimes it seems to me that I have never really been a Negro, that I have been only a privileged spectator of their inner lives" (153). The way in which he positions himself further increases the sense of aloofness which dominates his dispassionate commentary about the progress of the race despite the adverse circumstances dictated by racist hegemony. From this moment onwards he maintains a neutral and distant point of view toward the members of his race.

The life of the novel's protagonist, therefore, can be said to incarnate the critique of double consciousness by means of a continuous process of racial mutation, passing from a white to an African American identity on many different occasions. This series of mutations or alternating personalities precisely manifests the impossibility of integrating both identities in one body, and hence, the impracticability of the Duboisian third self. Johnson utilizes the parodic paradigm to consciously subvert the basic guidelines of double consciousness, specifically the positive representation of race, the inversion of the racist canon, and the participation in a bicultural society. In this way, Johnson achieves his purpose of destabilizing the concepts of race and African American identity as well as its white counterpart.

*   *   *

A Positive Image and the Inversion of the Racist Canon

With reference to the claim for a positive image and the subsequent challenge to the racist canon, Johnson chooses a rather awkward way in which to deal with the subject: he employs a utopian tone to render the vision of both races illusory and dreamlike.[24] The irony works both in the description of the white identity as well as in that of the African American. The idealization of the white way of life and idea of beauty inverts the pattern proposed by Du Bois in the same way in which the sublimation of the prototype of the African American way of life subverts the white racist ideal. The dialectic opposition that the text stages between

---

[24] A utopian tone can be attributed to Johnson's indebtedness to the sentimental novel that many critics have noticed (Fleming, "Irony" 87; Ross 202; Brooks 26-7). I have accounted for it previously as part of the autobiographical legacy, but now I analyze the parodic component of Johnson's appropriation in depth.

idealization and frustration is a clear illustration of the scathing critique that Johnson directs at both communities and the rigid stratification and separation between them.

The utopian element is prominent in the narrator's description of his childhood as some kind of nebulous or blurred world: "I dwelt in a world of imagination, of dreams, and air castles . . ." (32). The presence of the imaginary universe invented by the protagonist in the first period of his life is essential to the later development of the novel. Indeed, a great part of the narration is imbued with an atmosphere of dream fantasy, especially in its relation to the theme of his racial belonging. The narrator's depiction of his childhood is therefore idealized as the happiest time of his life, clearly identifying it with belonging to the white race. A white identity is equated to a life-style which he himself terms as the "aristocratic" ideal: "My mother dressed me neatly, and I developed that pride that well-dressed boys generally have. She was careful about my associates, and I was myself quite particular. As I look back now I can see that I was a perfect aristocrat" (4). The tone that dominates this period is intensely paradisiac, insisting over and over again on the idealization of that part of his existence—"My mother and I lived together in a little cottage which seemed to me to be fitted up almost luxuriously" (4), disclosing an early inclination toward an existence of luxury and comfort.

Throughout the novel this ideal is heightened through the nostalgia the character feels for its loss, especially in his first days in the South: "When I thought of the clean, tidy, comfortable surroundings in which I had been reared, a wave of homesickness swept over me that made me feel faint" (39). Here the comfortable life of his first years as white is presented as the archetype to which the narrator always aspires, and which is in obvious contradiction with his actual position as an African American. As the novel progresses, the rest of his experiences in his mature years tend to accentuate this nostalgia evident in the relationship the narrator establishes with the white millionaire, who seems to personify the aristocratic type *par excellence*, "I saw that I was in the midst of elegance and luxury in a degree such as I had never seen . . . the subdued tone, the delicately sensuous harmony of my surroundings, drew from me a deep sigh of relief and comfort" (85). The luxurious life of his patron leads the narrator to worship him openly: "[t]his sort of life appealed to me as ideal" (95).

Moreover, leisure and affluence are deemed a necessity at a crucial point of the book, when the narrator decides to "pass" for white on the train, justifying his action in the following words: "a certain amount of comfort and luxury had become a necessity to me whenever it was obtainable" (115). This need for material benefits becomes one of the main incentives for the protagonist to fix his racial identity as white. The "money fever" he catches on his arrival to New York is directed toward guaranteeing a carefree life: "[I]t required a good deal of money to live in New York as I wished to live and . . . I should have to find, very soon, some more or less profitable employment" (141). His desire assumes the shape of a lucrative job together with very profitable financial investments that ensure him the opulent life-style he has yearned for all his life.

But the parodic inversion of the Duboisian code can be elicited not only in the idealization of the white standard of living, but also in Johnson's investment in the preeminence of white standards of beauty. The protagonist himself is depicted as its embodiment:

> I was accustomed to hear remarks about my beauty; but now, for the first time, I became conscious of it and recognized it. I noticed the ivory whiteness of my skin . . . I noticed the softness and glossiness of my dark hair that fell in waves over my temples, making my forehead appear whiter than it really was. (11-12)

In the paragraph the narrator underlines the whiteness of his skin as evidence of his inclusion in the canon of racial purity. In contrast to this ideal, his mother stands for the other side of the coin, because the narrator finds in her "defects," which are simply features inherent in his mother's black race: "I could see that her skin was almost brown, that her hair was not so soft as mine" (12). The sudden awareness of the palpable differences between his mother's and his complexion make him realize his condition as mulatto, which he perceives immediately as irrevocably thrusting him into the black race, one of "the tragedies of life" (13). For the child narrator, then, the exclusion from the white ideal of beauty acquires tragic connotations that haunt him for the rest of the narration.[25]

In spite of the discovery of his true racial origin, the white ideal endures, evidenced by several later episodes of the novel. The first one takes place in adolescence, when the narrator falls in love for the first time with a white girl, for him the symbol of that white canon: "the escaping strands of her dark hair wildly framing her pale face . . ." (20), her whiteness interpreted as a sign of her great

---

[25] Sheeshy analyzes this mirror scene in detail applying the theories of Lacan and Gates (401-6).

beauty. Something strikingly similar happens in his sister's description: "she was so young, so fair, so ethereal" (98), in which whiteness predominates above all things and is automatically ascribed a certain degree of spirituality and fragility that complements ideal beauty. But the clearest example of the association beauty/whiteness is noticed in the portrait of his wife, where whiteness is sublimated:

> She was as *white* as a lily, and she was dressed in *white*. Indeed, she seemed to me the most dazzlingly *white* thing I had ever seen. But it was not her *delicate beauty* which attracted me most; it was her voice, a voice which made one wonder how tones of such passionate color could come from so *fragile* a body. (144; my emphasis)

Once more paleness and fragility are equated in a conception of feminine beauty as inherently white, meaning that only those who conform to the model can be considered beautiful. Moreover, as only those women who look fragile are regarded as beautiful, the narrator clearly subscribes to prevalent notions of femininity as well.

Despite the reiterative idealization of the white world and the internalization of the dominant canon of ideal beauty, the narrator's attitude is quite unstable through the different racial changes that succeed one another in the novel. It becomes especially poignant in the closing remarks, where the narrator sees himself as "an ordinarily successful white man who has made a little money" (154). The character seems to give vent to his frustration and disappointment because his dream of white aristrocracy never comes true. He even comes to discredit it as "a mess of pottage" (154) when compared to the ideal of African American identity he had rejected from the beginning. At this point the direct allusion to the biblical story of Esau is quite revealing because it establishes a marked opposition between "whiteness/pottage/materialism" and "blackness/birthright/spirituality" (Brooks 44). In this final opposition the materialistic vision upheld by the white way of life loses ground with respect to the African American, which is depicted as a serious alternative.

This unexpected twist has been nevertheless suggested by another undercurrent that pervades the text, consisting of the idealization of the African American identity. The sense of idealization can be perceived in certain key episodes in the narration and reaches its climax in the last statement in the novel in which African American identity is described as the narrator's "birthright." Contrary to what happens to the white identity, which becomes a source of greater disillusion as the novel unfolds, the African American counterpart progressively acquires more relevance. However, the idealized image of the black race that Johnson proposes is radically foreign to Du Bois' formulation, as there are two crucial differences: on the one hand, African American identity is conceived as possible only at a utopian level, that is, dissociated from reality; on the other, it is unable to integrate both identities—black and white—in an indissoluble whole. As in the case of the white aristocratic ideal, the narrator envisions African American identity as fanciful. There is an obvious tendency toward an imaginary archetype personified by the great leaders of the race he encounters in books while still a child and in which he blindly believes. On his quest for a model to follow, two figures are particularly symbolic: "Uncle Tom" and Frederick Douglass.

Concerning the former, the child narrator comments: "I was never an admirer of Uncle Tom nor of his type of goodness . . . however that may be, it opened my eyes as to who and what I was and what my country considered me; in fact, it gave me my bearing" (29). The statement undoubtedly discloses the unreality the narrator is living in, since he needs a literary character, a fictitious pattern, in order to understand the meaning of his new identity and its social status. This recourse to a piece of fiction corroborates the distance that the narrator feels with respect to the newly-found African American world, which increases even more the parodic overtones of the fragment. The character of Stowe's book constitutes a more valuable source of information with regard to his new social position than any history book which provides him, as he literally says, "very little information" (28). Kathleen Pfeiffer accounts for this apparent contradiction as follows: "[t]he history of being black in America is a history of slavery and . . . fiction is better able to provide him with a sense of political, social and civic identity than 'non-fictional' history texts" (416-7). Hence slavery is highlighted as a crucial interpretative clue to decipher his social bearing, and fiction is granted a very relevant role in the process of forging an identity.

But the influence of fiction is recurrent throughout the whole text. There is a particular instance worth noticing, because the passing from a white to an African American identity is effected through a substitution of heroes:[26] "My heroes had

---

[26] The importance the narrator grants to the vision of African Americans as heroes, in his early childhood as well as later on when he talks about the leaders of the race, derives from the

been King David, then Robert the Bruce; now Frederick Douglass was enshrined in the place of honor" (32). Douglass thus incarnates all the positive values to which the character aspires in his new life. Moved by the enthusiasm that his brand-new discovery awakens in him, the narrator listens to a speech by his classmate "Shiny," who becomes the model to follow as the African American counterpart of the white millionaire. His speech provokes a hitherto unheard-of reaction in him: "I felt leap within me pride that I was colored," which leads him once more to a state of reverie in which he begins to "form wild dreams of bringing glory and honor to the Negro race" (32). Thus, his first contact with the African American community is also marked by a utopian illusion, completely unaware of the harsh reality he has to face later in life.

He often associates a sense of heroism and pomposity with his African American identity, especially with his intention of becoming "a great colored man" (32). Particularly unequivocal is his desire to go back to the South after his stay in Europe, when he discovers the possibility of transforming "ragtime" into classical music: "From that moment my mind was made up. I clearly saw the way of carrying out the ambition I had formed when a boy" (104). Again there is a direct link between the idea of glory—musical in this case—with a more or less clear identification with the black race. But the statement is also ironic, since the way to reach that glory as an African American is through the conversion of a purely African American model, "ragtime," into the universally acknowledged white, classical music.

The doubts the narrator expresses regarding his real motivation to take up his African American identity once more are in consonance with his uncertain cultural project: "Was it more a desire to help those I considered my people, or more a desire to distinguish myself, which was leading me back to the United States? That is a question I have never definitely answered" (107). This passage is one of the rare instances in which the narrator unmasks in all its crudity that subversive component which is faintly perceptible in his views of his African Americanness, whereby insincere philanthropic motives to help the race are randomly intermingled with selfish reasons instigated by his personal ambitions. Despite his doubts, the idealization seems to gain ground and is ever-present in the reflections that close the novel. In the last sentences the narrator refers again to the leaders of the race

---

appropriation of certain features coming from the adventure novel, namely the heroic interpretation of the protagonist as mentioned above.

portraying them as examples: "Beside them I feel small and selfish . . . They are men who are making history and a race. I, too, might have taken part in a work so glorious" (154). Comparing his materialistic and anodyne life as white to the historical mission the African American leaders are undertaking, the narrator reproaches himself for not being part of such a task. It is clear that he cannot conceive of his African American identity without direct reference to the glorious enterprise of the leading class, that is, without belonging to the highest intellectual class devoted to the uplifting of the African American community.

The insistence on the idealization of service to the race as the only possible way to embrace an African American identity reiterates the subversive element inherent in the narrator's process of idealization, as condensed by Ross' words: "[O]nly on a romantic, story-book level does he really feel Negro" (204). In a certain way, it seems that the narrator stresses this idealization in order to protect himself from a reality that strikingly differs from the glorious mission of safeguarding the interests of the black race, or even, to mitigate the sense of inferiority he feels at being categorized as a member of a race he himself has repeatedly despised in the narration.[27] The sense of contempt he experiences appears first in the description the character offers of the African American children at school, which unmistakably demonstrates his distance and his feelings of superiority with respect to them all, including "Shiny." Although the narrator admits that the latter was recognized as "the best speller, the best reader, the best penman—in a word, the best scholar, in the class" (9), his inferior position as regards whites is also clearly specified: "[I]n spite of his standing as a scholar, he was in some way looked down upon" (9), implying that he also adopted that attitude. The narrator overtly identifies with the position of his white partners when he takes part in a fight against African American children and recounts the event to his mother, using the offensive word "nigger."

---

[27] Many critics have judged the narrator's rejection of the black race as undeniable proof of his feeling of "self-hatred" and have thus obviated the parodic nuances of the work. For instance, Fleming remarks: "Black self-hatred is another important theme employed by Johnson. Constantly told that he is a member of an inferior race, the black man may come to believe or fear that he really is inferior" ("Contemporary Themes" 122). In general, these critics revert to what Pfeiffer denominates a "racially correct" way of reading the text (403), which tends to identify with a definition of the black race as the authentic one and the white race as the wicked side of the binomial: Valerie Smith, "Johnson" (46); Collier (372), Kostelanetz (23), and Japtok (43). Particularly illuminating to understand the fate that had befallen Johnson as writer and critic is Richard Carroll's "Black Racial Spirit: An Analysis of James Weldon Johnson's Critical Perspective" (1971).

His repudiation becomes more palpable with the discovery of his mixed heritage. He openly states his refusal to replace his privileged racial status by that of the other African American children, explaining that "I had a strong aversion to being classed with them" (15), an aversion that drives him to a state of solitude he welcomes. His unwillingness to come into contact with other African Americans increases when he travels South and describes his impressions: "[T]he umkempt appearance, the shambling slouching gait and loud talk and laughter of these people aroused in me a feeling of almost repulsion" (40). At this point there seems to be no vestige left of the idealized image that has been formulated so far.[28] His hostility toward the black race culminates in the lynching episode:

> [I]t was not discouragement or fear or search for a larger field of action and opportunity that was driving me out of the Negro race. I knew it was shame, unbearable shame. Shame at being identified with a people that could with impunity be treated worse than animals. (139)

What is really distressing in the above paragraph is the fact that the narrator does not blame or recriminate the white race for performing such atrocities, but quite the opposite; he attributes the cause of the crime to the African American victim. The feeling of shame exhibited by the character at such a crucial moment greatly contributes to tarnishing the African American ideal promoted by Du Bois. The character clearly refuses to internalize the inferior status that the racist society assigns to the black race, and feels compelled to adopt a white identity in order to flee an abhorred fate.

Johnson, therefore, uses the device of dreamlike fantasy to reach several goals: first, challenging the idealization of the white race he subverts the dominant racial paradigm; second, using the same strategy with regard to the black race, he also subverts and destabilizes the racial representation supported by the Duboisian code; and third, using the same kind of idealization to deal with both identities on equal terms facilitates the deconstruction of the differences between them and the

---

[28] This passage in particular has been traditionally interpreted as another instance of Johnson's betrayal of the African American community and his own self-hatred. A more current view invokes a quite different effect towards the dehumanization of the victim: "the narrative's curious turn to a dehumanization of the victim rather than the perpetrators is part of an overall strategy by which we are led to judge both the narrator's and the nation's moral deficiencies" (Warren 274). Although fundamentally agreeing with Warren's idea, I will later argue that the narrator's reaction is, in fact, a symptom of his adherence to a definite social class rather than anything else.

impossibility of clearly separating them. In the end, Johnson signals the arbitrariness of all these categories and of their definitions. Starting with the Duboisian representation of African American identity, Johnson not only questions such representation, but also the very myth of neatly distinct and unrelated races, and ultimately the notion of race itself.

The character, then, poses his identity as a choice between two seemingly divergent models: the aristocratic pretension of the typical white upper-middle class, or the commitment and personal sacrifice of African American intellectuals and leaders. As Valerie Smith observes, the narrator feels divided between "the need to choose between raceless personal comfort and race-conscious service" ("Johnson" 223). Note, however, that Smith's statement can lead to misunderstanding, as the adjective "raceless" should read "white." To equate "racelessness" to "whiteness" is the result of a racist practice which pretends that whites do not constitute a race.[29] But what really stands out in Smith's statement is the fact that the protagonist feels obliged to commit himself to one of these possible options. The protagonist's predicament uncovers the strenuous social pressure to which he has been submitted throughout the novel and to which he finally succumbs. In order to maintain its hegemonic power, the dominant ideology strives to minimize the possibility of contact—either at a physical, social or cultural level—between their races. This hegemonic position is what Brooks terms the narrator's "tragedy": "the tragedy is that society has chosen arbitrary categorizations, constructed a meta-narrative of race that cannot be applied adequately to personal narratives of its individual members" (23). Therefore, the possibility of some space for a third category or third self is completely abrogated by the socially established canons.

*   *   *

---

[29] Werner Sollors in *Beyond Ethnicity* (1986) studies the fallacy that resides in a consideration of the concept of race or ethnicity as inherent in the "other" with respect to the dominant paradigm (24-5, 36-8). For an illustrative discussion of terminology, see chapter one in Bonnie TuSmith's *All My Relatives* (1993).

Biculturalism or an Uncertain Cultural Project

With reference to the notion of biculturalism that Du Bois proclaims as the basis for the coexistence of the two identities, Johnson also deconstructs it by means of the presentation of an ambiguous and incomplete cultural project that rarely contemplates the combination of both—black and white—cultures. This project develops along the same lines employed above to deal with the process of racial mutation, in an attempt to adapt cultural patterns to the racial identity of the moment and viceversa. Again, as verified before, parody is the dominant key that marks this third objective.

Turning once more to his childhood, a substratum of ironic connotations is also perceptible in certain allusions to the utter lack of knowledge of the character concerning any trace of his African American heritage. One good illustration appears in the "bottles" episode: "I became curious to know whether or not the bottles grew as the flowers did, and I proceeded to dig them up to find out; the investigation brought me a terrific spanking, which indelibly fixed the incident in my mind" (2). Stepto has astutely interpreted this episode as an "African survival in the New World" (100).[30] Thus, the protagonist's desire to remove the bottles attests to his total ignorance of any African American tradition. Indeed, the only thing he later recollects from the episode is the punishment that his action prompted, not the reason for his mother's anger.

A similar occurrence takes place in relation to music, which is an important subtheme of the novel. The type of music is relevant, as his mother sang "old Southern songs" (5) and played them on the piano. The songs obviously belonged to the rich African American folklore which originated in slaves' songs, but the character does not even hint at this possibility. He narrates the scene with the sole intention of giving evidence of the happiness he felt when sharing those musical moments with his mother: "Those evenings on which she opened the little piano were the happiest hours of my childhood" (5). Again he demonstrates his lack of awareness of his African American legacy through a casually expressed sentence which resonates with irony: "I remember that I had a particular fondness for the black keys" (5). The passage reflects an unconscious desire on the character's part

---

[30] Many African American contemporary artists known as "visionary artists" make use of this element in their works such as William Edmonson, Leslie Payne, etc., An interesting introduction to these artists' universe can be found in *What It Is: Black American Folk Art* by Regenia Perry (1982).

to identify with the African American side through his musical talent. Indeed, this talent unknowingly becomes the most suitable means of approaching that heritage.

The narrator's talent is also his main incentive for travelling from Europe to the South. As stated above, the narrator's ambivalence toward undertaking the trip is finally resolved when he recognizes that his decision is based "on purely selfish grounds": "I argued that music offered me a better future than anything else I had any knowledge of, and . . . that I should have greater chances of attracting attention as a colored composer than as a white one" (107-8). In this passage the character acknowledges that music is for him a way of life, a "mine" (Japtok 40), to which he often resorts in the narration, as, for example, during his stay in New York. There he becomes "the best ragtime-player," an employment that provides him "a rather fair livelihood" together with "a friend who was the means by which I escaped from this lower world" (84). The protagonist instrumentalizes his musical abilities right from the beginning in order to have access to an agreeable, comfortable way of life not only in New York, but also in Europe. The innovative feature of his return South is the fact that he regards his identity as an African American composer to be a real advantage to him.

Despite his willingness to be identified as a black composer, the character profits from his musical talent on multiple occasions without considering it part of his African American legacy. Early on in his adolescence, he establishes this notion quite clearly when he forms a duet with the white girl he is in love with: "It makes me laugh to think how successful I was in concealing it all; within a short time after our duet all of the friends of my dear one were referring to me as her 'little sweetheart,' or her 'little beau,' as she laughingly encouraged it" (21). Although the character connects the word "conceal" to the secrecy of his loving feelings for the girl, it can also suggest the possibility that the author was "passing" for white. That possibility is further stressed by the intimacy that exists between them. But this is not the only instance of the protagonist's use of his musical talent within a "white" context. Again in his relationship to the millionaire and, especially during his sojourn in Europe, the character deploys it to "pass" for white. The millionaire himself tellingly confirms his tendency to "pass": "[y]ou are by blood, by appearance, by education and by tastes a white man" (105). In addition, he also says that the character should devote himself to music as a white man, since "music is a universal art; anybody's music belongs to everybody; you can't limit it to race or country" (105). The millionaire's opinion practically coincides with the narrator's at that point as far as a "universalist" vision of music is concerned.

However, problems emerge when he tries to transform African American "ragtime" into "universal" or classical music, which the dominant ideology appropriates as its own. His project outlines a cultural "passing," very similar to his racial "passing."[31]

Even during his period in New York, in which his identification with the black race is quite evident, the protagonist becomes famous using a method that can be considered a type of reversed cultural passing: "It was I who first made ragtime transcriptions of familiar classic selections" (84). These examples demonstrate the ambiguity of assigning cultural models to certain racial categories and, hence, represent the irony implicit in such classifications. Despite the allusions to some sort of biculturalism that should be the implied product of the novel's cultural project, the character instead deconstructs that paradigm in the end, when his decision to definitely "pass" into the white race includes his abandonment of his musical ambition in favor of "white" materialism:

> It would be useless to try to establish myself as a teacher of music . . . since I was not going to be a Negro, I would avail myself of every possible opportunity to make a white man's success; and that, if it can be summed up in any one word, means "money." (141)

Therefore, though only at the end of the work, a distinct dichotomy is established between two ways of life which are diametrically opposed: on the one hand, the African American option, with its emphasis on the service to the race through culture and, on the other, the white one, whose value system is determined by capitalist gain. The deconstruction of the bicultural pattern proposed by Du Bois leads Johnson, once more, to an ample questioning of the cultural parameters of both races, and the forced separation between them. For the narrator of *The Autobiography* it is not easy to neatly ascribe a cultural model to a specific identity. The fact that in the end he must choose one of the two possible alternatives proves the existence of racial and social pressure towards homogenization in opposition to any idea of a biculturalism which could threaten the established order.[32]

---

[31] Several critics have indicated an attitude of cultural "passing" in the relationship between the character and music: Japtok (39-40, 42-43), Gayle (94), Stepto (119), and Sundquist, *To Wake* (12-13).

[32] Aldon Nielsen comments specifically on this aspect stating that "[i]n America it appears one must choose aesthetic legacies appropriate to one's race" (181). Sollors agrees when he says, "He sacrifices to the bipolar world of race the artistic vitality that could come from interracial sources" (*Neither White* 269).

Ultimately, the character himself is revealed as the central source of the subversive subtext in the novel, wavering between two worlds and identifying with one or the other according to his personal advantage. The ambiguity that characterizes him has encouraged an interpretation of the protagonist's nature as that of a "white-oriented Negro" (Collier 367), but the opposite label of "Negro-oriented white" could also apply. Actually, the narrator seems to be present in the two worlds without belonging to either of them, thanks to his special skills for passive observation and advantageous "racial mutation." This ability was highlighted in the alternative title that Johnson's brother had advised for the novel *The Chameleon* (*Along the Way* 238), which Johnson rejected in favor of the more impressive but misleading *Ex-Colored Man*. The lack of accuracy in the latter lies mainly in the fact that the protagonist is not simply a black man who ceases to be black, but a person who suffers from different transmutations throughout the novel, passing from white to black on many occasions. In consequence, the metaphor which most accurately portrays him is that of the iceberg the character encounters on his journey to Europe:

> The sun was shining full upon it, and it glistened like a mammoth diamond, cut with a million facets. As we passed, it constantly changed its shape; at each different angle of vision it assumed new and astonishing forms of beauty. (93)

The multiple forms of the iceberg symbolize much more adequately the phenomena manifested by the continuous racial and cultural transformation of the protagonist during his life, a metamorphosis that considerably expands the limits of double consciousness to convert it into multiple and heterogenous.

*   *   *

The Social Coordinate: A Revision of the Concept of the "Talented Tenth"

The sense of diversity underlying the novel can be better addressed on a social than on a racial plane, as it is the result of an unmistakable attitude of the social class to which the character belongs, and not merely a racial consideration. So far the protagonist seems to accept one race or the other on the condition that his social status remains immutable. That is, white aristocrat or African American leader are up to one point interchangeable as they are both ascribed to a high social condition. This fact introduces the parodic treatment that Johnson reserves for the other key idea in the Duboisian code: the significant role played by the so-called "talented tenth" in the uplifting of the African American community. The importance of the inclusion of a social perspective in the novel is stressed by several critics, who remark that the novel perpetuates the typical "tale of class" of the nineteenth-century literary production.[33] Collier defines the protagonist as "extremely class-conscious" (368) while Faulkner qualifies him as "an insufferable snob" (150). Other critics catalogue *The Autobiography* as elitist, because it advocates the concept of class instead of that of race as "the valid yardstick for any caste system" (Ross 207). However, this criticism deliberately ignores the parodic component present in the description of the social medium of the novel, which serves to question both the notion of class itself and its implications, and inaugurates a reelaboration of the Duboisian concept of "talented tenth."

The process of reformulation of this concept is mainly effected through references to the differentiation among the social classes that abound in the text. The best example is probably the classification of the African American community in the three groups already mentioned (153), in which the protagonist frankly identifies with the third or high class. Another illustration is provided by the protagonist during his Jacksonville period, when he states, "I became acquainted with the best class of colored people in Jacksonville. This was really my entrance into the race. It was my initiation into what I have termed the freemasonry of the race" (54). These words demonstrate that the significance of the black race for the narrator is concentrated on "the best class," an exclusive social position that is distinguished by its distance with respect to the rest of African Americans. In this vein the protagonist devotes a great deal of time of his sojourn South to outlining the way of life of the African American upper-middle class, their ideals and activities. This social group finds its spokesman in the figure of the doctor, who protests against the custom of taking the most degraded part of the African American community as reference and representative of the whole, when the best

---

[33] Basically the term corresponds to a series of novels written between the end of the Civil War and the beginning of the twentieth century, whose main objective is the eradication of racist attitudes by means of the depiction of issues of color and social class. The protagonists of these novels are usually members of the middle class who suffer from racial prejudice and discrimination. Among the best known representatives of this trend are Frances E. W. Harper, Paul L. Dunbar, and especially, Charles Chesnutt. So the "tale of class" can be understood as a direct antecedent to the production of the Harlem Renaissance.

exponents should bear such an important responsibility: "We are the race, and the race ought to be judged by us, not by them" (114). Moreover, the character also shows his dissatisfaction, even his despisal toward that lower social class echoing feelings already voiced by the narrator himself: "'You see those lazy, loafing, good-for-nothing darkies; they're not worth digging graves for; yet they are the ones who create impressions of the race for the casual observer'" (114), in which the social distance is quite obvious.

However, in justice to the social perspective of the novel, the narrator also finds positive features in this lower class when he notices, "I have since learned that this ability to laugh heartily is, in part, the salvation of the American Negro" (40). He reproduces almost literally the opinion articulated by Johnson himself in *Along the Way*: "We of the vanguard often look with despair at these very characteristics of the masses . . . but I believe it involves an underestimation. It takes no account of the technique for survival that the masses have evolved through the experience of generations" (120), overcoming the adverse circumstances of slavery and racism.[34] Thus, the portrait is not altogether negative, although a certain paternalistic tone may be perceived on the author's part as representative of the upper class. Johnson translates the social problem to the literary terrain by propounding that the perpetuation of the literary concept of the "darky" "constitutes an obstacle in the way of the thoughtful and progressive elements of the race" (122).[35]

The problematic nature of the social attitude taken by the narrator is heavily influenced by the Duboisian ideology of the "talented tenth" which Johnson shares. Within the general framework of double consciousness, it is precisely the educated class who are painfully aware of their conflicted character because they are capable of reflecting on the injustice of their position. Riddled with the contradictions that their complex situation generates in their everyday lives, they feel the moral duty to take up the burden of the totality of the race on their shoulders in order to put an

---

[34] In this case, the protagonist is echoing Johnson's ideas about the ambivalent relationship with the masses that the writers of the so-called "Old Guard" uphold. Although Du Bois warns that the "talented tenth" obviously "depends upon the relations that develop between these masses and the cultural aims of the higher classes" (*Dusk of Dawn* 189), he and the other "Old Guard" intellectuals are unable to fill in the great gap between both classes.

[35] The figure of the "darky" was popularized by the so-called "plantation school" to foster the idea of the happy, carefree slave, also identified as the comic type of minstrel shows. According to Bell, this school included a group of white writers before the Civil War, such as William Caruthers, Caroline Ingraham, George Tucker, and John Kennedy. Their novels depicted an idyllic vision of the life on slave plantations, a vision that was also part of the Southern myth intensified after the conflict in the racist prose written by Joel Harris, Nelson Page, and Thomas Dixon (*Afro-American Novel* 33).

end to the racist practices that render their social integration difficult. From all this derives the protagonist's constant desire to become "a great colored man" to show the white world the real possibilities of the black race through the achievements of its best members. What is interesting from this social perspective, and where the parodic factor lies, is the fact that the significance of the progress of the race is synonymous with becoming like the white race in all possible senses. Perhaps the most controversial aspect is what the narrator terms "the peculiar inconsistency of a color question" (113) that has to do with the phenomenon known as "intra-caste prejudice" or intraracial prejudice within the African American community itself.[36] Indeed, the strict social differentiation that is verified between the upper stratum and the masses of the race is not only the product of the process of education and acculturation to which the "talented tenth" is deeply committed. It also springs from a preference toward a lighter skin color, less negatively marked by white ideology.

The protagonist testifies to this social pressure as follows: "So far as racial differences go, the United States puts a greater premium on color, or, better, lack of color, than upon anything else in the world" (113). Moreover, the narrator promotes the concept of Eurocentric beauty and its internalization on many occasions throughout the book. One of the outstanding examples of his internalization takes place during his visit to Atlanta University, when he undertakes the description of some African American students: "I could not help noticing that many of the girls, particularly those of the delicate brown shades, with black eyes and wavy dark hair were decidedly pretty" (44). Their beauty is measured according to the degree of proximity to the white ideal. The parodic component inherent in his affirmation seems to be registered even by the narrator himself, who acknowledges it as a generalized phenomenon within the African American community, whose effect is "a tendency towards lighter complexions, especially among the more active elements in the race" (113). Thus, the character justifies his own attitude from an alleged African American viewpoint, adopting the perspective of the upper class to which he belongs.

---

[36] Intraracial prejudice has been subject of analysis and controversy for many critics and writers. During the Harlem Renaissance the work that tackled the issue and its devastating effects head-on was *The Blacker The Berry* by Wallace Thurman (1929). As Therman O'Daniel contends in his introduction to the 1970 edition, the publication of the book "embarrassed many Negroes, at that time, and made them resent the novel in which such details were so openly displayed" (x). Their reaction confirms that the intraracial problem was still considered taboo at the time. The fact that Johnson approaches the theme earlier, in 1912, makes him a pioneer writer. In contemporary literature, the topic is again a matter of debate in *The Bluest Eye* by Toni Morrison (1970).

The tendency towards lighter complexions signals, more than any other characteristic of the "talented tenth," the problematic position occupied by the black upper class: while their ultimate objective is the breakdown of all barriers to do away with the distinctions at a racial level and, hence, to foster the complete integration of the African American community in American society; those same barriers exert such an influence on the configuration of their thoughts that they end up accepting them unconditionally and reproducing the same intolerant attitudes toward the members of their own race. Although the narrator tries to excuse their behavior as "the question of earning a livelihood" (113), that is to say, for merely material reasons, its existence is a source of frequent intraracial friction. Conversely, it creates in the upper class a state of continuous frustration resulting in an erroneous admiration precisely for the race that manipulates them. This is the main pretext the character offers for one of the most criticized opinions in the novel: his favorable view of certain racist attitudes which even awaken admiration in him.[37] An illustration is found in his encounter with the Texan on the train who acts as a mouthpiece for racist ideology: "I was sick at heart. Yet I must confess that underneath it all I felt a certain sort of admiration for the man who could not be swayed from what he held as his principles" (120). The passage continues the line to which the narrator resorts every time he is faced with a particularly racist situation: for him the white side seems to be always right, an acceptance that foregrounds the subversion of values even more.

The same kind of response is elicited when the character takes up the issue of lower-class African Americans: "I could not but appreciate the logic of the position held by those Southern leaders who have been bold enough to proclaim against the education of the Negro. They are consistent in their public speech with Southern sentiment and desires" (124). The statement is clearly controversial, as it seems to deny the right to education to a great part of the African American population, one of the most sacred and inalienable rights for any human being, and to argue in favor of the consistency of racist arguments intended to maintain these people in complete ignorance. The person who is able to voice such opinions can be called racist, but what seems to be at stake here is the ambiguous position of the members of the "talented tenth," caught in the middle, unable to decide which side

---

[37] Many critics pronounce the narrator's attitude as the supreme example of the character's above mentioned self-hatred. To cite an example, Skerrett rates him as "a psychological sellout" because "he expresses admiration for traits of the oppressor(s) which are directly related to their mastery and his subjugation" (555).

they should take, between the defense of the values of the African American community and the attraction to the dominant system that nevertheless discriminates against them.

Finally, in relation to the black race in general, most of the opinions proclaimed by the narrator are in consonance with the ideology of the "talented tenth" brought to its extreme consequences. It unveils to what extent the protagonist has internalized white ideology, which has taught him to see himself as inferior for not complying with all the requirements of the dominant race. This sense of inferiority leads him to abandon his African American identity, as in the climatic scene of the lynching he excuses the criminal action perpetrated by the whites. At that precise moment Johnson reflects on the results, logical up to a certain point, of the upper class' ambiguous position unmasking their subversive content. Thus, Johnson inverts the established canons of the so-called "tale of class," exposing the most sinister side of the relationship between class and power, thereby deconstructing the racial myths on which the dominant system is grounded. The identification between the protagonist and the white world is the last link in the racist chain, as it leads educated and bourgeois blacks to distance themselves from the rest of the black race, and, then, to negate the existence of racial differentiation in favor of homogenization at a social level. The most direct consequence is the narrator's decision to "pass" for white, whereby he escapes into the alleged anonymity of the white race.

The act of passing at the end of the book cannot, therefore, be judged as authentic, since the only difference between this and the previous states lies in the character's willingness to make it permanent: "I finally made up my mind that I would neither disclaim the black race nor claim the white race; but that I would change my name, raise a mustache, and let the world take me for what it would" (139). As mentioned before, the ambiguity that surrounds his decision to pass seems to suggest the desire to transcend racial divides, though he is well aware that the social and racial milieu in which he lives will define it in one direction or the other.[38] Immediately after he adds: "[i]t was not necessary for me to go about with a

---

[38] Judith Berzon agrees with this idea when she observes:

> He is not being honest with himself . . . the hard lesson that he had learned in school and during the intervening years, where he had lived as a black man, was surely that he *would* be categorized as either black or white. And since he does not look like a Negro, according to the conception of most whites, he must know that he will be treated as a white man . . . so the Ex-Colored Man would seem to be lying to himself and to us. (156; author's emphasis)

label of inferiority pasted across my forehead" (139), reiterating the sense of inferiority ascribed to the black race commented at the beginning of the chapter. The refusal on the character's part to be considered inferior once more ratifies the impossibility of maintaining a double consciousness as well as of confronting a society in which he is going to be necessarily categorized under one of the two main racial headings.

Consequently, statements like that of Richard Kostelanetz—"The novel's theme is the many ambiguities of passing—moral, political, emotional" (20)—lose significance when set side by side with the intentional deconstruction of the categories of race, identity, and class detected in the text. The novel not only poses the consequences of passing, nor even those of the multiple "passings"—genetic, social, cultural, and even generic—that pervade the narration; it also attempts the investigation and deep analysis of the relations that are established between the two races by means of a liminal figure, who tries to belong to both at the same time but must finally choose one.

In fact, the parodic purpose of the novel focuses precisely on the fact that, starting from the previous autobiographical and Duboisian tradition, it creates a sort of kaleidoscope with different levels of racial and social significance that destabilizes the rigid white/black dichotomy but does not solve it. In this way, Johnson's work revises and updates that tradition, while simultaneously inaugurating an ironic and multivocal vision of the racial myths that it intends to deconstruct. The destabilizing effect initiated by Johnson's parodic reading is located at the core of the novels of passing of the nineteen-twenties. As they focus on a subversive process of definition for the notions of race and identity, these novels search for a valid resolution of the representation of the multiplicity inherent to a new conception of these two terms. In sum, the project of deconstruction initiated by Johnson in *The Autobiography* bears fruit in subsequent novels, thanks to the reelaboration of these two key concepts, both essential for the literary discourse of the Harlem Renaissance.

THREE

Black No More *or Chaos on the Other Side*

> Because I am the white man's son—his own,
> Bearing his bastard birth-mark on my face,
> I will dispute his title to the throne,
> Forever fighting him for my rightful place.
> There is a searing hate within my soul,
> A hate that only kin can feel for kin,
> A hate that makes me vigorous and whole,
> And spurs me on increasingly to win.
> Because I am my cruel father's child,
> My love of justice stirs me to hate,
> A warring Ishmaelite, unreconciled,
> When falls the hour I shall not hesitate
> Into my father's heart to plunge the knife
> To gain the utmost freedom that is life.

Claude McKay
"Mulatto"

Perhaps the most controversial figure within the African American cultural and literary framework of the twenties, George Schuyler seems to embody a radical antagonism toward the values upheld in Du Bois' work through his systematic questioning of the categories of race and African American community. Rejecting both categories, Schuyler manages more than anyone else to destabilize the validity of the parameters that sustain a racist ideology and, consequently, to deconstruct the racial myths that it generates. To this end, his novel *Black No More* (1931) takes as its premise the progressive disappearance of the African American community and the consequences that this disappearance would provoke in American society at all levels: economic, social, political, and racial.

In order to analyze the elimination of African Americans as a group and its aftermath, Schuyler resorts, as did Johnson before him, to a multilayered cover. This disguise is tripartite in nature, as it combines two literary traditions which were practically non-existent in the African American canon up to then—satire and science fiction—together with a parody of the sub-genre to which the novel belongs, the passing novel. While the introduction of satiric and science fiction elements is itself a significant innovation in African American letters, its analysis also throws light on the parody of the novel of passing, *raison d'être* of Schuyler's novel. As we shall see, Schuyler intentionally subverts the parameters of the passing tradition, stressing his intention of turning *Black No More* into the epitaph of the passing motif, a function similar to that of *Don Quixote* with respect to tales of chivalry.

Thanks to the conscious subversion of the three traditions cited above, Schuyler is able to unmask the internal mechanisms, usually occult, of the racial code imposed by the dominant white majority and accepted, even internalized, by the victimized African American minority. Therefore, the novel has a twofold target: on the one hand, to expose the racist convictions of the white community and, on the other, to criticize the hypocrisy of the African American community which tends to favor an assimilationist attitude due to an internalization of the prevailing racial order. This double target derides each of the subtle but treacherous methods employed by both communities to maintain the social *status quo*, denying the possibility of a sense of African American identity that could liberate itself from the constrictions imposed by such a regime.

THE CRITICAL RECEPTION

For most critics the double target that Schuyler intentionally foregrounds has served to discredit the legitimacy of his novel and to justify the defamatory campaign launched against him. Their focus has been especially on the direct mockery of the hypocritical attitudes of African Americans which Schuyler brilliantly portrays in his writing. Critics have equated this caricature to an intentional rejection on Schuyler's part of his own community. The most representative spokesman for this critical trend, Robert Bone, inaugurates it, affirming that *Black No More* is "a classic study in assimilationism" (91). Following his lead, Charles Larson in his introduction to the 1971 edition of the novel designates it as "a plea for assimilation, for mediocrity, for reduplication, for faith in the American dream" (12). This kind of criticism became so widely accepted that it determined the complete omission of both the novel and Schuyler himself as an influential writer of the period in many critical treatises until very recently, as Michael Peplow confirms in 1974: "[i]t is curious that, in this era of renewed interest in the Harlem Renaissance, George Schuyler's *Black No More* is virtually ignored" ("George Schuyler" 242). What is equally remarkable about the last statement is the fact that it can be easily applied to the nineties, a time when critical attention to the Harlem Renaissance was flourishing.[1] Hence the derogatory vision of the author has dominated, compromising the critical reception of the novel as mere assimilationist propaganda and overlooking its subversive intention.[2]

There are other reasons which have hindered a different interpretation of Schuyler's objectives, but they could be condensed into two main points: external factors frequently associated with Schuyler's political and ideological evolution, and internal elements that characterize the novel itself, namely its satiric and science fiction components. The external factors that ground the traditional accusations of assimilationism are related directly or indirectly to the impact of Schuyler's political and ideological views. His peculiar political evolution—from fervent defender of Communism in the twenties to conservative militant in the forties, passing through a phase of militant anti-Communism in the decade of the thirties—gave way to predictable attitudes of rejection and critique within the African American intellectual community.[3] According to Rayson, the principal problem lies in the fact that Schuyler is a forerunner of his own generation since he

---

[1] The increasing interest in this period can be seen in the growing number of publications on this topic. However, most of these monographs avoid Schuyler; to name a few *A Spy in the Enemy's Country* by Donald Petesch (1989), *The Harlem Renaissance: Revaluations* edited by Amritjit Singh (1989), or even *Black American Prose Writers of the Harlem Renaissance* edited by Harold Bloom in 1994. It is also noticeable that other works do mention him, but only in passing, and generally in association with the controversy stirred by *Nigger Heaven* (Kramer 204; Wintz, "Black Writers" 99). Among recent contributions Sollors' *Neither White Nor Black Yet Both* registers the critical void: "to my knowledge, Schuyler's novel has not received much critical attention" (note 96, 437).

[2] For instance, Arthur Davis (*Dark Tower* 104-6) and Bell (*Afro-American Novel* 142-4) refer to this type of criticism, which accentuates the assimilationist message as the pillar for the organization of the novel.

[3] Ann Rayson outlines Schuyler's evolution in the article "George Schuyler: Paradox among 'Assimilationist Writers'" (1978). Likewise, Peplow advocates a concept of evolution in his monograph. Nevertheless, other critics like Arthur P. Davis believe that Schuyler always maintained the same assimilationist and conservative position from the beginning of his career stating that "whatever else he has been, George Schuyler has been consistent, and he has defended his position stoutly in hundreds of newspaper columns, editorials and volumes" (*Dark Tower* 104). In view of the fact that Schuyler only adopts a conservative stance from the thirties onwards, it is clear that such opinions do not hold. Moreover, even more contemporary critics like Kuenz argue

"anticipates the general black rejection of the Communist Party in the 1940s and '50s" (106). In this sense, Schuyler seems to be out of step with the rest of the intellectuals of his age.[4]

Furthermore, the author's difficult personality has to be added to the general sentiment of rejection, since he raised tensions by addressing his criticism explicitly against the African American leaders of the period on multiple occasions, as for example in a 1932 *Pittsburgh Courier* editorial where he accounts for his attitude:

> I am tired of the cant, ignorance, blindness and lack of humor of most of the radicals, especially the extreme radicals. I am tired of a diet of slogans and catch-phrases that mean nothing. I am tired of these so-called radicals' assumption of omniscience. Indeed, I have about come to the conclusion that most of them are not radicals at all, but are maladjusted sentimentalists. It is not surprising that they have been able to corral a whole lot of Negroes, including many of our so-called intelligentsia. (qtd. in Rayson 105)

Through his harsh criticism of radicalism evident in the passage, Schuyler is obviously alluding to the Communist leaders of his time from whom he distanced himself from the thirties on. Rayson justifies this type of statement as part of the author's desire to create controversy in the African American community, concluding that "Schuyler was less interested in consistency of position than he was in stirring up argument" (105). Rayson bases her defense on Tolson's words, which in 1933 depicted Schuyler as a controversial author: "He stimulated more differences of opinion than any other Negro writer" (qtd. in Rayson 105). Tolson's affirmation could function as a sort of summary of Schuyler's critical intent. A last, somewhat trivial detail aggravated Schuyler's situation: he married a white woman, regarded as "an indication of conflict" by some African American psychologists

---

that "critical attention has often responded solely to the conservative crank rather than the complicated and contradictory social satirist" (172).

[4] Indeed, Schuyler seems to uphold a contradictory position especially in the thirties, a period of great political and social commitment for most African American intellectuals, generally united to their belonging or congeniality with the Communist Party, with Richard Wright as their main representative. To illuminate the links between African American intellectual thought and Communist ideology in the thirties, see Anderson 281-3; Davis, *Dark Tower* 147-57; Bell, *Afro-American Novel* 150-67. Even some of the most prominent figures of the Harlem Renaissance like Langston Hughes or Claude McKay also committed themselves to the Communist Party around that period (Wintz, *Black Culture* 193-200, 204-5; Lewis, *When Harlem* 282-307).

also cited in the article (105). What stands out is that, throughout the years, all his attitudes and declarations favored the widespread belief in the controversial nature of both his political career and his work. In sum, Schuyler could be defined as a writer who held at times ambivalent positions with respect to his racial and cultural allegiances, but who always suggested different possibilities for debate and discussion, a characteristic of all his literary production, including *Black No More.*

But apart from these external factors which clearly influenced the critical reception of the novel, there are elements within the text itself that provoked a general disapproval after its publication. In short, the critical rejection of the novel was due to a misunderstanding of its main purpose, arising from its resistance to generic categorization. As a result, its important subversive substratum remained unexplored and the lack of appropriate parameters brought about an assimilationist interpretation. However, recent reassessments have deciphered the real nature of *Black No More,* essentially by investigating the rich subversive character of Schuyler's double critique. As with Johnson's text, the use of a tripartite cover—satire, science fiction, and passing—prompted an ambiguous reading that failed to reveal the rich subversive substratum of the work. It is therefore essential to analyze the contribution of each of these traditions to the novel's racial and social critique and to the far-reaching effects of Schuyler's interrogation of the biracial system in *Black No More.*

SATIRE OR THE TRUE PURPOSE OF *BLACK NO MORE*

Taking satire as the initial reference for the analysis, it is clear that the employment of a satiric model, practically unknown in African American letters in novelistic form up to then,[5] decisively influenced the reception of the work by its contemporary readers. As a matter of fact, the lack of clues for a correct reading of these satiric ingredients fostered the rejection of the novel from its outset. W. E. B. Du Bois had already detected this problematic aspect of the novel as early as 1931:

---

[5] Locke acknowledges the novel as pioneer in this tradition ignored up to that moment: "[o]ne of the great new veins of Negro fiction has been opened by this book—may its tribe increase!" (qtd. in Lewis, *When Harlem* 252). I cannot devote the sufficient space or time here to the controversy over satire as a genre, but a very illuminating discussion on the topic can be found in Leon

"The book is extremely significant in Negro American literature, and it will be—indeed has been—abundantly misunderstood [because] a writer of satire is always misunderstood by the simple" ("Black No More" 522). That is to say, Du Bois points out the equivocal character inherent in satire as one of the main reasons for which the novel has been an object of discrimination, thus underlining the transcendence of the satiric component as a key to understanding the true objective of the work. Moreover, the problematic nature of satire itself and the misconceptions that it has engendered for the decoding of the novel are reiterated by Peplow in 1974, when he argues that "*Black No More* has been misunderstood, perhaps, because its critics have not been familiar with the purpose of satire and with the rhetorical devices employed by the satirist" (*Schuyler* 242), clearly hinting at the need to revise the critical instruments employed up to then for its exegesis.

Although from the beginning the root of the conflict was located in the novel's satire, its analysis was not directly addressed until recently.[6] Reconsidering each of the most relevant satiric elements in the novel dispels some of the controversy about it, while it also unveils the racial conception on which Schuyler bases his work and the deconstruction of racial myths that *Black No More* implies, especially concerning two controversial issues: the concepts of race and African American community. In the end, Schuyler advocates the total abolition of racial differences on the thesis that "color has no reality apart from the socially created one" (Reilly 107). For Schuyler racial prejudice is merely a social construction, independent of any actual distinguishing feature between races. As a result, he takes up the issue of miscegenation as irrevocable proof to refute racism, because it ranks both races—white and black—equally, and outwardly expresses the intimate relation that unites them.

To begin the analysis of the satiric component, a useful starting point is Northrop Frye's classic definition of satire: "[S]atire is militant irony: its moral norms are relatively clear, and it assumes standards against which the grotesque and the absurd are measured" (*Anatomy of Criticism* 223). Probing into each of these—militant irony, clear moral norms, and the absurd/grotesque—allows the

---

Guilhamet's *Satire and the Transformation of Genre* (1987), whose introduction provides a useful distinction between modal and generic satires.

[6] The only critics who treat satire as a main motive in Schuyler's production are John Reilly in "The Black Anti-Utopia" (1978), Ann Rayson in the article already mentioned and Michael Peplow in his article "George Schuyler, Satirist: Rhetorical Devices in *Black No More*" (1974) and in his later monograph *George Schuyler* published in 1980. More recently, see Kuenz's "American Racial Discourse, 1900-1930: Schuyler's *Black No More*" (1997).

identification of the satiric pattern of the novel, along with the subversive and parodic function implicit in its satiric practice. The elucidation of the satiric pattern also accounts for the motives that have led to a contorted interpretation of the racial message contained in the novel.

*   *   *

Black No More and Schuyler's Satiric Articles

Schuyler's irony is articulated by means of the direct relationship between the novel and the satiric articles that the author wrote throughout the years, especially those issued in the nineteen-twenties. Indeed, most of them seem to be connected in some way with the genesis of the novel,[7] but two could be regarded as its direct antecedents: "Our White Folks" and "Our Greatest Gift to America," both published in 1927. In them Schuyler makes reference to the themes that he later tackles in the novel: the attack on both white and black communities, the denunciation of the absurd biracial system, the praise of the black race, and the import of the African American presence in American society.

In the first article, "Our White Folks," Schuyler makes use of the same critical paradigm that he avails himself of in *Black No More,* ranging from the attack on the racist attitudes of the white community to the censure of the assimilationist tendency in contemporary African American leaders. His principal purpose is to denounce the absurd biracial system that allows physical features to become the defining factor for the classification of human beings in different categories. This parameter of classification is not valid for the so-called "intelligent Aframerican" who claims that "to judge an individual solely on the basis of his skin color and hair texture is so obviously nonsensical that he cannot help classing the bulk of Nordics with the inmates of an insane asylum" (388). The passage is revealing for two main reasons: on the one hand, it anticipates the attitude of superiority with respect to the white population that Max Disher, the protagonist of *Black No More,* upholds as an embodiment of the intelligent African American. On the other, it precludes the vision of American society as a sort of lunatic asylum in which the obsession with color reaches extreme proportions, leading obsessive

---

[7] For a detailed analysis of these articles, I recommend Peplow's monograph, especially chapters two and three.

whites to the most illogical and ridiculous reactions.

Moreover, the article also envisions one of the central topics in the novel, intimately linked to such color mania: miscegenation. The patent reality of miscegenation emphasizes the incoherence implied in the division into two separate races even more, as Schuyler systematically asserts: "Indeed, an examination of family trees will reveal that a large number of the whites and blacks are really related, especially in the land of cotton, where most of the hue and cry is raised about Anglosaxon purity" (388). The critique launched against the biracial system that these sentences comprise, and especially the reference to mixed family trees, is a clear premonition of the novel, acknowledged in the dedication that opens it:

> This book is dedicated to all Caucasians in the great republic who can trace their ancestry back ten generations and confidently assert that there are no Black leaves, twigs, or branches on their family trees.

Finally, in the article Schuyler's racial allegiance is shown in his defense and exaltation of the "Aframerican" as a counterpart to the stereotype of the white racist: "The fact is that in America conditions have made the average Negro more alert, more resourceful, more intelligent, and hence more interesting than the average Nordic" (391). The same kind of praise of African Americans is reiterated in the figure of Max Disher in the novel. Basically characterized by his artfulness and his intelligence, he is able to mock the racist system making use of its own strategies both to destabilize it and to obtain personal benefit. In addition, the praise of the black race in opposition to the white is highlighted on multiple occasions throughout the novel, as, for example, in the nostalgia that Disher himself feels for his previous African American existence—"despite his happiness Max found it pretty dull . . . he felt a momentary pang of mingled disgust, disillusionment and nostalgia" (40), and in the sentimentalism which marks the end of "the good old days" (147) and leads to the enormous success of many emotional songs dealing with the disappearance of the African American community.

Such a laudatory attitude can be also perceived in another peculiarity that both texts share, namely the constant allusion to African American beauty:[8] "[T]he

---

[8] In this sense, Schuyler shares with Johnson his preoccupation with the dominant canon of beauty and its relation to the construction of African American identity. However, Johnson seems to be more ambivalent, simultaneously exalting and condemning the existence of that dominant canon; whereas Schuyler is much more straightforward in his reproval of the harmful effect caused by the

Negroes possess within their group the most handsome people in the United States, with the greatest variety of color, hair and features. Here is the real melting pot, and a glorious sight it is to see" (392). For obvious reasons, in the novel such an eulogy cannot be manifested because of the thematic content of the work—African Americans that want to leave their race; in spite of this, the references to African American beauty and its variety are recurrent in the text, from the so-called "high yaller," the type of woman Disher prefers, to certain incidents that recall that beauty, culminating in the ending of the novel: "America was definitely, enthusiastically mulatto-minded" (222). This conclusion confirms then that mulatto, and not white, beauty reaches the level of dominant social model, gesturing toward Schuyler's attempt to replace the dominant canon with an alternative shaped by African Americans.

With regard to the second article, "Our Greatest Gift to America," the main similarity to the novel is related to a positive vision of the presence of African Americans in America at all levels, but most of all, psychological: "[O]ur presence in the Great Republic has been of incalculable psychological value to the masses of white citizens" (364). This psychological value is centered primarily on the concept of "flattery" that Schuyler pronounces as the best gift that African Americans can offer to the white majority, defining it as "inflation of the racial ego of the dominant group by our mere proximity, by our actions and by our aspirations" (362), that is, the majority of whites feel flattered by the noticeable attitude of admiration on the part of the repressed minority. Their reverence takes diverse shapes, but the most significant is the assimilationist tendency of the latter and their imitation of the former's behavior. The fact that the African American minority internalizes the dominant values is the most direct way of approving of the dominant value system and thus perpetuating it.[9]

This reasoning paves the way for two crucial ideas in the novel, the first being the significance of the presence of the African American minority for the well-being of the white majority. As the narrator observes when he comments on the situation in the Southern areas of the country: "[T]he blacks had really been of

---

internalization of this "ideal" and in his proposal of an alternative African American standard of beauty.

[9] In his study about interracial relationships in the United States entitled *They & We* (1964), Peter Rose substantiates the existence of this kind of interaction between the white dominant group, for whom "it is often surprising . . . to learn that all that they do is not thought worthy of emulation" (74); and the racial minorities that, in general, assume "the cultural patterns of the dominant racial groups" (58) even to the extent of internalizing "the dominant group's ranking system" (76).

economic, social and psychological value to the section" (132). This comment echoes the premise of the article. The second idea is a direct consequence of the previous one and has to do with the chaos that the absence of that minority creates, which is basically the hypothesis on which *Black No More* is based. Therefore, from the examination of the articles some of the fundamental satiric guidelines can be inferred: the denunciation of the absurd racial system through an African American character superior to the racist whites; the incoherence of this system due to the fact that it is grounded in fallacy; the so-called racial purity, which ignores the reality of miscegenation; and, last, the devastating effect of the obsession with racial purity on American society, which transforms it into a mental asylum where whites need an African American minority in order to reaffirm their self-esteem as a dominant group.

*   *   *

Satiric Elements in the Novel

The same ideas can be traced in the novel by means of a detailed analysis which elucidates Schuyler's militant irony through the recurrence of satiric elements. The first one, the absurd racial system, constitutes the target of the intentional attack that appears in the description offered by Max Disher. When Max becomes white, the illusions about his new life do not last long: "He was not finding life as a white man the rosy existence he had anticipated," and his critique appears immediately thereafter, "there was nothing left for him except the hard, materialistic, grasping, inbred society of the whites" (63). Max's opinion of the white world is thus very negative, since he foregrounds its relentless materialism and the manifold derivations that affect white society.[10] Of these racial prejudice is the worst: "the unreasoning and illogical color prejudice of most of the people with whom he was forced to associate infuriated him" (63); the enduring presence of racial prejudice dictates the lives of those whites that surround him. The harsh picture that Max paints of white society, then, is not the kind that would be

---

[10] Schuyler's image of the white world is similar to that devised by Johnson in the previous chapter, as both define this community with respect to its most characteristic trait, its overwhelming materialism.

expected from a supposedly assimilationist narrative because it does not idealize the white world in the least.[11]

In addition, the critique of the white world is perhaps more effective because it is *precisely* Max who undertakes it. That is, the fact that an African American who decides to pass for white condemns the same community he has chosen to belong to implies a sharper indictment of this community. It is worth noticing, however, that Max not only criticizes the white position, but makes use of different strategies to show off his superiority with respect to whites, embodying the figure of the "black picaro" *par excellence*.[12] Indeed, Max does not need long to grasp the "money-making possibilities" (63) involved in the racial situation of the country, and adopts a motto that is quite telling—"enjoy life and laugh at the white folks" (48)—following the prototypical desire of any black picaro. Once he realizes the various paths open for him to satisfy his material and personal ambitions, his actions pursue a premeditated trail and reveal a comprehensive understanding of the internal workings of racial prejudice. He exploits this to obtain a fortune ironically through his prominent position in the racist organization "The Knights of Nordica," a direct descendant of the Ku Klux Klan.

This organization is described by Max, now Matthew Disher, as consisting of "the lower stratum of working class people" (78). The speech that he addresses them testifies to the accuracy with which Max has analyzed the racist creed of his audience and to his understanding of the best way of manipulating them in order to achieve his purpose:

> For an hour or so Matthew told them at the top of his voice what they
> believed: i.e. that a white skin was a sure indication of the possession of
> superior intellectual and moral qualities; that all Negroes were inferior to
> them; that God has intended for the United States to be a white man's
> country and that with His help they could keep it so; that their sons and

---

[11] I agree with John Reilly when he states that the novel "does not provide an image of white society which would encourage those assimilationist goals" (108). In spite of recognizing this, Reilly insists on admitting the possibility that "Schuyler's novel may represent racial assimilation as an ideal" (108), a possibility that does not seem to account for the very disdainful way in which Schuyler depicts white society, never postulating it as a model to follow.

[12] According to Peplow, Max Disher symbolizes the perfect figure of the "picaro-trickster" following two different traditions: the European tradition of the picaro and the African version of the god Esu-Elegbara. Peplow exemplifies the African American variant of both traditions in the typical tales whose main protagonist is "Brer Rabbit," who always manages to outwit his opponents thanks to his wit and cleverness (*Schuyler* 67-8).

> brothers might inadvertently marry Negresses or, worse, their sisters and
> daughters might marry Negroes, if Black-No-More, Incorporated, was
> permitted to continue its dangerous activities. (78)

In the speech the three most common racial myths and fears prevalent in white
society are schematically delineated: the belief in the inferiority of the black race,
thereby upholding the superiority of the white race; the use of religion as an
instrument to support this belief; and, finally, miscegenation as a serious threat
because the company "Black No More, Incorporated" devotes itself to whiten
African Americans. The line of argumentation employed by Max secures the trust
of the organization and his acceptance in it. Once a member, he can use racial
prejudice as a weapon against the same community that generates it.

A practical example of the way in which Max operates is found in Paradise,
a small town in South Carolina, where the workers are exploited cruelly under very
grievous conditions. The ironic tone is noticed in the name itself, since Paradise
could be identified with anything *but* a paradise. When the workers begin to get
organized, Max arrives to spread the news that the leaders who want to go on strike
are really "whitened Negroes." The workers' reaction is immediate: "The erstwhile
class conscious workers became terror-stricken by the specter of black blood . . . it
was better to leave things as they were than to take a chance of being led by some
nigger" (127). With this subtle means, Max succeeds by making use of racial
prejudice for his own benefit and substituting the class struggle by the racial
struggle "that made the worker race conscious instead of class conscious" (110).
Thus Max calms the white working class who prefer exploitation at the hands of
white people rather than better living conditions led by supposed blacks, reiterating
once more the illogical nature of the racist order.

The case of Paradise is particularly significant because it conveys a specific
illustration of the way in which Max consciously manipulates the white racist code,
emphasizing his superiority over the white leaders who also benefit from it. It is
thus quite interesting to consider Max's own point of view with regard to the social
position he occupies, as he still defines himself as an African American despite his
success as a white man. When his friend Bunny—another whitened Negro—tells
him that he sometimes forgets who they really are, Max's answer is conclusive: "I
know I'm a darky and I'm always on the alert" (138). The fact that Max identifies
with his previous African American identity indicates the fact that Max is not
fooled by external appearances. Despite his unmistakable white complexion, Max

never abandons the double position he occupies as "a black trickster opposing the white man" (Peplow, *Schuyler* 70). For him this double status is very advantageous, since it allows him to judge white society from a privileged position of insider/outsider and grants him access to what he desires, especially money and power.

The protagonist's ambiguous position, a given in narratives of passing, illustrates the second characteristic that Frye enumerates as essential to any satire, the moral norms: "Of course the moral norm is inherent in satire: satire presents something as grotesque: the grotesque is by definition a deviant from a norm: the norm makes the satire satiric" (*Satire Newsletter* 9). Therefore the degree of deviation from the norm in a literary work is what denotes the greater or lesser presence of satiric content. This second feature also awakens controversy, since Frye asserts that it is the reader, and not the author, who is "responsible for 'putting in' the moral norm" (*Satire Newsletter* 9). The satiric interpretation is placed on the reader's shoulders, with the subsequent risk that it may not be accurate. In fact, the absence/presence of moral norms has raised a persistent debate among theorists of the satiric mode, as discussed by Peter Petro in his 1992 introduction.[13] Petro himself never solves the problem, insisting on the possibility of imagining that "a reader could dispute the positive value of this inherent, implicit norm" (20), again stressing the reader's active role.

Nevertheless, Booth questions such assumptions on the grounds of the "fantastic explosion of controversies about readings that has occurred in the last few decades" (qtd. in Petro 21). It is precisely within the framework of those controversies that the critical history of *Black No More* can be placed, as it has been rejected on the basis of its implicit moral norm. Dustin Griffin takes up the issue of moral norms in satire much later, in 1994, stating that "the notion that clear moral standards are at the center of satire is likewise open to challenge" (37), and that the satirist is better conceived as "playfully exploring a moral topic" (38) in "an open-ended inquiry" (41). I suscribe here to Griffin's view about the nature of satire, because *Black No More* responds to Elkin's definition as "valuable for the insights it gives into moral problems, not for providing solutions to them" (qtd. in Griffin 204, note 30). I wish to demonstrate here that the novel could be deciphered as an inflexible critique of both white and black communities for their acceptance of the

---

[13] Petro refers concretely to a symposium organized in 1964 by the magazine *Satire Newsletter* around the question: "Is reference to moral norms essential to satire?" The great variety of responses generated by the question attests to the lack of critical agreement on this point (18-20).

dominant racist philosophy, without making any distinction between them. Thus, Griffin's line of inquiry and provocation is more appropriate for the novel's challenge to received ideas about race.

Schuyler's critique is mainly manifested in the description that he offers of the white community, which is neither idyllic nor exemplary, as mentioned above. The materialistic and sordid picture that Max draws, especially regarding its absurd racist bias, reaches a climax in the sacrifices that white society is ready to undertake in order to maintain its complete hegemony. This despicable portrayal is completed with the idea of boredom, as Max repeatedly states: "He was forced to conclude that it was pretty dull and that he was bored" (63). Moreover, Max actually specifies the main causes that lead him to consider his life as a white man as tedious, lacking the freshness and sophistication of his previous black existence: "As a boy he had been taught to look up to white folks as just as a little less than gods; now he found them little different from the Negroes, except that they were uniformly less courteous and less interesting" (63). Max thus confesses his disillusion in finding out that whites are like blacks, or what is worse, sensibly less attractive.

This kind of statement cannot spring from an assimilationist attitude; quite the opposite, it bears witness to the subversive intention prevalent in the work. Such a critical viewpoint can be tracked in numerous episodes in which white society is characterized as radically ignorant and full of racial prejudice. A good example of such characterization is provided by the figure of Reverend Givens, the head of the "Knights of Nordica":[14] "[Givens] was a short, wizened, almost-bald, bull-voiced, ignorant ex-evangelist" (67). His scarce intellectual abilities are exposed when Schuyler recounts the way in which Givens feels compelled to look up the word "anthropology" in the dictionary and is unable to understand its definition: "He read over the definition of the word twice without understanding it, and then cutting off a large chew of tobacco from his plug, he leaned back in his swivel chair to rest after the unaccustomed mental exertion" (71). The irony implicit in this depiction of the leaders of racist organizations such as the Klan or the "Knights of Nordica" informs the harsh critique aimed at these racist associations and, by extension, at the whole white population. The irony is again emphasized by the detective Max

---

[14] Many critics identify this character as inspired in a figure of real life, William K. Simmons, a failed evangelist who revived the Ku Klux Klan in 1919 (Lewis, *When Harlem* 253). Other critics suggest a combination of Simmons and another leader of the Klan in the twenties named Edward Clark Young (Peplow, *Schuyler* 64).

visits to find out about Givens: "[T]hese damn, ignorant crackers will fall fer anything fer a while" (72). Ignorance is the same incentive used in the political campaign in which Max becomes involved, since he has many chances to verify the incompetence that characterizes white society. Max is very successful in this campaign because he avails himself of a principle that he explains to his friend Bunny: "How often must I tell you that the people never remember anything?" (146), highlighting once more his knowledge of white psychology.

The criticism becomes even more evident when Givens is invited to deliver a speech on the radio, rated as a "scholarly and inspiring address," and summarized as follows: "[H]e cleared his throat and talked for upwards of an hour during which time he successfully avoided saying anything that was true, the result being that thousands of telegrams and long distance telephone calls of congratulation came in to the studio" (149). Clearly falseness and ignorance occupy center stage. Even worse is the examination of the content of the speech:

> In his long address he discussed the foundations of the Republic, anthropology, psychology, miscegenation, coöperation with Christ, getting right with God, curbing Bolshevism, the bane of birth control, the menace of the Modernists, science versus religion, and many other subjects of which he was totally ignorant. (149; sic)

In this passage very diverse areas—anthropology, psychology, biology, religion, politics, and even literature—are called upon to sustain the racist code that Givens tries to inculcate in his listeners. The logical conclusion of such a confusing blend is that Givens demonstrates his complete lack of ethics by publicly discussing disciplines of which he has no knowledge at all. As a consequence, the racist ideology that Givens transmits is shown to lack any solid foundation and to be mere fanaticism resting on a pseudo-scientific creed.

In another episode two white leaders confront each other in the national elections. On the Republican side Goosie is reelected as candidate for President of the United States,[15] and for the Democrats, Givens is nominated. What Givens' nomination entails for the Democratic party is symbolized by his ambiguous political programme: "[A] platform was again adopted whose chief characteristic was vagueness. As was customary, it stressed the party's record in office, except

---

[15] Peplow ventures that this character could be Herbert Hoover (*Schuyler* 64)

that which was criminal; it denounced fanaticism without being specific" (164), such that the Democratic option is presented as very uncertain and imbued with notions of corruption and criminality. Goosie's intention is to put forward his programme as a radical alternative to the Democratic ideal: "As the Democratic slogan was White Supremacy and its platform dwelt largely on the necessity of genealogical investigation, the Republicans adopted the slogan: Personal Liberty and Ancestral Sanctity" (164). But his intention and the entire political system are compromised when the text insinuates that, in fact, there are no great differences between both candidates who even resort to "the same speech" (165).

Schuyler treats other white leaders similarly, as, for example, Arthur Snobbcraft, president of the "Anglosaxon Association,"[16] who is nominated as Givens' vice-president. His main obsession is the so-called "genealogical law" which consists of "sterilization of the unfit: meaning Negroes, aliens, Jews and other riff raff and an abiding hatred of democracy" (154). Or again, Dr. Samuel Buggerie who incarnates the paradigm of the scientific expert greatly respected by his colleagues and society in general.[17] Despite his popularity, everything he has published is completely absurd, markedly illustrated in the title of his most famous treaty: *The Fluctuation of the Sizes of Left Feet among the Assyrians during the Ninth Century before Christ*. This book "had been favourably commented upon by several reviewers, one of whom had actually read it" (155), emphasizing again the poverty of knowledge that defines the intellectual and political leaders of the white community. In this way, Schuyler's satire includes attacks on white intellectuals represented by the figure of Buggerie as the most ignorant among the ignorant.

The depiction that Schuyler furnishes of the white ruling class is quite estranged from any idealized vision of it. It is never proposed as a model as it lacks moral or ethical qualities. On the contrary, each of the characters that makes up this class is systematically dissected by Schuyler's satire with the firm intention of uncovering the absurd racist code that controls their every thought and action. Indeed, in their racist convictions the upper class is likened to the profile of the working class already sketched in the analysis, in which racial consciousness prevailed over their own self-interest. Their similitude is also emphasized in the novel in the description of the events that precede the elections, where both classes

---

[16] Also in this case Peplow speculates that a possible correlative for this character is John Powell, who belonged to the "Anglo-Saxon Clubs" of Virginia (*Schuyler* 64).

[17] In this case, too, critics suggest an actual correspondence: Frederick L. Hoffman, defined by Lewis as "a senior racist among early twentieth-century social scientists" (*When Harlem* 254).

are involved: "For the first time in American history it seemed that money was not going to decide an election" (175), since racial prejudice wins the battle even over the patent materialism in which white society is immersed.

Thus, the negative image presented by Schuyler the satirist distances itself from any assimilationist intent. Instead, it is conceived as an open attack against it, so the moral norm here should leave no room for doubt. Indeed, the problematic aspect of the text's moral norm is not actually located in the description of the white community, but in its African American counterpart. In other words, the real question lies in the representation of the latter community,[18] even though Schuyler clearly targets white society as his main objective by devoting more time and energy to its critique. Despite his efforts, his attack against his own community has provoked the accusations of assimilationism that pervade the critical reception of the novel. According to many critics, the fact that Schuyler treats both communities in the same way undermines the most sacred African American assumptions. What Schuyler tries to demonstrate with the deployment of a double target is that in the end there is an underlying similarity between both communities, a principle that constitutes his most polemic opinion: "The Aframerican is merely a lampblacked Anglo-Saxon" ("The Negro Art-Hokum" 662).[19] This affirmation acquires its full dimension in the project of deconstructing racist myths that the author undertakes in *Black No More*.

Max expresses the parallelism between both communities in a very significant quote that refers to his experience with women: "Since I've been white I've found out they're all the same, white or black" (174). This statement could be easily applied to the whole of society, since racial differences lose importance when both white and black people seem to function according to the same code or seem

---

[18] Reilly refers to the critique of the African American community asserting: "[B]lack characters are more easily identified with actual persons than are white characters, so the Black satire hurts more" (108). The same point has been made by Kuenz (183). It seems that Schuyler made the mistake of employing too personal a perspective when alluding to African American leaders, a danger that the critic Arthur Pollard warns of in so-called "personal satire" (4). Despite the consistency of Reilly's argument, I contend that this is not the only pretext for the rejection of the novel, but just one more excuse critics have resorted to in order to ignore the subversive content of the text.

[19] In this article Schuyler defends the total equality between whites and African Americans to the point that he denies the existence of the so-called "negro art 'made in America'" (662), consistent with his premise that the concept of race or color does not constitute a valid parameter for classification. Obviously, Schuyler's article was criticized and taken as an example of the assimilationist attitude of its author, even by his own contemporaries like Hughes, who wrote his famous "The Negro Artist and the Racial Mountain" as a direct response to the implications of Schuyler's essay.

to be motivated by the same things, namely ambition and power. As James Miller points out in the preface: "[H]is characters, black and white, are all rogues, hustlers, and opportunists who seem to be driven by sex, greed, and the desire for social status" (6). Schuyler, then, analyzes and deconstructs each of the myths created by a dominant system that proposes differences at a racial level as conclusive principles for the division of society into two layers.

The most important of all these racist myths is the so-called biological or genetic differentiation which propounds that each race possesses certain intrinsic physical characteristics that distinguish it from the others. The biological myth implies that physical differences correspond to others at either a mental or behavioral level, as was explained above (chapter one). This stereotype is questioned in the text when the distinctions between races are said to respond more to an "exaggeration about the contrast between Caucasian and Negro features" (31) rather than to a clear-cut disparity. The text also makes clear that the origin of such diversity lies mainly in the conscious overstatement of certain racist groups for comic effect: "[T]he cartoonist and the minstrel men have been responsible for it very largely" (31). The problem arises when the intention behind this comic effect is finally disclosed as a desire to discredit and stigmatize the black race. This deliberate comic style covers up an important substratum of derogatory connotations that has nothing to do with physical or genetic characteristics.

Apart from this condemnation of the racist myth of white superiority, the fact of miscegenation indisputably repudiates any categorical differentiation between both races:

> When you consider that less than twenty per cent of our Negroes are without Caucasian ancestry and that close to thirty per cent have American Indian ancestry, it is readily seen that there cannot be the wide difference in Caucasian and Afro-American facial characteristics that most people imagine. (32)

Considering the long-term and on-going racial mixing within American society, Schuyler establishes once more that differentiation on the grounds of appearance or genetics lacks any validity or legitimacy.

Another myth that is usually invoked to establish a neat differentiation between both races is the so-called "Negro dialect," identified with the African

American distinct way of speaking, long a target for many white racists.[20] Schuyler also deconstructs this myth when the doctor declares that "there is no such thing as Negro dialect, except in literature and drama" (31). Schuyler not only intends to demolish yet another myth, he also displaces the attention from a racial to a social distinction, proving that dialects depend on both the area and the social class one belongs to: "[I]t is a well-known fact among informed persons that a Negro from a given section speaks the same dialect as his white neighbors" (31). With this statement Schuyler both challenges the existence of a dialectal difference, and introduces into his inquiry a social component that is crucial to comprehend the satiric parameters of the novel.

Although some of the same characteristics can be found in all the social classes that appear in the novel,[21] social differences become key instruments of analysis. Focusing on the working class, the protagonist of Schuyler's novel observes on more than one occasion that there is a straightforward similarity between the white and the African American working classes. An example of their resemblance is illustrated in the episode of Max's speech before the "Knights of Nordica," when Max "was amused because of the similarity of this meeting to the religious orgies of the more ignorant Negroes" (77). Another image of this ignorant lower class has been presented in the Paradise community. However, the image becomes more caustic in the depiction of the community of Happy Hill that perfectly fits the typical profile: ignorant and fanatic, centering all its social and labor unrest on its hatred of African Americans.

The profile of this working class is tellingly articulated: "[O]ther things of which the community might have boasted were its inordinately high illiteracy rate and its lynching record" (203), parameters that mark the daily life of the village of Happy Hill as a model of any authentic white community. But, in fact, Happy Hill is used as a microcosm of both Caucasian and African American societies in another illuminating quotation: "[N]ow there was nothing left to stimulate them but

---

[20]Among the writers who have used "Negro dialect" for comic effect, those of the well-known "plantation school" have taken it to its maximum level. To cite an example, in popular post-bellum works such as *Uncle Remus: His Songs and His Sayings* by Joel Chandler Harris (1880) the so-called "black dialect" is employed as the patent illustration of the inferiority of blacks with respect to whites.

[21] I differ here from Howard Faulkner's analysis up to a certain point because he contends that there is a clear differentiation between both classes ("Vanishing Race" 277). On the contrary, the rules of behavior are very similar and widely operative in both lower and upper classes. Nevertheless, Schuyler's critique is primarily directed toward the upper class, and specifically toward the African American upper class, because its members can achieve more in the fight against racism thanks to their education and positions of power.

the old time religion and the clandestine sex orgies that invariably and immediately followed the great revival meetings" (205). Here Schuyler directly alludes to the analogy between the illiterate white and black lower classes, since both combine orgies/religion as a means to liberate themselves from the social oppression to which they are submitted. The systematic critique of the support that religion provides for the dominant racist system and the prevalence of sexual desire are constant objects of satire in the description of both communities—black and white—throughout the novel. Hence, Happy Hill represents both working classes in the total ignorance and intolerance that make them such easy prey of racist manipulation.

Just as Happy Hill stands for a microcosm of white society, so Harlem is displayed as the prototypical African American community. Controlling racist practices often determined that African Americans would live in Harlem: "[T]he mechanics of race prejudice had forced them into the congested Harlem area where, at the mercy of white and black real estate sharks, they had been compelled to pay exorbitant rents" (58). The consequences of racial segregation condition the lives of African American inhabitants, who are obliged to pay "one hundred per cent more" (58) than their white counterparts in order to rent a house of questionable quality.[22] The racist practice of making blacks pay more than whites is carried out by both whites and blacks alike, who take advantage of the chaotic situation created by the growing demand of African Americans arriving from the South to Harlem.

Apart from the profit that a certain segment of the African American population obtains by exploiting the rest, the distinct feature of the Harlem population is an obsession with color, which causes a state of disharmony and rupture that characterizes their daily life. The internalization of the racist code which motivates this lack of unity can be explained in three basic ideas: a lack of racial awareness, the persistent presence of the so-called "intracaste prejudice," and their belief in white superiority. In fact, one of the black characters sums up the passing phenomena in these terms: "I always said niggers didn't have any race pride" (47). The lack of racial awareness is added to the inward division which

---

[22] The situation of Harlem during the twenties is accounted for in a number of publications that deal with the origins and later development of the area. Even in the first period of optimism, some signs unmistakably prove the fact that Harlem was not a paradise, as the iconography of the time would have it, but a slum, as it turned out to be during the economic collapse of the thirties. Gilbert Osofsky in his detailed study *Harlem: The Making of a Ghetto* (1963) explains its evolution step by step, and also James Weldon Johnson, *Black Manhattan* (1930) and Jervis Anderson, *This Was Harlem 1900-1950* (1981). A summary of Osofsky and Johnson is found in Makalani 10-13; Wintz, *Black Culture* 17-29 and in "Harlem: The Culture Capital" by Johnson (301-11).

afflicts the community and encourages the desire to pass in order to belong to the dominant majority. Indeed, the only element that finally unifies the whole community is precisely their desire to leave behind their African American identity:

> Those who had always maintained that it was impossible to get Negroes together for anything but a revival, a funeral or a frolic, now had to admit that they had coöperated well in getting white. The poor had been helped by the well-to-do, brothers had helped sisters, children had assisted parents. (131-2; sic)

Only in the crucial moment of passing as white does the entire community become one in their effort to abandon blackness. The sense of unity affects not only the members of the same family but also the different social classes that compose it. In their vivid eagerness to forsake their inferior racial condition, their shared determination leaves no space for any vestige of racial pride.

Schuyler also unmasks the so-called intracaste or intrarracial prejudice as another palpable example of the internalization of the racist model, in which lighter complexions are privileged over darker ones. Max and his partner, Bunny, exemplify this phenomenon, affirming that "there were three things essential to the happiness of a colored gentleman: yellow money, yellow women and yellow taxis" (19). The case of women with lighter complexion is especially revealing, because, on the one hand, they are vital to African American men as icons of their social and economic status, since "they were so sought after that one almost required a million dollars to keep them out of the clutches of one's rivals" (19). On the other hand, because of the symbolism that these women acquire within the African American framework of reference, it is evident that they are mere objects of consumerism and ostentation.[23]

Finally, blacks' belief in the superior life-style enjoyed by whites is a result of their own experience since "a lifetime of being Negroes in the United States had convinced them that there was great advantage in being white" (57). The moral norm implicit in the novel portrays the internalization of the dominant value system, but it subverts it by criticizing the outcome of such an internalization

---

[23] The objectification to which women are generally subjected is part of the usual process of consumerist society, since they are conceived as objects for use and abuse. However, this fact is even more explicit in the case of African American women, whose humanity and femininity have been systematically denied by the racist society that has commodified them.

through the presentation of the disunity and lack of common objectives that pervade the African American community in all its social strata. Certainly the majority of characteristics that define the African American working class are also part of the picture of the upper class.

Within this context, the idea of profit for a part of the African American population is perhaps the most direct goal of the satire contained in the novel. This critique is even more mordant when centered on the world of cosmetics, a very successful industry within the African American community, with astronomic sales of products that whiten skin color or smooth down kinky hair, or, in other words, suppress some of its most predominant characteristics.[24] The character that embodies the cosmetics universe is Mme. Sisseretta Blandish, "who owned the swellest hair-straightening parlor in Harlem" (47).[25] Her prestige in the community runs very high: "[S]he had been doing very well at her vocation for years and was acclaimed in the community as one of its business leaders" (59). For her the disappearance of her African American clients into the white race signifies a real tragedy, the destruction of her most precious dream: to hold a prominent social and economic position.

Perhaps for the same reasons, Mme. Blandish is much more realistic and sincere than the rest of the characters in her thoughts about what awaits her if she decides to pass to the other side of the racial barrier: "[H]ere at least she was somebody. In the great Caucasian world she would be just another white woman," whose import she herself specifies: "[S]he had seen too many elderly, white-haired Caucasian females scrubbing floors and toiling in sculleries not to know what being just another white woman meant" (61-2). The character is able to voice convincingly what the dream of becoming white might actually mean, foreseeing how the dream could turn into a nightmare because it would bring along the loss of the distinguished social and economic status she now possesses. This is one of the few moments in the text when the actual situation of many poor white women, for whom their Caucasian attributes are of no help, is treated in all its horror and anguish. Mme. Blandish is aware of her own superiority in her eminent status as

---

[24] This aspect of the novel reaches absurd proportions, corroborating the extremes to which the obsession with color leads African Americans in their attempt to be what they are not, that is, in their attempt to fit the dominant canon of beauty. Color mania becomes extremely disturbing because it manifests rejection and contempt for their own physical appearance.

[25] An obvious reference to Madame C. J. Walker, "the richest self-made woman in America" (Lewis, *When Harlem* 110), who made her fortune thanks to her hair-straightening business.

"vice-President of the American Race Pride League" and "head of the Woman's Committee of the New York Branch of the Social Equality League" (59).

Mme. Blandish thus belongs to the African American social elite defending the ideals of race pride and equality but, concurrently, making a fortune through her beauty parlor which exalts the white canon of beauty. She represents the flagrant contradiction of all the members of the upper class, who live off the fight against the racist system proclaiming the equality of all races while simultaneously imitating and perpetuating the ideals of the white world through their actions. Such is also the case of Dr. Shakespeare Agamennon Beard. Founder of one of the most important organizations in favor of the rights of the African American population, he writes biting editorials "denouncing the Caucasians that he secretly admired and lauding the greatness of Negroes whom he alternately pitied and despised" (90). Obviously, Beard personifies the majority of his social class trapped in a great dilemma,[26] caught between their social duty to criticize white attitudes while defending their own race's interests, and their attitude of praise toward those same whites with the subsequent rejection of their own.

Beard and his class constitute the most direct attack on the Duboisian idea of the "talented tenth." Although their education would enable them to play leading roles in their community, they continue to function according to the same value system as that of the ignorant working class:

> In limpid prose he told of the sufferings and privations of the downtrodden black workers with whose lives he was totally and thankfully unfamiliar. Like most Negro leaders, he deified the black woman but abstained from employing aught save octoroons. He talked at white banquets about "we of the black race" and admitted in books that he was part-French, part-Russian, part-Indian and part-Negro. He bitterly denounced the Nordics for debauching Negro women while taking care to hire comely yellow stenographers with weak resistance. (90)

Several elements are worth mentioning in this excerpt, most of which originate in the color obsession that also distinguishes the upper class: the intrarracial prejudice manifest in a preference for light mulatto women; the use of the African American

---

[26] In fact, the magazine he publishes is entitled "The Dilemma," clearly alluding to W. E. B. Du Bois and his publication *The Crisis.*

woman, and particularly of mulatto women, as visible icons of a high social position, and the elitism that singles out this social class as compared to the more humble component of the African American community.

The features listed above can be applied to all African American organizations and their leaders, repeatedly satirized by Schuyler for their employment of racial prejudice as their way of life and means to obtain benefit: "While the large staff of officials was eager to end all oppression and persecution of the Negro, they were never so happy and excited as when a Negro was barred from a theater or fired to a crisp" (88). These words convey the cruel irony that the sense of these organizations lies in the perpetuation of racist practices against African Americans. If complete equality were to be obtained, such organizations would cease to exist. For the same reason, the leaders of those associations contest the project of "Black No More, Incorporated," because it would mean the end of their profitable existence. This possibility encourages them to meet for the first time in history to try to agree on the most suitable strategies to stop the large-scale exodus of African Americans into the white race. The only agreement they manage to reach, however, is manipulated by Max himself who cunningly realizes that all these leaders "were too old or too incompetent to make a living except by preaching and writing about the race problem" (117). So he persuades them to work for the "Knights of Nordica," thus completing one of the most ironic turns of the novel in which the so-called "race leaders" end up supporting their traditional enemies.

The novel's most acerbic critique of the African American community, therefore, lies in Schuyler's insistence on the racial prejudice that affects the entire social, political, and economic network of the community. The moral norm implicit in the novel rejects a vision of the world that internalizes the inferiority of blacks and unveils the terrible consequences wreaked on the African American conscience. In the final section of the novel, Schuyler proposes a total rupture of the established order, promoting a new mulatto society based on the amalgamation of the races. To present this new social order as a result of the subversion of the previous one, Schuyler resorts to the absurd, which is a key element in satire according to Frye. Because of his double focus "of morality and fantasy" (*Anatomy of Criticism* 224), Schuyler's novel could also be understood as a dystopia.[27]

---

[27]According to Matthew Hodgart, a dystopia can be defined as "a grotesque version of our world with a logical extrapolation" (185) [Its most important illustrations in the twentieth century are *Brave New World* by Aldous Huxley (1932) and *Nineteen Eighty-Four* by George Orwell (1949)]. But as dystopias fall within the scope of both satire and science fiction, both perspectives are

Dystopia: Between Satire and Science Fiction

Some critics like Tom Moylan regard utopia and its counterpart, dystopia, as a genre in itself, although closely related to both satire and science fiction. The present analysis fuses the three traditions because in *Black No More* they form an indivisible whole, whose function is basically subversive. As the subversive role of satire has been discussed above, the absurd component of the novel is now examined using the framework of science fiction and utopia as direct referents. Kathryn Hume suggests an illuminating distinction between satire and dystopia. She argues that serious satire "may alienate its audience and may, in its wrath, fail to provide a clear plan for improvement," whereas dystopias have more chances "to hint at possible patterns of reform" (110). *Black No More,* therefore, could be viably analyzed as a dystopic work which opposes the dominant contemporary ideology and presents possible alternatives.

Especially relevant for this purpose is Anne Cranny-Francis' study of H.G. Wells, as his work constitutes what she denominates "socially and politically conscious science fiction" (41), origin of the utopian or dystopian novel. Indeed, Wells' novels inaugurate the investigation of the social effects of scientific discourse in which "futurist technology was primarily an estrangement device allowing Wells to confront the reader with allegorized versions of her/his own reality" (45). This "estrangement device" is what best defines science fiction and, by extension, fantastic modes in general. According to Moylan's interpretation, this distancing mechanism or alienation[28] "is identified as central to the subversive

---

useful for expanding the signification of the novel. Most critics use this term "dystopia" to represent the opposite way of approaching utopia, although some others like Hodgart and Reilly refer to this phenomenon as "antiutopia" and still others like Pollard use the term "negative Utopias" (34). According to Jeffrey Tucker, "it is important to realize that the satiric and utopian impulses are not mutually exclusive" (143).

[28] This concept was developed by Russian formalists as one of the most important functions of any kind of art, outlined in Victor Shklovsky's illuminating article "Art as Technique" (1917): "The technique of art is to make objects 'unfamiliar,' to make forms difficult, to increase the difficulty and length of perception because the process of perception is an aesthetic end in itself and must be prolonged" (24). The idea of rendering something unfamiliar is, thus, an aesthetic objective and it becomes the artistic aim *par excellence*. The study of this mechanism in science fiction literature has been fundamentally undertaken by Darko Svin who describes science fiction as "cognitive estrangement" (qtd. in Cranny-Francis 60).

quality of the genre [because] it focuses on the given situation but in a displaced manner to create a fresh view" (33). It presumes to reflect critically on the reader's world through the presentation of a different reality. Such a device is often accompanied by a futurist extrapolation through the construction of a very different society in which "that difference [is] signified by its alien technology" (Cranny-Francis 60). The distance existing between the futurist society and the actual society in which the reader lives creates an ideal framework for a social and political critique.

In the case of dystopias, however, the estrangement device is a bit more complicated, as it may not be used to describe a society temporarily or even geographically displaced, but rather a hitherto unheard-of vision of the reader's society. As Cranny-Francis suggests about the dystopias written by Orwell, Huxley or Zamyatin: "Their dystopias are not projections of the future of their own societies; they were representations of the present of those societies" (125). Hence, the employment of the distancing technique has to be regarded as even more subversive, because it not only presents a different social paradigm but also scrutinizes the present world in a very blunt manner. In this way, the deconstruction of that world is prominent at each step of the narration.

Such a deconstructive strategy is perceptible in the dystopic elements Schuyler introduces in *Black No More*, because the novel is based on a fairly reliable reconstruction of the social and racial processes that mark the society of his time.[29] In this reconstruction several elements are easily recognized by the reader: the bases for the preface, the description of African American leaders, and the phenomenon of miscegenation. Schuyler's satire and futuristic projection of these realistic ingredients create the alienating effect that characterizes dystopias. Despite this estrangement device, it is still possible to recognize the American society of the nineteen-twenties that Schuyler depicts in his work in order to subvert the racial and social code.

It can be argued that Schuyler tried to depict his society truthfully, taking his cue from an article published in *The Pittsburgh Courier* in 1929 October titled "Racial Metamorphosis Claimed by Scientists: Japanese Says He can Change Black Skin into White . . ." (Peplow, *Schuyler* 57). In this article, a doctor named Yusaburo Noguchi claims that he "could change the Japanese into a race of tall,

---

[29] This would justify Tucker's claim that "it is important to recognize Schuyler's *Black No More* and *Black Empire* as the first published examples of speculative fiction by an African American" (149, note 30).

blue-eyed blonds," an affirmation that Schuyler transcribes almost literally into the preface (14). The idea of "whitening" black people is not original,[30] then, but seems to have been suggested to Schuyler by this and other articles published in the twenties. The other contemporary source for the idea was the sale of cosmetic products such as "Kink-No-More" (13) that Schuyler also mentions in his preface. While the actual existence of a similar product is difficult to corroborate, the importance of the cosmetic industry within the African American community of the period is significant.[31]

Consequently, through the estrangement device, the scientific-technological discourse on which the novel depends is exaggerated into mysterious industrial transformations. In fact, the description itself of the process whereby African Americans are "whitened" incorporates all these ingredients in a conscious combination of the real and the absurd. The set of instruments employed "resembled a cross between a dentist's chair and an electric chair. Wires and straps, bars and levers protuded from it and a great nickel headpiece . . . hung over it" (34), leading Max to perceive the place as "quiet, swift, efficient, sinister" (35). This portrayal helps to create an atmosphere of mystery and death recalling the sinister vision of science and technology that fills the pages of *Frankestein* by Mary Shelley (1818). The indirect allusion to this precedent for contemporary science fiction is of great significance; Shelley's novel is also considered to be subversive in that it deconstructs the dominant cultural patterns of the early nineteenth century by means of systematically substituting the patterns for "a series of ambiguities" (Aldiss 42) that filter constantly in the text.[32] Just as *Frankenstein* is constructed around a network of ambiguities, so *Black No More* is built on an ambiguous nucleus, especially when it refers to the racial indetermination as an instrument for

---

[30] Indeed, it is interesting to note that this idea can be traced back to the Renaissance, when "to wash an Ethiopian" was considered impossible (see emblem LIX in *The English Emblem Tradition* edited by Peter Daly et al.).

[31] Its importance is still noticeable today in any popular African American magazine like *Ebony* or *Upscale*, where cosmetic advertisements abound, especially those designed for skin and hair care. According to a market study, "black women will spend up to $625 million on cosmetics by 1995," out of which "more than 40 percent . . . are under 40, the younger consumers spend three times the amounts of Caucasians on personal care products" ("Black Radiance Cosmetics" 108). Also radiation treatments for whitening skin were advertised much earlier.

[32] As Brian Aldiss observes, the source for these ambiguities in *Frankenstein* is located in the dramatization of "the difference between the old age and the next, between an age when things went by rote and one where everything was suddenly called into question" (40). Such questioning modifies the content of the work until it is transformed into a symbol of what Aldiss calls "modern predicament" that he himself specifies as "the post-Rousseauvian dichotomy between the

questioning social and ideological categories.[33] Like Shelley's novel, *Black No More* breaks with established literary molds with the purpose of creating an adequate space for the confrontation between past and present, between the ideal and the real, between the dominant and the subversive.

Apart from its pseudo-scientific discourse, the novel's acerbic critique is directed toward real characters who populate the cultural and political sphere of the time and who are more or less easily identifiable. Once estranged through satire, they are transmuted into hideous creatures who only care about their personal interests. This is particularly true of the caricatures of the African American leaders belonging to the political and social panorama of the Harlem Renaissance. For instance, Dr. Shakespeare Agamemnon Beard is an obvious allusion to W. E. B. Du Bois as mentioned above, "the venerable lover of his race" (91) as Schuyler qualifies him. His hypocritical attitude and "double consciousness" as an *African American* leader who exalts the white world makes him the prototype for other leaders. Dr. Napoleon Wellington Jackson is also quite significant, a portrayal of one of the most representative intellectuals of the period, James Weldon Johnson. At first Schuyler's presentation of the character seems to confirm his great worth as a leader—"you know of his scholarship, his high sense of duty and his deep love for the suffering black race" (92), but this presentation is immediately undermined by the ambiguous racial allegiance reflected in his cultural preferences:

> You have doubtless had the pleasure of singing some of the many sorrow songs he has written and popularized in the past twenty years, and you must know of his fame as a translator of Latin poets and his authoritative work on the Greek language. (92)

There are recurrent references in the novel to the "sorrow songs" as a way of exploiting the disappearance of the black race for personal benefit; the fact that Jackson participates in this exploitation diminishes him as a leader and part of the

---

individual and his society, as well as the encroachment of science on that society, and mankind's dual nature" (51).

[33] For a brief account of the diverse influences that form Shelley's creative universe, see the introduction to the 1992 edition by Maurice Hindle. Shelley's narrative is also a hybrid narrative, in between the Gothic novel and science fiction, with innumerable influences ranging from *Don Quixote* to the Prometheus myth, through Rousseau, Godwin (to which it is dedicated), and many others. Muriel Spark interprets the novel as inaugurating a new genre "in which the influential currents of two minds—Godwin representing the scientific empiricism of the eighteenth century, and Coleridge, the nineteenth century's imaginative reaction—meet" (159).

"talented tenth," according to the Duboisian code. Likewise, his interest in classical culture puts his leadership to the test since he identifies with an eminently white cultural pattern.

Two other leaders, Mr. Walter Williams and Dr. Gronne, also stand for important intellectuals of the time: Walter White and Booker T. Washington. Both caricatures continue the previous line, questioning their racial allegiances and their liminal position. In Williams' case his dual position is revealed through the narrator's comment immediately after the character has declared the pride he feels for belonging to the black race: "Mr. Williams was known to be a Negro among his friends and acquaintances, but no one else would have suspected it" (95). Actually, the writer Walter White's skin was so white that his mixed parentage was not readily perceptible.[34] On the contrary, Dr. Gronne does not need a light skin to obtain access to both communities because of the prestige he enjoys in both. As Schuyler comments: "Much of his popularity was due to the fact that he very cleverly knew how to make statements that sounded radical to Negroes but sufficiently conservative to satisfy the white trustees of his school" (95), a major criticism of Washington at the time.[35]

One more concept directly influences the perception of the novel as a mixture between realism and absurdity: miscegenation. In his dedication of the work, Schuyler repeatedly describes American society as unmistakably and irrefutably amalgamated. The emergence of "Black-No-More, Incorporated" only intensifies the consequences of the constant presence of miscegenation throughout the history of the United States. The narrator notes the increasing number of headlines such as "Wealthy White Girl Has Negro Baby," ironically reflecting that: "For the first time the prevalence of sexual promiscuity was brought home to the thinking people of America" (117). Obviously, the irony stems from the deliberate blindness of American society to a reality visible in each of its mulatto members.

---

[34] Despite Schuyler's suggestion, Walter White became well-known for his unceasing struggle against lynchings, going to the extreme of passing for white in order to carry out his investigations, as reflected in his autobiography titled *A Man Called White* (1948). White published the results of his experiences in his impressive *Rope and Faggot: A Biography of Judge Lynch* (1929), where he delves into the causes and history of lynching in the United States.

[35] The first three characters are clear, but the one who represents Booker T. Washington is less explicit: Dr. Gronne or Colonel Mortimer Roberts. The latter, Colonel Roberts, could be inspired in Russa Motton from the Tuskegee Institute according to Miller's introduction (8-9). Washington's ideology is basically delineated in his autobiography *Up from Slavery* (1901), where the two key ideas are "self-help" and "industrial education" or a type of education oriented for practical purposes. W. E. B. Du Bois and the Niagara intellectuals opposed Washington's model (Rampersad 91-115).

The social alarm stirred by the "sudden awareness" of this reality produces comic effect because miscegenation obviously did not originate with the activity of "whitening" black people; "Black-No-More, Incorporated" is just its logical consequence.

The resulting uneasiness makes no sense when confronted with the possible racial ramifications that permeate the American social fabric. From this perspective, many expressions recurrent in the text are mere exaggerations of the easily verifiable reality of miscegenation, as the following statement illustrates: "There was no way, apparently, of telling a real Caucasian from an imitation one" (118). The impossibility of discriminating between "races" does not emerge as a result of the activities of "Black-No-More, Incorporated," but is an observable pattern within the American society of the twenties; it is precisely this impossibility that facilitates the phenomenon of passing around which the novel revolves. What the company fosters is an increasing number of African American people who decide to pass to the other side of the racial barrier, exposing to public light the outcome of a long national history that challenges any notion of racial purity.

Such a process of deconstruction is completed by the genealogical investigation compiled by Dr. Buggerie, which constitutes the best proof of the high incidence of miscegenation in American society. Although this project at first intends to affect only the working class, the conclusions derived from it certify that all social classes without exception have been involved in the process, especially including the upper crust of white society because of its historical relationship with the black race:

> Most of our social leaders, especially of Anglosaxon lineage, are descendants of colonial stock that came here in bondage. They associated with slaves, in many cases worked and slept with them. They intermixed with the blacks and the women were sexually exploited by their masters. Then, even more than today, the illegitimate birth rate was very high in America. (178)

Miscegenation cannot be denied as these observations strongly refute the "genetic purity" used by racists to justify their actions. Racial division becomes a mere social construction. The phenomenon of miscegenation together with the evidence of the elevated number of people who have passed, which Buggerie estimates "close to fifty million souls" (179), are the most conclusive arguments against the racial segregation of American society, demonstrated to be a sectarian strategy devoid of any legitimacy.

Hence, the expression "we're all niggers now" (193), the logical consequence of all the above, needs to be understood as applicable to both the society depicted in the novel and Schuyler's society of the nineteen-twenties. Indeed, the last pages of the novel are deeply invested in the inversion of the racist paradigm: now a darker skin symbolizes the *status quo* previously ascribed to white or light skin. Ultimately, Schuyler the satirist manages to transgress the remaining racist taboos by constructing a mulatto society as ideal:

> Everybody that was anybody had a stained skin. A girl without one was avoided by the young men; a young man without one was at a decided disadvantage, economically and socially. A white face became startingly rare. America was definitely, enthusiastically mulatto-minded. (222)

Coming full circle, Schuyler solves the issue of the true foundation of the racist code. He propounds that what matters is definitely not the color of the skin, but the way society—either white or mulatto—functions, employing the same parameters of coercion as the main means of compelling all its members to accept its unjust rules. Thus, the dystopic present portrayed by the novel is easily identifiable with the social and racial universe of the twenties.

Nevertheless, as Cranny-Francis affirms, "[T]he problem with dystopias is that readers commonly fail to recognize the dystopian society as a representation of their own real" (125). In general, many dystopias do not achieve their purpose because they employ the technique of alienation so brilliantly that the real world is not recognizable. Schuyler's novel, however, probably produced the opposite effect: wholesale rejection produced by the recognition of certain real-life characters. Nevertheless, the source for the disapproval of the novel can best be located in the effect that the dystopian strategy pursues, identified up to now with the subversive critique pervasive in the text. Problems emerge when such a critique is too revolutionary and disturbing. It tends to achieve the opposite effect, that is, the neutralization of the seditious element in favor of the maintenance of a widely accepted value system. Moylan explains this phenomenon as follows:

> [T]he dystopian narrative itself has all too easily been recruited into the

> ideological attack on authentic utopian expression: commentators cite
> the dystopia as a sign of the very failure of utopia and consequently urge
> uneasy readers to settle for what it is and cease their frustrating dreams
> of a better life. (9)

Dystopia is concomitant with the expression of frustration over the impossibility of effectuating any social improvement. Thus, the present world is invoked as better than the dystopic one because it is more tolerable. With the acceptance of this reality, one of the fundamental values of dystopian discourse is lost, specifically the fresh approach to that reality and the possibility of deconstructing it in order to obtain a more objective vision and to attempt the correction of its mistakes.

The sensations of frustration and failure dominate the critical review that Faulkner wrote about the novel when he qualified it as "unsettling" ("Vanishing Race" 283): it does not try to improve the depraved society it portrays since, he says, "the human race is hardly worth the effort" (285). To the contrary, I have attempted to show here how Schuyler makes conscious use of subversion to expose the racist myths that back the dominant ideology of the society of his time. By deconstructing them one by one, he implies that the very concept of "race" is in itself racist. Social differentiations have replaced racial ones, as an individual's race is defined socially. The artificiality of these racial differences articulates, then, the concept of "race" itself as another social construction, leading to a clear destabilization of the traditional equation white/universal which loses significance in a fundamentally mulatto world. Schuyler's deconstruction of the notion of race enables the denunciation of racism as a mechanism that is very profitable for the leaders of both communities. And, as a result, the blunt refusal of a biracial division of society contributes to demonstrate beyond any reasonable doubt the artificiality and incoherence that characterize an ideology based on race.

In order to achieve his subversive objectives, Schuyler has resorted to a variety of strategies within the generic mixture that constitutes the novel. Satiric and dystopian elements combine to provide a negative vision which is, at the same time, extremely revealing and innovative. In a certain way, it is as if the novel itself were shaped around the central idea of miscegenation that pervades its content, displaying itself as a "mulatto" narrative able to integrate a great multiplicity of levels and interpretations. As mestizo, *Black No More* becomes the epitome of the passing novel: while "passing" as a deceptively simple story, quite improbable and grotesque, it contains an enormous discursive potential. The novel not only investigates the inner functioning of the motif of passing, but also widens the field of application of this canon, desmystifying the racial—and racist—concepts on which it depends.

Interrogating the notions of race and the phenomenon of passing itself, the novel calls into question the legitimacy of the discourse of passing, elaborating in its pages an informed and profound revision of the parameters that ground it. The protagonist is not a mulatto who decides not to be black anymore, but an entire community that chooses to "whiten" itself in an effort to avoid victimization at the hands of an absurd racist code. Likewise, *Black No More* is not a novel about passing, but a novel which "passes" in order to unmask such racism and to complete the circle which, starting from the Duboisian perspective of double consciousness, ends up definitely debunking any attempts at racial categorization. This novel represents, then, the end of the passing motif, which declines after the Harlem Renaissance, and the beginning of a frank understanding of the essential values of the African American community that was characteristic of the decades of the thirties and forties.

SECTION II

Female

Approaches

FOUR

'Ain't I a Woman' and a Mother?: Sexuality and Motherhood in Nella Larsen's Quicksand and Passing

> I have plowed, and planted, and gathered into barns, and no
> man could head me—and ar'n't I a woman? I could work as
> much and eat as much as a man (when I could get it), and bear de
> lash as well—and ar'n't I a woman? I have borne thirteen chilern
> and seen 'em mos' all sold off into slavery, and when I cried out
> with a mother's grief, none but Jesus heard—and ar'n't I a
> woman?
>
> Sojourner Truth
"Ar'n't I a Woman?"

During the nineteen-twenties African American women writers began to raise their voices to question the dominant racial *and* sexual order and to suggest alternative definitions of their black female identity. They encountered manifold obstacles especially because of their gender, which relegated them to a secondary category in the social and intellectual hierarchy of both communities—black and white. Since African American women have been systematically excluded from the feminine ideal embodied by white women, they have been forced to devise a series of strategies in their works to mask and disguise their blunt rejection of derogatory images of their femininity. Within this context, Nella Larsen articulates in her novels *Quicksand* (1928) and *Passing* (1929) questions of both race and gender in an attempt to reinterpret the traditional roles assigned to African American women, particularly the highly controversial issues of sexuality and motherhood.

In these novels Larsen tries to redefine both topics from the point of view of contemporary African American women who are actively engaged in the reconstruction of their own identity and history. This conscious process of reinterpretation offers a new vision of black women springing from their real life experiences and intentionally subverting externally imposed images. Hiding behind two unassuming and inoffensive genres, Larsen's novels "pass" for sentimental novels of passing, while the author actually delves into the more serious work of exploring the diverse stereotypes ascribed to African American women. In doing so, Larsen demonstrates how these images have undeniably limited the expression of African American femininity. A detailed analysis of the double façade of the two novels also allows the unraveling of the highly parodic and anti-conventional component that underlies Larsen's effort to shape a sense of self, estranged from any socially sanctioned definition. The multiple implications of the intimate association between racial and sexual discourses in Larsen's novels allow the author to develop the concept of "double double consciousness" as a valid alternative for the female African American identity.

⋙⋘

THE PASSING MOTIF OR THE SUBVERSION OF THE "TRAGIC MULATTO" TRADITION

In both *Quicksand* and *Passing* the search for an alternative way of defining the African American woman is effected by using the convention of passing with a mulatta figure as the protagonist. The significance of this character lies in her explicit transgression of the boundaries imposed by race and color, thereby calling into question the legitimacy of such barriers. Conversely, the mulatta figure may also provide an ideal framework for dealing with the topics of sexuality and motherhood as strategies for subverting preestablished assumptions and canons. Larsen's choice of the mulatta heroine also reveals her designs for her project of reconstructing the black female identity, aptly described by Hazel Carby:

> The mulatto . . . enabled the exploration in fiction of relations that were *socially proscribed*. The mulatto figure is a narrative device of mediation, allowing a fictional exploration of the relation between the races while offering an imaginary expression of the relation between the races. (171; my emphasis)

The exploration of social restrictions—racial as well as sexual—through the mulatta figure facilitates a redefinition of her position which breaks with, or at least destabilizes, the socially established confines. Caught between two opposing worlds—black and white—the mulatta never reaches a satisfactory conclusion. In this way, Larsen profits from, but at the same time deconstructs, the so-called "tragic mulatto" tradition.[1] As Jacquelyn McLendon explains, Larsen deploys the mulatta figure as an "organizing metaphor" (154) in her novels "to explore the concept of doubleness as it inheres in the experience of African-Americans" (153). This use is indicative of Larsen's need to revise the mulatta trope in order to dismantle the traditional biological interpretations of divided legacy and inscribe it as "a psychological reality, an angle of vision" (Dean 3). The mulatto protagonists of Larsen's novels move beyond the stereotype, becoming "Du Bois' 'double consciousness' made feminine" (Dean 3), that is, a psychological embodiment of "double double consciousness" in their search for self-definition and self-expression.

Thanks to the representativity commanded by the mulatta women and to the dialogue that they establish with the "tragic mulatto" precedent, the racial discourse of both novels is transmuted into a suitable metaphor for interrogating the real motivations that lead these women to the act of passing. At this point it is necessary to make an important differentiation within the "tragic mulatto" paradigm. Although many critics regard it as monolithic, there are actually two main trends in "tragic mulatto" novels: the so-called "antebellum narrative" or pre-emancipation narrative, with *Clotel or the President's Daughter* by William Wells Brown (1853) as a good illustration; and the "postbellum narrative" or reconstructionist narrative, exemplified by *The House Behind the Cedars* written by Charles Chesnutt (1900).[2] The tragedy of Brown's Clotel is precisely the discovery of her mixed racial condition which is instrumental in turning her into a slave after the death of her father, supposedly president Thomas Jefferson. Ultimately the impossibility of

---

[1] A great number of critics argue that the use of the tragic mulatto on Larsen's part does not imply a process of deconstruction. On the contrary, they affirm that Larsen is loyal to this tradition in order to depict the divided racial heritage of her protagonists. Barbara Christian qualifies her novels as "the quintessence of the tragic mulatta image" (*Black Women* 48). See also Bone 103-6; Huggins, *Harlem Renaissance* 157; Singh, *Novels* 102; Gayle 111; Davis, *Dark Tower* 96-98. Countering this critical tendency, Cheryl Wall has remarked that "the tragic mulatto was the only formulation historically available to portray educated middle-class black women in fiction," but Larsen's protagonists "subvert the convention consistently" ("Passing for What?" 97-8). I follow Wall's lead, investigating the author's subversive intent from a parodic viewpoint.

[2] I take the main difference between both trends from *Neither White Nor Black* by Judith Berzon (54-61), and mention the exemplification of relevant aspects in these two novels when necessary.

achieving freedom either for herself or for her daughter leads her to suicide. Chestnutt's Rena, on the other hand, deliberately renounces her family to complete her integration into the white community, following her brother Warwick's advice, who exhorts her to obtain "the glory" (*House* 20), as he terms his life as a white man.

On first sight, it seems that the main reason for Larsen's protagonists to pass is dictated by their desire to leave behind the social restrictions linked to their African American identity and to take advantage of the relative "freedom" promised by an identification with whites. After reconsidering their identities and racial allegiances with respect to their "blackness," both protagonists choose to abandon it in order to pass to the other side. However, they do so in two distinct ways: while Clare in *Passing* opts for a conventional passing, that is, using her light skin to integrate into white society; Helga in *Quicksand*, whose skin color does not allow that kind of passing, departs from the United States to settle in Copenhagen. From the very beginning, Larsen inverts the canon of the antebellum tragic mulatto, who passes from a white identity to the discovery of his/her black blood. In this tradition the discovery scene constitutes the first tragedy of his/her life from which all misfortune derives. Larsen's novels, instead, follow the line of the reconstructionist romance, when the protagonists voluntarily decide to forsake their community of origin in search of new horizons in the white world.

Cheryl Wall explains the subversion of the tragic mulatto as exemplified in the two protagonists: "[T]hey are neither noble nor long-suffering; their plights are not used to symbolize the oppression of blacks, the irrationality of prejudice or the absurdity of concepts of race generally" ("Passing for What?" 98). Even though Wall hints at the presence of a parodic revision, her analysis focuses only on the pre-emancipation conventions that portray a mulatto protagonist moved by noble intent. Ready to face any kind of adversity for the well-being of the race, this figure is elevated to the category of martyr for the entire race. But Larsen's protagonists do not fit the abolitionist ideal; their decision to pass is the result of a combination of reasons, never clearly stated, but among which social and material ambitions are prominent.

In Clare's case the causes for her determination to pass are materialized in her yearning for middle-class privileges denied to her because of her humble origins within the African American community. Clare expresses this idea in the term "things," whose vagueness underlines an important feature of her personality, particularly her lack of definition, of identity: "I wanted things. I knew I wasn't bad-looking and that I could 'pass'" (159). Convinced of the necessity of escaping from her difficult situation, she makes use of the only thing she has: her own skin. her own body. The importance ascribed to the female body in the discourse of passing as instrumental for belonging to the white race, is noteworthy; it is the text where the protagonist's assumed identity is inscribed.[3] However, it is not only material or social expectations which lead Clare to cross the so-called "color line," using her light-skinned body as passport, but another. even more pressing motivation frequently found in narratives of reconstruction: a disenchantment with the black race because of the multiplicity of problems they must face on a daily basis. In *The House Behind the Cedars,* Rena shows her contempt especially in her aloof attitude towards other members of her race. This disparaging attitude on her part is reflected in the use of standard English instead of dialect, in her solitary existence, and in the feeling of self-pity suggested by her behavior. Clare admits it openly on different occasions. "I was determined to get away, to be a person and not a charity or a problem, or even a daughter of the indiscreet Ham" (159).[4] Clare repudiates her "black blood" and rebels against the social stereotypes that block her way.

Although Helga in *Quicksand* does not cross the color line, the desire for material possessions is also a major motivation: "All her life Helga Crane had loved and longed for nice things" (6). The consumerism that characterizes Helga is an integral part of her aspirations for stability and security, translated into an obsession for accumulating objects on which she spends all her wages: "Most of her earnings had gone into clothes, into books, into the furnishings of the room which held her" (6). Several critics have interpreted her materialism as part of the complicity that Larsen supposedly maintains with a middle-class value system.[5] However, direct critiques of the materialism of the African American bourgeoisie constitute the

---

[3] This use of the female body will be taken up below as a clear referent in the discussion of the expression of female sexuality and the right to maternity.

[4] Ham was the ancestor of the Canaanites and Noah's son in the story that appears in Genesis 9: 18-27. Ham finds his father drunk and naked in his tent and does not cover him, so the father curses him condemning him and his descendants to be slaves to his brothers and their tribes. Ham's episode justifies the enslavement of the Canaanite tribe, known for their black skin. As Pieterse confirms, this biblical tradition has had great impact on Western racist ideology, since "until well into the nineteenth century . . . this remained the most popular explanation of slavery" (44).

[5] Bone (1958), Ford (1936), and Singh (1976) evaluate Larsen's novels as imitations of white middle-class standards and, thus, stress the use of the "tragic mulatto" figure as the embodiment of Larsen's will to pass, likening her to the characters she portrays in her novels (See also Bell, *Afro-American Novel* 109; Vashti Lewis, "The Mulatto Woman" 58; Gayle 111; Christian, *Black Women* 49).

manifold contradictions in Helga's personality and reveal Larsen's attack on their obsessive preoccupation with property and social position.[6] Helga also voices the same disdain for the black race as does Clare but in more extreme terms: "Why, she demanded in fierce rebellion, should she be yoked to these despised black folk? . . . she didn't, in spite of her racial markings, belong to these dark segregated people" (55). Both women, then, refuse to be categorized within a race they do not claim and from which they are alienated. This estrangement has led critics to insist on the racial ambivalence found in Larsen's novels.[7]

The two protagonists' repudiation of the black race might also be understood as an adaptation of both novels to the "tragic mulatta" convention. Unable to feel a part of the African American community, they try to belong to a white world which allures them with opportunities denied to the black race. The assimilation into the white community is handled differently, depending on the character, but in both novels it amounts to a total rupture with the restrictions imposed upon the "tragic mulatta" figure facilitating a new development away from this stereotype. For Clare, it means a complete adaptation to the white way of life, culminating in her marriage to a white man and her subsequent engendering of a white daughter. These two facts constitute, perhaps, the major difference from the preceding tradition, in which interracial marriage could not take place and in which biracial couples were unavoidably destined to failure.[8]

For Helga, the complete identification with the white race is not possible, as she does not possess a skin as light as Clare's. Helga, therefore, decides to travel to Denmark where "there were no Negroes, no problems, no prejudice" (55). In a

---

[6] In "Freeze the Day: A Feminist Reading of Nella Larsen's *Quicksand* and *Passing*" (1985), Priscilla Ramsey articulates in detail this feature of Larsen's work in relation with the studies on the African American middle class undertaken in the seventies and eighties. Also Mary Mabel Youman bases her analysis of *Passing* (1974) on the combination between race and class factors and their influence on Irene's character. Berzon accounts for Larsen's indictment against black bourgeoisie (171-4). See also Mary Helen Washington's "The Mulatta Trap: Nella Larsen's Women of the 1920s" for constrictions and limitations of middle-class black women.

[7] An exemplification of this type of criticism is found in Bell, when he claims that "color and class restrictions in America also reinforced her feelings of ambivalence and 'a fine contempt for the blatantly patriotic black Americans'" (*Afro-American Novel* 111). Here he reiterates ambivalence and self-hatred as key elements for interpreting Larsen's novels.

[8] In "'Never Was Born': The Mulatto, an American Tragedy" (1986) Werner Sollors comments on this characteristic typical of "tragic mulatto" novels, concluding that "the Mulatto suicide is the cultural given in American settings; Quadroon and Octoroon lovers survive only if they remove themselves to Europe with their white suitors or spouses" (300). To illustrate this point, Rena's passing is almost complete until she must face the dilemma of marrying a white man, which she regards as an "irrevocable" step (74). However, her fiancé discovers her racial background and

certain sense, her trip symbolizes a kind of passing, as hers is similar to Clare's: to flee from the restraints that blackness places on her in order to find her self and make her dreams come true.[9] In the first place, her new life involves obtaining the material possessions she wishes for, as she herself puts it: "Always she had wanted, not money, but the things which money could give, leisure, attention, beautiful surroundings. Things, things, things" (67). So Denmark signifies "the realization of a dream" (67) and, at least for a while, she feels completely happy and satisfied. Her intense complacency makes her compare her new existence with the previous one in America, resolving "never to return to the existence of ignominy which the New World of opportunity and promise forced upon Negroes" (75), that is, affirming her resolution to forget the past and to completely pass into Danish society forever. Despite differences, Helga's sense of satisfaction with her new life and with the negation of her African American identity can be equated to most characters of reconstructionist narratives who, like Rena, feel perfectly adapted to their new condition. Rena also describes her new life as "a dream . . . only a dream. I am Cinderella before the clock has struck" (*House* 62).

In spite of their apparent contentment, and following the patterns in narratives of reconstruction,[10] both Helga and Clare end up acknowledging the bonds with other black people. As Clare says: "you don't know, you can't realize how I want to see Negroes, to be with them again, to talk with them, to hear them

---

repudiates her, even manifesting physical revulsion toward her. His slight will precipitate Rena's tragic ending.

[9] This argument is invoked by many artists who travel to Europe in the period between the twenties and the forties, as Jeffrey Gray testifies: "The African American's journey to Europe may be a flight *from* white and/or black Americans, but it is certainly a flight *to* a different or at least a differently perceived white people" (260; author's emphasis). Gray likens Helga's journey to those of several artists, among whom he includes Richard Wright, Josephine Baker, and James Baldwin, asserting that their reactions to Europe are strikingly analogous: a desire to forget other Americans and to live their difference without feeling marginalized. For instance, Baker, who left for Paris in the twenties, confesses: "I felt liberated in Paris. People didn't stare at me" (qtd. in Gray 262). Indeed, a great parallelism between Helga and Baker as a woman-spectacle can be drawn as exotic "others." Marilyn Elkins devotes her article "Expatriate Afro-American Women as Exotics" (1995) to delineate the objectification that African American women are subjected to in Europe and the way in which these women, especially Helga, strive to "convert themselves into art objects" (265), embodying the Exotic stereotype.

[10] In his brilliant analysis of the employment of the tragic mulatto/a figure in the twentieth century, Sterling Brown points out that "in our century, Negro authors have turned the story around; now after restless searching, she finds peace only after returning to her own people" ("A Century of Negro Portraiture" 371). Such an inversion is ascertained in Rena's case, whose belonging to the black race is revealed when she visits her sick mother out of her feelings of nostalgia for her family.

laugh" (200). The same fortune befalls Helga, who decides to settle down for good in Harlem, justifying her change of mind with her sense of racial belonging:

> These were her people . . . How absurd she had been to think that another country, another people could liberate her from the ties which bond her forever to these mysterious, these terrible, these fascinating, these lovable, dark hordes. Ties that were of the spirit. Ties not only superficially entangled with mere outline of features or color of skin. Deeper. Much deeper than either of these. (95)

Nevertheless, even in their most articulate expressions of loyalty to the black race, a certain distance can be perceived between these characters and the rest of the community. It is as if they saw themselves apart from the "Negroes," who are defined as "mysterious," "terrible" or "dark hordes," qualifications that imply the lack of a clear identification. Despite their final acceptance of their African American identity, both women are "outsiders," a characteristic inherent in their mulatto condition.

Indeed, racial dichotomies form the inescapable pattern of their lives, as Helga realizes: "Why couldn't she have two lives, or why couldn't she be satisfied in one place?" (93). Racial ambivalence prevails in the description of these two characters who continuously fluctuate between both identities, without truly belonging to either of them. They almost advocate an "in-between" space or a mixed category that can encompass both of them. The impossibility of completely living up to their aspirations allows them privileged insight, from which both women frankly analyze the sexual and racial restrictions that have been forced upon them. Therefore, Helga and Clare's problematic nature symbolizes the deconstruction of the essential conception of the tragic mulatto; their tragedy does not emanate from their indefinite racial condition but from instability in many different spheres of their lives, especially anchored in their role as women.[11]

A traditional reading concludes that both protagonists finally conform to the fate of the tragic mulatta: Clare dies and Helga experiences a death of her self at the novel's closure. But considerations of gender must also be factored into an analysis

---

[11] Judith Branzburg asserts that "the key to Larsen's ambivalence about blackness can be found in an examination of Helga's attitude toward sexuality" (91). She also adds that "Helga can accept her situation, can play at being black, until sexuality is included as part of the definition of

of this "conformity." Larsen is writing in the nineteen-twenties, when "depicting the tragic mulatto was the surest way for a black woman fiction writer to gain a hearing" (Wall, "Passing for What?" 110); she needs to capitalize on the popular tragic mulatta convention to ensure access to her readership. Moreover, as Wall also appropriately remarks, this character was "[t]he least degrading and the most attractive" (110) of all the fictional options available to her, so Larsen puts the mulatto heroine to good use in order to explore the muddy terrain of the sexual profile of African American women.

AFRICAN AMERICAN FEMALE SEXUALITY: BETWEEN PURITY AND PROSTITUTION

Larsen's writing not only presents the figure of the mulatta as a continuous transgression of the racial barrier, but also as the rupture of the last sexual taboo, miscegenation. The resulting product of the sexual encounter of two races, a mulatta becomes by definition "the sexual and racial 'other'" (Flitterman-Lewis 47), wherein gender and race are intimately united. The sense of double jeopardy and transgression inherent in a mulatta transforms her into an appropriate instrument for the exploration of the other infractions of the social code affecting the realm of sexual definition, with special reference to the expression of her own sexuality and the acceptance of the traditionally feminine roles of wife and mother. She thus becomes "a mask for exploration of a female sensibility" (McManus 16). This inquiry is not overtly undertaken in the texts, but needs to be "disguised" or concealed by the racial motif.[12]

*   *   *

---

blackness" (91). Helga's, and by extension Clare's, conflictive relation with her African American identity rests on her uncertain bond to her own sexuality.

[12] The first critic to notice the existence of a sexual substratum under the racial façade in Larsen was Deborah McDowell in her groundbreaking introduction to the 1986 edition: "'S]afe' themes, plots and conventions are used as the protective cover underneath which lie more dangerous subplots" (xxx). Important contributions in this sense are Thornton (1973), Hostletler (1990), and Blackmer (1995).

History of Representation

The main reason for Larsen's use of that kind of façade to tackle such a polemic issue lies precisely in the history of the representation of African American female sexuality from the era of slavery onwards. This representation is heir to an eminently racist legacy, symbolized by the so-called "plantation school," whose most significant result is the tradition of the "cult of true womanhood." Together with this racist perspective, another important point to take into account in that history is the revision and debate over representation that takes place during the decade of the nineteen-twenties within the African American intellectual community between two seemingly clashing codes: primitivism and the genteel tradition. These conflictive images of African American women comprise the legacy of the patriarchal and racist past that both protagonists actively seek to redefine.

At this point of the analysis, a brief overview of such a history seems appropriate to be able to better relate it to the texts. While in general, female sexuality has always been considered a social and literary taboo, the taboo has been greater in the case of African American women. The "cult of true womanhood" basically upheld white women as repositories of the qualities and virtues that made them worthy of the feminine category *par excellence*: piety, purity, submission and domesticity (Welter in Carby 23).[13] Among these qualities, purity or the complete absence of sexual desire became the *sine qua non* for the ideal woman. Welter specifically comments on it: "Purity was as essential as piety to a young woman, its absence as unnatural and unfeminine. Without it she was, in fact, no woman at all, but a member of some lower order" (qtd. in Carby 25). Such sexist ideology was particularly endorsed in the literature of the time, the "plantation school," which

---

[13] An important part of the analysis that follows draws from three crucial contributions to the understanding of the birth and social function of the "cult of true womanhood" and the stereotypes it fosters: *Reconstructing Womanhood* by Hazel V. Carby (1987), *Black Women Novelists* by Barbara Christian (1980), and *Women, Race & Class* by Angela Davis (1983), especially chapter one. In his study of the emergence of this ideological configuration, Ronald Takaki clarifies the process whereby in the mid-nineteenth century economic factors—mainly associated with the growing industrial development and the absence of husbands from households—were determining in the rise of a sharp dichotomy between work and home and the subsequent demand of the constant presence of women at home (140-1). These causes led to the establishment of an ideological patriarchy that needed to be continuously reaffirmed by means of an absolute control of the so-called "domestic sphere," where not only women but also slaves were included as beings "naturally" inferior to the white men who held the reins (Davis, *Women* 12; White, *Ar'n't I a Woman?* 58).

presented the figure of the "Southern belle" as the embodiment of all those feminine attributes.

Obviously, the essentialist notion of femininity propounded by this ideology is not only sexist, but it is also, and more profoundly, racist. The lack of adaptation to its model implies "no femininity," that is, African American women are defined as "no women," since they fail to comply with all the indispensable prerequisites: "[B]lack women were practically anomalies" (Davis, *Women* 5). As a counterpart to the sexless white women, African American women and, concretely, mulattas were conceived as the prototype of the "loose woman," women possessed by a kind of animal instinct that transformed them into "beasts" in search of sexual pleasure. As Christian puts it: "The image of the black woman as 'lewd' and 'impure' develops partially in response to the lady's 'enforced' chastity and partially as a result of the planters' myth about the sexuality of blacks" (*Black Women* 13).[14]

This conception of African American women is so ingrained in the racist and sexist mentality of the time that it remained one of the most powerful literary tropes up to the nineteen-twenties. The third decade of the twentieth century is marked by a willingness on the part of African Americans to revise such a myth, postulating a new image of female sexuality diametrically opposed to the stereotype. Preoccupation with the topic during the Harlem Renaissance is enacted in the conflict between the so-called "primitivism" or the most popular literary trend of the time that capitalizes on African American sensuality in general, and the more conservative side identified with the "genteel tradition."

The representation of African American women's sexuality in primitivist works is characterized as lascivious and uncontrollable despite the sexual liberation primitivism seems to assure them. The derogatory image of their sexuality is evident even in the works by artists such as Picasso, despite their admiration. In these works black women still personified the sexuality of prostitutes, although Pieterse grants that "the attitude towards sexuality itself was different—not hostile; nor was the prostitute made a criminal" (183). Even acknowledging the fresh

---

[14] Undoubtedly, the fallacy about the exaggerated sexuality of the black race and, concretely, of black women justified the reiterated abuse female slaves were subjected to by white planters. These men clearly projected onto their female slaves the sexual fantasies that they refused to admit in themselves, profiting from "the natural craving of the black woman for sex" (Christian, *Black Women* 13). Conversely, the belief in the uncontrollable sexuality of black women favored the maintenance of the enslaving patriarchal power and of its racist ideology, since women slaves constituted the basis for the reproduction of new slaves, new labor force. However, it was precisely this animal nature which also served as the perfect excuse to deny African American women their right to motherhood, since only chaste white women could claim that prerogative.

perspective and sexual tolerance promised by the primitivist movement, the direct nexus between sexuality and African American women implies the perpetuation of a vision that configures both as the "Other" *par excellence.* This process of redrawing the boundaries to exclude the "Other" means the rejection of that otherness, and simultaneously, of the sexual discourse as marginal and thus dangerous for the continuity of the social and racial *status quo.*

In opposition to the primitivist school, the so-called "genteel tradition" basically proposes the development of the conservative virtues characteristic of the nineteenth century. Special emphasis is conferred to the established moral code in contrast to the racist image of African American animality and, particularly, that assigned to black women. They, more than men, must carry the moral burden placed up on them and prove racist assertions false. Ultimately, they are also responsible for the affirmation of the bourgeois and demure character ascribed to the middle class, which is erected as the only valid representative of the black race.[15]

So sexuality is proposed within the confines of a third coordinate: social class. The inclusion of this new parameter responds to historical conditions, since the existence of an African American middle class is not possible until after the Civil War. What is relevant, though, is that this middle class is intent from the very beginning on appropriating white middle-class ideology, even absorbing its cultural and sexual patterns. The representation of African American women is intimately linked to the idea of purity intrinsic to the concept of "true" women. The accusations of lust are therefore rejected as socially determined, as Elise Johnson McDougald puts it: "Sex irregularities are not a matter of race, but of socio-economic conditions" (379). Upholders of the genteel orientation defend the right of the intellectual middle class to represent the rest of the race, basing their claim

---

[15] Both Monda and Wall mention Elise McDougald and her defense of African American women's morality in her article "The Task of Negro Womanhood" (369-82) as a good illustration of the rupture with preestablished stereotypes and affirmation of the conservative character of the genteel tradition. Wall initiates her study on women poets of that time in this telling way: "Part of the conservatism found in the writings of the poets of the period reflects a determination not to conform in even the slightest manner to the hateful stereotypes. Certain subjects, particularly sex, were taboo and the language was mostly genteel" ("Poets and Versifiers" 76). In the quote these poets' intentionality, and that of African American women writers' in general, is related to an attempt to do away with any racist myth surrounding their sexuality. The problem is that another myth is molded to replace the discarded one, the genteel image. For many critics Larsen contributes to the configuration of the latter myth: when "outraged by prevailing concepts and stereotypical images of African Americans during the Harlem Renaissance" (Williams 165-6), Larsen becomes "aggressively bourgeois" (Fuller 18). This kind of critique, however, fails to notice to what extent Larsen engages in a direct attack on that same bourgeoisie.

on an almost Puritan value system. African American women are compelled to respect a moral and sexual criterion of purity that does not leave any possibility for expression or control of their own sexuality.

Thus, there are two sets of images that emerge out of the long historical development briefly delineated: the prostitute or exotic woman versus the lady or genteel middle-class woman. I contend that Larsen's protagonists deconstruct each of these prevailing stereotypes while conversely searching for self-definition and independence.[16] Besides the racial ambiguity dealt with above, both women also experience a patent insecurity as regards their sexuality. This sense of insecurity derives from the tension between the internalization of the different demeaning stereotypes about their sexuality and the need for self-expression. Both Helga and Clare reject stereotypical images in favor of a self-definition based on their own experiences, which enables a less repressive reading of their own sexuality and, consequently, could actually become representative of African American women of the time.

*   *   *

Sentimental Tradition and Sexuality

In addition to the narrative of passing and in order to deal with the sexual innuendo in both novels, Larsen makes use of another genre, which is supposedly more appropriate for writing a feminine narrative: the romance or sentimental novel. This connection clearly affiliates her with a female tradition which, according to McLendon, "does not preclude her inclusion in a black tradition" (112). Larsen's allegiances to both canons—female and African American—confirm her adherence to the concept of "double double consciousness" personified in her protagonists. However, a problem emerges in her use of the sentimental tradition because usually "these texts also assume an Anglo-Saxon background for the main characters" (Cranny-Francis 187). Larsen's work is at odds with this trait, but I want to demonstrate that the author appropriates the sentimental model intentionally in order to subvert the conventional image of women and to parodically revise it.

---

[16] Several critics have noticed Larsen's depiction of the dichotomy between these two opposite images, without delving into the profound implications of such a portrait (Lewis, "The Mulatto Woman" 85; Branzburg 77; McLendon 119; Wall, "Passing for What?" 102; McDowell, "Introduction" xix).

Despite Larsen's determination, her manipulation of a markedly white standard has awakened great controversy in critical responses to her novels, read as offensive to the African American value system.[17] Claudia Tate accounts for this critical standpoint very discerningly: "They [critics in general] see instead a writer who chose to escape the American racial climate in order to depict trite melodramas about egocentric black women passing for white" ("Nella Larsen's *Passing*" 146). The combination of the passing convention, of which many critics disapproved, with "trite melodramas" in their view diminishes her value as a writer. However, none of these critics seems to take into account what Tate calls "the psychological dimension" (146). Tate alludes to this dimension with regard to the sentimental component found in *Passing,* which serves to increase the insurmountable distance between the aspirations of the protagonist (Irene, in Tate's view),[18] and the reality of her life. Such discrepancy, according to Tate, is mainly of an emotional origin: "The real impetus for the story is Irene's emotional turbulence" (143). Although agreeing with Tate on locating a frankly romantic component not in one but in both novels, I intend to expand what Tate terms the psychological dimension in order to include the analysis of the psychological impact that the historical representation of African American female sexuality has had on these characters. Likewise, I would like to account for the way in which they try to renegotiate the parameters that rule their definition as African American women and the many limitations they need to come to terms with.

Within African American literature the sentimental tradition dates back to the period of abolitionist propaganda.[19] The employment of the sentimental novel to

---

[17] As mentioned above, Robert Bone inaugurated this critical train of thought about Larsen's literary production, characteristic of the fifties and sixties under the auspices of the so-called "Black Arts Movement." Nevertheless, critics contemporary to Larsen judged it very favorably, as Du Bois' praise evinces: "the best piece of fiction that Negro America has produced since the heyday of Chesnutt" ("Passing" 522). To study the historical development of the critical reception to Larsen's works, see a summary in "Desire and Death in *Quicksand*, by Nella Larsen" by Claudia Tate (1995).

[18] Several critics concur with Tate in pointing Irene as the true protagonist of *Passing*, among them Youman (1974), McMillan (1992), Vashti Lewis (1990), Little (1991), and Blackmer (1995). Despite the importance of Irene as narrative voice of the story, I grant protagonism to Clare in this analysis due to the fact that she sparks the narrative interest and triggers the novel's action.

[19] This literary tradition originates in the "novel of manners" or "tale of seduction" typical of the English eighteenth-century production, whose main exponent is *Pamela; or Virtue Rewarded,* published by Samuel Richardson in 1740. Its influence is already felt in American literature a few years later with novels like *The Power of Sympathy: or the Triumph of Nature* by William Hill Brown (1789), considered the first American novel; *Charlotte Temple* by Susana Rowson (1791 in England and 1794 in the United States) or *The Coquette* by Hannah Foster (1797). Despite their popularity, the characteristic critical reaction to this type of novel can be exemplified in the scant

undertake the defense of abolition is pervasive in all antebellum tragic mulatto narratives (*Clotel* by William Wells Brown or *Iola Leroy* by Frances Harper), heavily influenced by the most popular abolitionist novel of the period: Harriet Beecher Stowe's *Uncle Tom's Cabin* (1852). The impact of this trend during the abolitionist era has been studied by Christian (*Black Women* 19-34), who asserts that "by presenting an image of the black woman that would elicit sympathy and appreciation for her and therefore for black people as a whole, Brown and Harper sought to soften as many differences as possible between the images of the black woman and the white woman" (33). From the beginning the heroine of the African American sentimental novel is intent on achieving two main objectives: first, the representation of her race in a positive light and, second but no less important, the approximation of her image to that of white women. The method devised to attain this second aim is, nevertheless, ambivalent at times because of the difficulties involved in the deconstruction of the "cult of true womanhood," which has always excluded and marginalized black women.

Larsen's two novels are inscribed within this literary framework as archetypes of the sentimental trend.[20] However, Larsen's instrumentalization of this tradition responds to two diverging needs: on the one hand, Larsen seems to feel compelled to accept the prevailing model of this convention and, in consequence, its conception of women; on the other, the historical specificity of African American women leads her to break away from the limitations imposed by this tradition, expanding the focus of her narration to incorporate racial and sexual factors.[21] Hence, a double process of parodic revision and reelaboration of the conventions of the sentimental tradition is at work in Larsen's novels, with the

---

attention that critics like Ruland and Bradbury pay to it in their history of American literature *From Puritanism to Postmodernism* (1991), which reveals "a tacit dismissal of the tradition," having been labeled "women writing about women's lives" (Brothers, "What is a Novel of Manners" 1).

[20] In "The View from the Outside: Black Novels of Manners" (1990), Mary Sisney recognizes the propagandistic purpose behind African American novels in general, and the similarities between them and the sentimental tradition, namely "the fight for acceptance, the loss of identity, and the sense of oppression" (172). Her study is illustrative because it tends to belittle any trace of Larsen's intention of revising the sentimental novel, concluding that she "is simply following the novel of manners tradition," whose main message is that "no lady can survive outside society" (180). To the contrary, I intend to give evidence of an intentional revisionist attitude in Larsen.

[21] In this sense, Larsen would occupy a similar position to her predecessors, Harper and Hopkins, who must also seek to reconcile the romanticism inherent in sentimental novels with the necessity of continuing with the African American antebellum imperative to tell the truth. But as Arlene Elder has stated, "in no other body of American writing are form and content so fiercely at war" (qtd. in Washington, *Invented Lives* 76).

purpose of adapting them to the particular definition of African American female sexuality.

In a preliminary approach, Larsen's novels could be interpreted merely as simple variations of the prototype, which, according to Nina Baym, all sentimental novels follow: the heroine, deprived of any help, has to negotiate her journey from adolescence to maturity to achieve independence and self-sufficiency.[22] In Helga's case, the journey would be not only psychological but also literal, since the protagonist's unceasing geographical mobility is read as a tenacious search for that independence. However, as she is never successful, the end of the novel could be taken to represent the inversion of the sentimental pattern. With respect to Clare, the passage from adolescence to adulthood takes place outside the narration; the protagonist presented by Larsen is already the result of her fight to acquire self-sufficiency, which she only attains after her marriage to a white man. It could be argued that, up to a certain point, both novels adapt to the sentimental tradition, but with specific nuances. Indeed, Larsen's main contribution to the parodic subversion of the sentimental code is, precisely, the inclusion of this sexual discourse.

Within the context of sentimental novels, the thematization of female sexuality is practically non-existent, as Cranny-Francis corroborates: "[W]omen must deny their own sexuality in order to achieve a satisfactory marriage" (183). This lack, however, surprises in a type of narrative whose final objective is the maturity of the heroine at all levels "who, beset with hardships, finds within herself the qualities of intelligence, will, resourcefulness, and courage sufficient to overcome them" (Baym 23). Despite the alleged autonomy promoted by the sentimental discourse, female sexuality is still regarded as inadequate because it is too disruptive. Nevertheless, its subversive presence is highlighted in Larsen's works: "[I]ts [Larsen's *Quicksand*'s] sexual politics tore apart the very fabric of the romance form" (Carby 168). Carby's statement about *Quicksand* can be also applied to *Passing*, as both protagonists face the history of the representation of African American female sexuality in specific ways.

*   *   *

---

[22] For the study of the structure and fundamental traits of the sentimental tradition, I take Nina Baym's classic book *Women's Fiction: A Guide By and About Women in America 1820-1870* (1978) as main reference.

Staging Sexuality in Larsen's Novels

Centering on the dichotomy between lady and prostitute, Helga is repeatedly perceived as the latter throughout the narration, which provokes her utmost indignation. The first hint at this kind of possibility is given when she first arrives in New York from Naxos: "[A] few men, both white and black, offered her money, but the price of the money was too dear" (34). Helga's refusal to be defined as such is articulated in her abrupt reaction to the indecent proposal by a famous Danish painter, Olsen: "In my country the men, of my race, at least, don't make such suggestions to decent girls" (86). At this point Helga herself establishes a clear-cut division between her self-definition as a pure woman, following genteel conventions, and the external vision that brands her as a prostitute and projects onto her the convenient cliché of irrepressible sexuality.

This stereotype is also used by Olsen, who represents, up to a certain point, all white men, projecting his sexual desires onto Helga: "You know, Helga, you are a contradiction . . . You have the warm impulsive nature of the women of Africa, but, my lovely, you have, I fear, the soul of a prostitute. You sell yourself to the best buyer" (87). The contradiction does not arise from Helga herself, but quite clearly from Olsen's impossibility of reconciling his vision of Helga as a primitive woman, identifying her with his own fantasies about black women, and the reality he must face in her rejection. Helga very astutely acknowledges these implications in Olsen's strategy. For this reason, Helga chooses to switch from a sexual discourse to a racial one when she declines his marriage proposal: "I couldn't marry a white man . . . It isn't just you, not just personal, you understand. It's deeper, broader than that. It's racial" (88). With this gesture Helga undermines the historical relationship between white men and black women, disallowing the stereotype of primitive women.[23]

Moreover, Helga's reaction against the primitive image not only responds to the kind of treatment she receives from Olsen, but also to the way in which Danish society conceives of her. From her arrival in Denmark her aunt and uncle encourage

---

[23] Monda mentions an essay under the title "White Men and a Colored Woman: Some 'Inter-racial' Activities," in which Larsen tackled the racist assumptions behind that relation which were still operative in 1930. These were reflected in the "painful confrontations with white-male assumptions about her sexual availability" that she herself had to systematically withstand in her encounters with white men (25). Missy Dehn Kubitschek offers an enlightening description of Helga's experience with Olsen as "a cross between that of the American black women on the auction block and that of women sold as mistresses at the Creole balls" (99), later adding that Olsen represents "the full measure of white modernism's racism" (188).

her to visually display her difference wearing bright colors that stress the contrast with her dark skin. This attitude on their part makes her feel at a certain point "like a veritable savage" (69). The scene that follows, in which her relatives literally exhibit her to their friends, recalls the role Hottentot women played in European salons during the nineteenth century (Pieterse 179-82). Helga is aware of this similarity: "Here she was, a curiosity, a stunt, at which people came and gazed" (71). However, she seems to enjoy it until she goes to watch a "minstrel show."[24] Her reaction is immediate: "She felt shamed, betrayed, as if these pale pink and white people among whom she lived had suddenly been invited to look upon something in her which she had hidden away and wanted to forget" (83). In that instant Helga grasps the significance of the role assigned to her by Danish society; the "something" she alludes to is undoubtedly her sensuality. Although she had previously deceived herself, now Helga suddenly realizes her tacit acceptance of the stereotype, as her dismissal of Olsen's picture demonstrates: "It wasn't, she contended, herself at all, but some disgusting sensual creature with her features" (89).

As far as Clare is concerned, the motif of the "loose woman" is even more explicit than in Helga's case. Indeed, many descriptions in the text made through Irene's eyes evoke Clare's sensuality with adjectives like "appealing," "seductive," "caressing," "attractive" and, above all, "so daring, so lovely and so 'having'" (174). These qualities turn Clare into a danger for her friend, who even warns her she could be taken for a prostitute if she went to a charity ball on her own: "Anybody who can pay a dollar, even ladies of easy virtue looking for trade. If you were to go there alone, you might be mistaken for one of them" (199). Irene, on the other hand, personifies the other face of the binomial: the educated and elegant lady who devotes her life to answering letters and organizing social events within the African American community of which she is a prominent member, that is to say, the living embodiment of the genteel lady. Irene advises Clare to find company with in the genteel cicles.

As her counterpart, Clare confesses to her friend that she can be dangerous: "It's just that I haven't any proper morals or sense of duty . . . to get the things I want badly enough, I'd do anything, hurt anybody, throw anything away. Really,

---

[24] Although originally this musical and comic kind of entertainment was performed by white people who painted their faces black to imitate African Americans, black minstrels replaced them becoming the soul of African American comedy in the last decades of the nineteenth century. For a

'Rene, I'm not safe" (210). Clare confirms Irene's perception of her lack of security and her potential risk, the internalization of a stereotypical image of African American women's sexuality as uncontrollable. Clare seems to personify that image, whereas Irene refuses to confront it. Despite this alleged difference between these characters, they share the inner fight to express their own sensuality/sexuality overtly; both feel the weight of social restrictions, which prevents them from acknowledging their real desires. They appear to have internalized the racist assumptions that define them as lacking any moral principle, an internalization that leads them to self-repression and subsequent negation of desire. In consequence, the description of their sexual life is plagued by lack of definition and ambiguity.

From the beginning, Helga is concerned about the lack of something indefinite, something she cannot name, which she attributes to "a lack somewhere" (7). That something is later specified as "something vaguely familiar, but which she could not put a name to," which leads to her discovery that "it was of herself she was afraid" (47). The main reason for her feeling of fear is later disclosed as the sexual attraction she experiences for Dr. Anderson. That sexual desire is always hidden in the text by conveniently vague expressions like "aching delirium" or "indefinite longings" (51) that seem to allude to her racial insecurity. Helga's reaction to her passionate feelings is downright negation and rejection, to the point that she usually runs from Dr. Anderson's disturbing presence. For instance, when she encounters him in a cabaret, dancing with another woman:

> While she still felt for the girl envious admiration, that feeling was augmented by another, *a more primitive emotion*. She forgot the garish crowded room. She forgot her friends. She saw only two figures, closely clinging. She felt her heart throbbing. She felt the room receding. She went out the door . . . At last, panting, confused, but thankful to have escaped . . . A taxi drifted toward her, stopped. She stepped into it, feeling cold, unhappy, misunderstood, and forlorn. (62; my emphasis)

This passage is highly illustrative as it furnishes details about the mixed feelings of passion and jealousy Helga experiences, not only with respect to Dr. Anderson, but also to the woman who dances with him. She apparently admires the woman for

---

study of their evolution and significance during the Harlem Renaissance, see Lewis' *When Harlem* 30-41.

two reasons: first, because she is able to transgress racial boundaries, "she goes about with white people" (60). Although she is condemned by the African American community for this reason, Helga gives her credit for it. But, secondly, Helga's feeling of admiration increases because she also transgresses sexual restraints in her sensual dance with Dr. Anderson. Watching the provocative scene produces very contradictory impulses in the protagonist: on the one hand, she is jealous of her, jealousy being one of the possible interpretations of that "primitive emotion" the text refers to; on the other, Helga is possessed by a strong sexual passion that seizes her and makes her flee. The final description of her sentiments of unhappiness, lack of comprehension, and helplessness articulates Helga's need to give vent to the passion that she constantly denies in herself.

Clare's lack of definition reveals a strategy of ample sexual questioning, even positing a lesbian relationship with her friend Irene.[25] This possibility is suggested through Irene's narration, though it is never clearly stated. Clare's true intention is always blurred, and her only admission is her lack of "proper morals" mentioned above. Such a lack can be decoded even as a reference to her lesbianism in the eyes of Irene, who feels fatally attracted to her. But that hint is as indefinite as Helga's description of her sexual desire: "and something else for which she could find no name" (176). The omission of an appropriate name indicates a clear predisposition on Irene's part to read Clare's behavior as a deviation from the established rules. But the implications once and again signal the presence of a lesbian subtext, as many examples in the novel foreground. For instance, Clare explains the anxiety she felt while waiting for a letter from her: "I'm sure they were all beginning to think that I'd been carrying on an illicit love-affair and the man had thrown me over" (194). Irene tries to bring the argument back to the less unsettling terrain of passing, reminding Clare of the unnecessary risks she runs when going to Harlem, but Clare's answer is evident: "You mean you don't want me, 'Rene?" She

---

[25] Deborah McDowell is again the first critic who ventured that such a substratum existed: "Having established the absence of sex from the marriages of these two women, Larsen can flirt, if only by suggestion, with the idea of a lesbian relationship between them" ("Introduction" xxiii). David L. Blackmore in his article "'That Unreasonable Restless Feeling': The Homosexual Subtexts of Nella Larsen's *Passing*" (1992) explores Clare's sexual significance for Irene, showing evidence of a possible homosexual relationship between them. For both critics lesbianism and marriage are intimately connected since "lesbianism offers an alternative to repressive middle-class marriage" (Blackmore 478). For a psychoanalytic reading of lesbian desire, see Judith Butler's "Passing, Queering: Nella Larsen's Psychoanalytic Challenge" (1993).

thus corroborates that substratum of sexual connotations that has nothing to do with the racial question Irene uses as her excuse.

Once again there is an obvious disparity between Helga's and Clare's behavior: while Helga refutes the feelings that overrun her, Clare tends to accentuate their presence. Intent on denying her own sensuality, Helga reacts violently against her feelings in the cabaret:

> When suddenly the music died, she dragged herself back to the present with a conscious effort; and a shameful certainty that not only had she been in the jungle, but that she had enjoyed it, began to taunt her. She hardened her determination to get away. She wasn't, she told herself, a jungle creature. (59)

The allusion to the metaphor of the jungle to symbolize a certain state of animality related to sexual desires equates "unnatural" sexuality with a lack of moral standards. This definition of sexuality also corresponds to the genteel tradition in which women must be pure and thus deprived of any and all sexual feeling. The above episode takes place after she has witnessed Dr. Anderson's dance, highlighting Helga's repulse of her primitive side which she associates with her sexual passion for him. What is even more relevant here is that these feelings of shame and fear lead her to evade an unbearable situation. The same holds true of her leaving for Denmark. Helga justifies her departure on racial grounds, idealizing Copenhagen as a paradise away from racial prejudice where the dichotomy white/black disappears. In light of the above reflections on Helga's sexual anxiety, this justification could be taken as just another pretext to disguise the true reason that lies in the repression of her sexual desires.

However, in Clare's case such a restraint does not spring from herself, but from Irene who regards her as a very disturbing, potentially disastrous, force in her own life. Irene herself admits that she has built her life on the basis of the social and personal stability that marriage has provided her, which she will not easily renounce: "to her, security was the most important and desired thing in life. Not for any of the others, or for all of them, would she exchange it" (235). When she feels cornered by emotions she is not ready to acknowledge and that could do away with the stability she has worked so hard to achieve, she decides to project those sexual feelings onto her husband imagining an adulterous affair between him and Clare (Blackmore 482). With this choice, Irene again confirms her total adaptation to the code for upper middle-class women, "who accept the culturally prescribed popular genteel image of themselves" and, therefore, "are not only sexually repressed, but will also destroy anything or anyone who threatens their way of life" (Lewis, "Nella Larsen's Use" 41). Irene's positing of an adulterous relationship between her husband and Clare facilitates the repression of her own sexual desires, while it simultaneously makes her aware of the absolute necessity of destroying Clare, who represents a terrible threat to the continuity of her comfortable way of life.

Unable to repress the sexual desires that relentlessly torment her, Helga also considers the possibility of an adulterous relationship with Dr. Anderson, now married to her friend Anne. Her attitude of self-denial crumbles into pieces when Dr. Anderson kisses her and "a long-hidden, half-understood desire welled up in her with the suddenness of a dream" (104). That desire makes her fall prey to tumultuous feelings that take her by surprise and force her to accept a side of her self that she has preferred to ignore. Even then she feels divided between her burning desire and her identification with the genteel society's ideas of a decent woman: "Only then had uneasiness come upon her and a feeling of fear for possible exposure. For Helga Crane wasn't, after all, a rebel from society. Negro society. It did mean something to her" (107). It is at this crucial point when the conflict is laid bare between the social values upheld by the middle class, which constrain her to a genteel mold, and her own longings that lead her to forget its rules and responsibilities.

Despite her doubts, Helga decides for the first time to break away from social restrictions: "But these late fears were overwhelmed by the hardiness of insistent desire" (107). Rejected by Dr. Anderson, she suffers not only from her damaged pride, but from the awareness of her own powerful sexual desire and of the sacrifice she was ready to make in order to satisfy it. The outcome is her feeling of loneliness and her search for reconciliation with the society she was ready to reject. Such reconciliation takes the shape of a religious conversion and an acceptance of the image of prostitute forced upon her as fair punishment for her contemptible behavior: "A scarlet 'oman. Come to Jesus, you pore los' Jezebel" (112).[26] From this moment onwards Helga feels seized by a powerful force that prevents her from leaving the spectacle, a great "Bacchic vehemence" (113) arising from her acceptance of her identity as a sinful, lost woman. That she stays within

---

[26] Lewis coincides in analyzing this episode as the acceptance of the prostitute stereotype on Helga's part ("The Mulatto Woman" 99).

that atmosphere of religious fanaticism suggests that Helga comes to internalize this alleged identity.

Likewise, Irene finally accuses Clare of adultery without any kind of evidence. Clare and her sexual potentiality are deemed dangerous for Irene's social and personal identity. That lurking danger provokes a panic in Irene that is very similar to Helga's and leads her to wish for Clare's destruction. As McDowell writes, "Irene must destroy Clare because she 'is both the embodiment and the object of the sexual feelings' which threaten her safe middle-class existence" (qtd. in Blackmore 482). Consequently, Clare's destruction represents the final repression of Irene's sexual desires and her continued acceptance of the genteel code which calls for the sacrifice of the object of her desires. In this case as well, the prudish and pure lady has triumphed over the primitive woman.

Therefore, up to a certain point both Helga's and Clare's attitudes embody the dilemma of African American women between an external definition of their own sexuality, which offers the two limiting images of prostitute versus lady, and their own efforts for self-definition and self-expression. The fact that both of them succumb to those images and adopt the prevailing moral code implies failure in reconstructing their own identity in favor of the reestablishment of social harmony. Although in both cases Larsen seems to prefer the stability ensured by the dominant value system, certain signs of change are evident under this conventional cover, conducive to a rupture with the system. The main change that I seek to underline in this analysis is precisely the claim for women's control over their own sexuality and the subsequent questioning of the preestablished canons and images. Within this general framework, there seems to be some space for the development of relationships not socially sanctioned, such as affairs out of wedlock or with other women, although they must be sacrificed in the end in favor of social standardization and the maintenance of the *status quo*.

AFRICAN AMERICAN MOTHERHOOD: FROM "MAMMY" TO PERFECT MIDDLE-CLASS MOTHER

Larsen's vision of motherhood also responds to the revision of the dominant racial and social parameters undertaken in the novels as a logical consequence of the problematizing of sexuality described above. A parodic reelaboration of the sentimental conventions is also at work, especially those concerned with the establishment of what Baym calls "a self-made or surrogate family," that is, a family that replaces the biological family, seen as an impediment to the integral development of women. The new family is understood within the framework of the so-called "cult of domesticity" as an alternative to the dominant patriarchal order, a very positive enviroment for women, as this framework "bolstered her self-esteem, supported her inclinations towards self-fulfilment, and justified a search for means of exerting influence that were compatible with her woman's nature" (Baym 29). Despite Baym's exaltation of this cult as an appropriate means for female liberation, the sentimental tradition is still circumscribed to the limited domestic sphere granted by patriarchal rule, and the family is still envisioned as the primary objective in women's lives. The emphasis on the family in sentimental novels in Tate's view means that: "[T]hese narratives not only culminate in marriage; they also idealize the formation of the family unit. Moreover, the marriage story and resulting domestic ideality assume discursive dominance in female narratives" ("Allegories" 106). From this premise, Tate revises the critical attention that has been paid to this tradition, concluding that the sentimental novels written by African American women during the nineteenth century are, in fact, "discourses of liberation" (107), reiterating Baym's description of the sentimental tradition.[27]

So far a study of the sentimental trend in general, and of nineteenth-century African American novels in particular, depicts marriage and maternity as the ideal discourses for the formation of female subjectivity, because women can develop in a nurturing enviroment, away from the negative influence of the patriarchal ideology of the time. However, in the case of Larsen's novels, the idealization of marriage and motherhood is never evidenced. On the contrary, Larsen inquires into the limitations and constraints of both institutions in the lives of the protagonists,

---

[27] Tate as well as Baym seem to answer the need to counteract the traditional derogatory vision of the sentimental code. For a summary of this kind of critical evaluation, see "What Is a Novel of Manners?" by Barbara Brothers and Bege Bowers (1990).

which lead both of them to reject motherhood. Their attitude generates a controversy between the polemic history of the representation of African American maternity and Helga and Clare's attempt to define themselves, even advocating at the end of the texts a kind of "voluntary motherhood" (Davis, *Women* 202).[28]

Traditionally, the definition of African American women's maternity has been also dictated by the previously mentioned literary codes: the "cult of true womanhood," on the one hand, which denies them their right as mothers characterizing them only as "breeders";[29] and the "genteel tradition," on the other, which views them as the epitome of the perfect middle-class wife and mother. In the latter one, the predominant role of the mother as bringing harmony and religious cohesion to the family denotes the adaptation of the genteel role to the non-white middle-class family. This code was transferred to sentimental novels, which can be divided in two groups according to Tate: those written before Emancipation, in which African American women express their "moral indignation at the sexual and maternal abuses associated with slavery" ("Allegories" 107), and those after Emancipation, which "construct, deconstruct, and reconstruct Victorian gender conventions in order to designate black female subjectivity as a most potent force in the advancement of the race" (107). The genteel tradition, therefore, revalues the matriarchal figure following the parameters promoted by the middle class in an attempt to vindicate African American women's rights to marriage and maternity. Within this paradigm, maternity is intimately related to marriage in such a way that both are defined as the compendium of security and stability to which a middle-class woman may aspire.

At first sight, both protagonists seem to personify the genteel pattern because they picture themselves as happy wives and mothers despite class differences. Thus, they seem to break definitely with racist stereotypes that deny them both roles: they are neither "mammies" as they take care of their own children full-time, nor "black

---

[28] Davis devotes chapter eight to explaining the intimate relationship between the feminist claim for voluntary motherhood and the campaigns in favor of contraceptives.

[29] The denial of their maternity does not negate the biological fact of procreation, so "the cult of true womanhood" transforms African American motherhood into something negative through the invention of two stereotypical images secondary to the prominent role of the white mother: the "mammy" and the "black matriarch." Although different, both images are intent on alienating African American women from both their femininity and their subsequent maternal prerogative, exculpating the inhuman treatment to which they are submitted, which often includes separation from their own children. Deborah White details the origin and evolution of the figure of the "mammy" as a necessary counterpart to the Jezebel image, in which the ideology of slavery and the cult of domesticity converge (46-61). For a discussion of these stereotypes see Christian (*Black Women* 11-12) and Carby (39); see also Pieterse on its persistence (228).

matriarchs" as they live with their husbands and display typically feminine attributes. In fact, in this first moment, both of them seem to constitute the perfect example of a fulfilling motherhood, well beyond any limitations imposed by external representations. A more detailed study reveals, however, the way in which Larsen makes use of both conventions—"cult of true womanhood" and "genteel tradition"—to critique the construction of African American motherhood and to explore "the need for black women to create new forms of self-representation" (Hostetler 44). Their need is especially related to their self-definition as mothers, which is a problematic issue for both protagonists. The two women share an internal struggle to establish their own perception over forced definitions of their sense of motherhood—either racist denial or genteel idealization. This struggle leads them to ambiguity, an ever-present characterization of these heroines.

The ambiguity and questioning of their motherhood starts from the very notion of which race they have chosen to reproduce. From this standpoint, both women symbolize very different attitudes towards their role as mothers: while Helga sticks to the code established by the African American community, involving herself in its reproduction and expansion; Clare destabilizes such a code, preferring to reproduce the dominant race as the culmination of her integration into the white world. Both decisions imply a very definite positioning with reference to conventional images of their value as mothers. In the first case, Helga subverts the racist notions and chooses to reproduce her own race, showing her willingness to contribute to the African American cause for independence from the dominant ideology. In the process, though, she submits to the genteel notion of motherhood. With respect to Clare, her choice to have a "white" child could be understood as twofold: on the one hand, it represents a submission to the racist construction of her motherhood as a possession of the whites and thus a betrayal of her own race, because, as another character says, "[N]obody wants a dark child" (168); but, on the other hand, it also marks a clear subversion of conventions constituting an act of freedom and agency that ridicules restricting dominant laws and calls into question the mere existence of racial and social boundaries.

Analyzing the motives that impel both women to accept their roles as mothers and wives, it is possible to discover the reasons for so much of their ambiguity. Certainly, for Helga, maternity and marriage represent at first the definitive acceptance of the genteel social and moral order, as she puts it: "[I]t was a chance at stability, at permanent happiness, that she meant to take" (117). But it also provides her with a sense of security with regard to her sexuality, redeeming her from any possible undertone of "looseness." Indeed, this seems to be one of the main motivations for accepting her new way of life: "it had brought this other thing, this anaesthetic satisfaction for her senses" (118). The fact that she marries a minister devoted to his community down South ratifies her in a double sense, erasing any doubt at a social and sexual level (McDowell, "Introduction" ixi). She ensures the satisfaction of her sexual needs within a socially sanctioned framework, in which the expression of her sexuality is channelled to a less dangerous terrain, justified and even sanctified in a Christian marriage for its main objective of reproduction. This triple function—racial, social, and sexual—of her motherhood and marriage makes Helga come to terms with the initial rejection that she feels for both institutions.

Exactly the same reasons seem to motivate Clare to consider both marriage and maternity as indispensable elements to consummate her final passing into the white race. Her need for racial and social status leads her to regard marriage and her subsequent maternity as desirable. Marrying a white man automatically transforms her into a member of the privileged race and bestows upon her the right of inclusion in the canon of purity and the subsequent right to maternity reserved for white women. To achieve the status of respectable white middle-class woman, she is ready to sacrifice everything, even her personal security threatened by the birth of her daughter: "I'm afraid I nearly died of terror the whole nine months before Margery was born for fear that she might be dark. Thank goodness, she turned out all right" (168). To beget a white descendant elevates her symbolically to the motherly ideal in the dominant ideology and erases any doubt of her racial identity. The fact that she actually undergoes this torment to bring a white child into the world emphasizes the vision of maternity as a social imposition to which she submits in order to complete her social and racial integration, but which is in no way fulfilling at a personal level.

Both women, however, show a profound rejection of their maternity as forced upon them by social pressure. In both cases the objection seems to be grounded in a compound of racial, social, and gendered circumstances which reveal their struggle against stereotypical categorization. Helga's objection to a conventional way of life has been influenced by the experience of her mother who defines marriage and family as "a grievous necessity. Even foolish, despised women must have food and clothing; even unloved little Negro girls must be somehow provided for" (23). Helga's original rejection of motherhood, moreover, is also affected by her vision of racial prejudice and its effect on her unborn children:

> How stupid she had been ever to have thought that she could marry and perhaps have children in a land where every dark child was handicapped at the start by the shroud of color! She saw, suddenly, the giving birth to little, helpless, unprotesting Negro children as a sin, an unforgivable outrage. (75)

Helga affirms here her rejection of her own possible maternity because she feels helpless to defend her future children from racist pressures, recalling the image of the slave woman unable to exert control over her own family. In a way, by rejecting her role as mother of these hypothetical children, she is showing her unwillingness to become part of the social game that perpetuates the dominant racist society and the stereotypes about her motherhood that this society forces upon her. Her beliefs are articulated more clearly in a conversation with her ex-fiancé James, in which she equates marriage and maternity: "Marriage—that means children, to me. And why add any more unwanted, tortured Negroes to America?" (103). However, this excuse occults other reasons that have to do with Helga's perception of motherhood as a dead end, as a prison for life.

The fact that in the end Helga capitulates and marries signifies the impossibility of fighting against conventions and the necessity of adapting to middle-class moral and social standards. Indeed, as Hostetler points out, "the images of claustrophobia that close the novel have little to do with racial self-hatred and everything to do with gender constructed as a biological prison" (40).[30] Helga is trapped by her maternity, which accounts for the "quicksand" (the more she struggles, the deeper she sinks) from which the title of the novel is taken: "The children used her up. There were already three of them, all born within the short space of twenty months" (122). In fact, Helga falls victim to her own body which she is unable to control. As Hortense Spillers affirms: "[T]o lose control of the body is to be hostage to insufferable circumstances; it is also in the historical outline of black American women often enough the loss of life" ("Interstices" 93); in fact, the end of the novel is prefigured by the mention of death, the lot assigned to Helga.

---

[30] Many critics in addition to Hostetler consider her gender to be the main reason for her claustrophobia and tragic ending, to name a few, McLendon (1995), McMillan (1992), Christian (1980), and Thorton (1973).

The definition of maternity and marriage as veritable "quicksand" for African American women makes Helga rebel against the socially established rules and criticize both institutions as subtle means to enslave women. Similarly, Helga questions marriage as the source of stability for women according to the genteel code, even considering it immoral: "Marriage. This sacred thing of which parsons and other Christian folk ranted so sanctimoniously, how immoral—according to their own standards—it could be!" (134). In the end, Helga rejects marriage as the solution to her sexual anxiety, because it brings undesirable pregnancies that destroy her both physically and mentally. She is unable, however, to find a positive sense of her motherhood outside conventional images. Her sexual and racial quicksand drags her lower and lower.

Similar feelings are articulated by Clare, who considers marriage and family as a constraint for women, admitting repeatedly that she also feels trapped by her husband: "Damn Jack! he keeps me out of everything. Everything I want" (200). Clare profits from these institutions to obtain racial and social stability (just as Helga does). But the sacrifice involved is too great: her own sense of self. Her unhappiness, as in Helga's case, is quite imprecise in the novel, but her position as mother and wife seems to be one of the main causes for dissatisfaction in her life. Unlike the image of the respectable white middle-class woman that she seems to personify, her behavior transgresses this genteel model because her blunt rejection calls into question her own sense of motherhood. For her, maternity is equated to cruelty, as she herself affirms: "I think . . . that being a mother is the cruellest thing in the world" (197). This statement echoes Helga's in her initial refusal to fulfill the expectations of motherhood imposed upon her. From the beginning Clare's refusal is united with her fear as to which skin color her child would have, because it could represent the betrayal of her passing: "But I'll never risk it again. Never! The strain is simply—too hellish" (168). Although both characters refuse at first to comply with the socially imposed model of perfect mother on racial grounds, this rejection is more complicated in Clare's case due to the psychological horror of her pregnancy.

In addition, her rejection is also connected to her sexual ambiguity, identified by some critics with the alleged lesbianism of the character, a trait that would definitely shatter the stereotypical image of perfect wife and mother. The possibility of a lesbian subtext in the novel subverts, then, the genteel idealization of marriage and maternity. At the same time it challenges the role that both institutions play in the patriarchal domination of women, who are taught to aim at both as the only possible source of happiness. Clare's behavior, however, transgresses that model especially on the sexual plane. The fact that, despite her feelings, Clare subjects herself to the suffering her pregnancy entails in order to bring into the world a white heir underlines her view of maternity as an imposition, unrewarding in any sense.

According to Deborah McDowell, maternity becomes a symbol of "death in life" ("Introduction" xxii), and marriage an equivalent to moral and sexual degradation for these women. They attempt to fight against conventional definitions of their role as mothers but end up trapped by them. Nevertheless, the way in which each of them faces it is quite different: whereas Clare gives in only once in order to ensure her complete integration into the white race and therefore instrumentalizes her maternity in accordance with the spirit of "voluntary motherhood," Helga finds no way out of her endless pregnancies. Despite these differences, the price that both have to pay for their rebellion against the established social order, as both stories suggest, is very high, amounting to their final destruction. Although it takes diverse shapes, the message is similar: both women have to yield to social rules which ultimately destroy them.

Indeed, both novels close with images of death: in *Passing* Clare falls out of the window and *Quicksand* leaves Helga pregnant for the fifth time, a pregnancy which will trap her even more securely in her death in life. Maternity as a metaphor of death in life is clearer with reference to Helga, who cannot break her vicious cycle of pregnancies. The middle-class quicksand has sucked her into extreme physical and mental deterioration.[31] Also for Clare death is the inevitable end. Even if her death were merely symbolic, it would mean discarding what Clare represents at two levels: first, as the embodiment of lesbian desire, inappropriate according to the genteel code, which denies sexual desire in women at all, much less desire for other women; and second, her anomaly as a wife and mother who declines to beget any more children. In this sense, her death would represent the same resolution to the conflict indicated in Helga's; that is, both of them must surrender to the pressure exercised by the social order, which kills any deviations from the norm. The tragic endings that both protagonists meet confirm the social reality that these women face. In their flight from racist manipulations, they must accept a model of security, stability, and respectability based on marriage and maternity that does not allow the

---

[31] Although in "Nella Larsen's 'Moving Mosaic': Harlem, Crowds, and Anonymity" (1997) Mary Esteve upholds that due to the nature of quicksand, "she may indeed resurface" (282), I align myself with other critics like Carby or Ann DuCille who see the ending of the novel as a clear representation of death.

free expression of their desires and dreams. Even at a symbolic level, their deaths stand for the inability of both women to confront the constraining and suffocating definitions of their motherhood and to devise ways to free themselves from their effect.

Nella Larsen's novels enact the conflicting traditions that interact in the interpretation of the key issues of sexuality and maternity. In this reading, coordinates grounded in race, gender, and social class converge in order to redefine these two key concepts through a multiple vision that allows the analysis of the diverse images generated by these conventions. Hence, Larsen's purpose is twofold: to account for the deviations from the norm African American femininity entails, and to reformulate it in consonance with the real experience of contemporary women engaged in a process of self-definition and self-validation. In order to do so, both novels make use of the figure of the mulatta as an effective instrument for exploring the different kinds of transgressions in the novels, thereby justifying the leit motif of passing, or the debate over "race," as a crucial cover to deal with the controversial issues of African American sexuality and motherhood.

Throughout the chapter I have foregrounded two key ideas: first and foremost, the affirmation of sexuality as an integral part of the everyday life experience of African American women in open contradiction with the prevailing contemporary preconceptions that regard it as anti-natural or anti-feminine; and second, the denunciation of marriage and maternity as restrictive institutions that hinder the personal development of these women. Apparently because of the innovative, possibly offensive, nature of these considerations, Larsen seems to have felt compelled to hide them under the cover of the protagonists' final destruction. Despite the fact that they lose their fight against the social machine, these novels inaugurate the feminist debate that deconstructs the monolithic male literary tradition and creates some space for other possible interpretations. These interpretations hint at new ways to be a woman without having to adapt to racist or idealistic codes of behavior, and propound a valid, although problematic, feminine vision as an alternative for the definition of African American womanhood.

FIVE

Female Fancy in Jessie Fauset's Plum Bun

Keep sleeping:

I'm not a prince,
I have no sword
nor have I time
to cut the hedge
to climb the wall
to give a kiss
or marry you . . .

Tomorrow
I must start work early
(or I'll be fired)

My dreaming must wait
till Sunday
My thinking till vacation
time

Keep sleeping
and dream another hundred years
until the right one
appears

Josef Wittman

"Sleeping Beauty"

The same racial and gender coordinates foregrounded in Larsen's novels are found in Jessie Fauset's *Plum Bun* (1928), in which the author's exploration of the dichotomy between appearances and reality also makes use of the mulatta figure as a convenient twofold metaphor: on the one hand, as the sublime symbol of the idea of double consciousness and of the social and racial implications derived from it; on the other, as a suitable representation of African American women and the problematic definition of both their identity and their sexuality. However, although they share common topics and interests and a similar woman-based perspective, the important difference between Larsen and Fauset lies in their choice of strategies for questioning the dominant racist and sexist ideology of the nineteen-twenties.

At first sight, both seem to opt for the conventionalism inherent in the passing and sentimental traditions as appropriate covers for masking the potent racial and gender critique in their texts. However, in Fauset's case the façade also includes two other literary traditions regarded as fundamentally inoffensive and, up to a point, naive: fairy tales and nursery rhymes. These four traditions are combined in the text to create a universe mainly dominated by female fancy, often mistaken for assimilation to the dominant white mythology. Because of its dreamlike atmosphere, Fauset's novel has been traditionally discarded as a mere African American version of a romantic tale. A critical opinion that has endured until quite recently, but which overlooks the presence of the subversive and parodic component.

⤞⬥⤝

THE CRITICAL RECEPTION OF FAUSET'S NOVEL

While all the writers discussed so far—Johnson, Schuyler, and Larsen—have been systematically condemned by certain critics, Fauset's case is even more poignant. Although intellectuals such as Du Bois proclaimed Fauset part of a chosen group of writers whose contribution proved crucial to the development of the Harlem Renaissance,[1] the traditional response to her work has objected to it on two main grounds, namely its emphasis on the middle class and its markedly romantic nature.

---

[1] Du Bois praises both Fauset and Larsen for their perceptive representation of African American women, especially for their treatment of the delicate topic of morality in consonance with his vision. Particularly laudatory is his review of Fauset's first novel *There is Confusion* (1924) which he describes as "a novel of the educated and aspiring classes" ("Younger Literary Movement" 162). Another contemporary critic of Fauset's, George W. Jacobs, mentions her novels as "delightful exceptions" to the primitivist tendency of the time, proposing them as models for "aesthetic truth" over passing fashions (710). Following their lead, W. S. Braithwaite depicts Fauset as "the potential Jane Austen of Negro literature" (26). According to Abby A. Johnson, the publication of Fauset's first novel was very significant, as Du Bois and Locke predicted that it would mark an epoch. George Schuyler also shared their enthusiasm: "I was like a traveler returning to familiar scenes, nodding with satisfaction and approval at the recognition of familiar landmarks" (qtd. in Johnson, "Literary Midwife" 143). The event of this publication led to the so-called "Civic Club dinner," which officially inaugurated the Harlem Renaissance era (Lewis, *When Harlem* 89, 93-4; Shockley 124).

The first view is exemplified by Addison Gayle who considers Fauset the representative of the middle class *par excellence:*

> More so than her contemporaries, [Fauset] spoke for the black bourgeoisie, past and present. The dream of Frank Webb, of a class midway between whites and poor Blacks, is now realized; the middle class has grown to maturity and received validation in the work of a talented writer. (119)

Gayle is seconding a critique that labels Fauset as "simply an apologist for the black middle class" (qtd. in McDowell, "Regulating Midwives" ix).[2] The problem seems to be located not in Fauset's *belonging* to the middle class, but in the assumption that she agrees with the attempts of the African American middle class to assimilate to white middle-class standards. Fauset fostered this conviction when affirming in the introduction to her third novel *The Chinaberry Tree* (1931):

> I have depicted something of the homelife of the colored American who is not being pressed too hard by the Furies of Prejudice, Ignorance, and Economic Injustice. And behold he is not so vastly different from any other American, just distinctive . . . his sons and daughters respond as completely as do the sons and daughters of European settlers to modern American sophistication. (ix-x)

This statement has been appropriated in order to denounce the author's tendency to equate white and African American middle classes, emphasizing the superiority that Fauset seems to assign to the former over the latter.[3]

---

[2] Examples of this kind of criticism can be traced back to one contemporary writer, Langston Hughes, followed by Robert Bone and Arthur P. Davis, among others. Bone's *The Negro Novel in America* (1958) plays a significant role in classifying her with the so-called "Rear Guard" or "Old Guard" (99). Leroi Jones in the sixties cements this rejection to the middle class that Fauset seems to symbolize, defining her as the main representative of "a group that has always gone out of its way to cultivate any mediocrity, as long as that mediocrity was guaranteed to prove to America . . . that they were not really who they were, i. e., Negroes" (qtd. in Johnson, "Literary Midwife" 144). See also Davis, *Dark Tower* 90; Berzon 170-1; Rampersad 195; Anderson 198.

[3] Hiroko Sato depicts Fauset's novels as "novels of manners of the Negro upper class," which emphasize "the similarity between blacks and whites, rather than the differences" (70). Another writer contemporary to Fauset, Rudolph Fisher, comments that "it is plain, as Miss Fauset intended it to be, that these Americans are not essentially different from other Americans" (qtd. in Bloom 37). Apart from other critics mentioned above, see also Branzburg 42; Bell, *Afro-American Novel* 107.

With regard to the second objection, Fauset's novels have been characterized as naive and romantic, endowed with scant artistic quality. Claude McKay was the first critic who judged Fauset as "prim and dainty as a primrose" and her novels as "quite as fastidious and precious" (qtd. in McDowell, "Regulating Midwives" xxx). David Littlejohn reiterates McKay's judgment when he qualifies Fauset's novels as "vapidly genteel lace curtain romances" (qtd. in McDowell, "Neglected Dimension" 86). Feminist critics have also obviated the highly parodic and suggestive substratum in Fauset's work. McManus seconds Barbara Christian's earlier arguments about Fauset's plots which, in Christian's words, "seldom rise beyond the level of melodrama," so her novels become "bad fairytales in which she sacrifices the natural flow of life to the thesis she feels she must prove—that blacks are as conventional as whites" (41). Likewise, McLendon also mentions Christian's disparaging criticism of Fauset for presenting an image of African American women according to predominantly white parameters (29).[4] This critical tendency, inaugurated by Christian, has even promoted the idea that Larsen is a much better novelist than Fauset.[5]

All the above responses demonstrate that the parodic and subversive intentionality in Fauset's work has been mainly overlooked perhaps, because it was very well hidden under a multilayered cover. Recent criticism, however, has begun to evaluate the "indirect strategies and narrative disguise [which] become necessary covers for rebellious and subversive concerns" (McDowell, "Regulating Midwives" xxi). Thanks to the work of critics like McDowell,[6] serious reevaluation has begun to determine the type of cover deployed by Fauset to disguise the racial and gender critique in *Plum Bun.* The multiple dimensionality of Fauset's work—the passing tradition, the romance, the fairy tale, and the nursery rhyme—is, in fact, quite

---

[4] Another instance of a feminist critic objecting to Fauset is illustrated by Carby who, even admitting the presence of a subversive intention in Fauset, concludes: "I would argue that ultimately the conservatism of Fauset's ideology dominates her texts" (167).

[5] Among the critics who suggest Larsen's superiority with respect to Fauset, see Singh, *Novels* (98); Gayle (110); Christian, *Black Women* (43); Branzburg (78), and Carby (168).

[6] Among these critics, the most relevant contributions by chronological order are the two articles by Joseph Feeney, "A Sardonic Unconventional Jessie Fauset: The Double Structure and Double Vision of her Novels" (1979) and "Black Childhood as Ironic: A Nursery Rhyme Transformed in Jessie Fauset's Novel *Plum Bun*" (1980); Carolyn Sylvander's monograph *Jessie Redmon Fauset. Black American Writer* (1981), the only monograph about the author so far; Carol Allen's chapter on Fauset in *Black Women Intellectuals* (1998); and some doctoral dissertations that have elucidated the subversive component of Fauset's work: Wintz (1974), Vashti Lewis (1981), Branzburg (1983), McLendon (1986) published in book form under the title *The Politics of Color in the Fiction of Jessie Fauset and Nella Larsen* (1995), McDade (1987), and McManus (1992).

innovative, able to sustain a critique that integrates both racial and gender perspectives.

THE GENRE OF PASSING AS A STARTING POINT

From the beginning of the novel, it is clear that *Plum Bun* "passes" for a novel devoted to the study of the circumstances and consequences surrounding the phenomenon of passing in the African American community. This view has been encouraged by the author herself, whose comments on the fidelity to the reality of passing have been taken literally: "All my novels have been taken from real life. Yes, as stories they are literally true" (qtd. in Starkey 219). Fauset also adds in an interview to the *Pittsburgh Courier* that approximately twenty thousand blacks passed in New York, motivated by "the advantages of the white race" and the escape "from the disabilities which are the heritage of the Negro" (qtd. in McLendon 9). These comments have contributed to the construction of the popular legend of Fauset as a traitor to her race and as a spokeswoman for an assimilated African American middle class. Despite such criticisms, Fauset continued to insist on the veracity of her work as the focal point of her writing, evident in her reaction to the novel *Birthright* published by T. S. Stribling in 1922:[7]

> A number of us started writing at that time . . . Nella Larson and Walter White, for instance, were affected just as I was. We reasoned, "Here is an audience waiting to hear the truth about us. Let us who are better qualified to present that truth than any white writer, try to do so." (qtd. in Starkey 218-9; sic)

Besides the emphasis on the realistic character of her work, Fauset's words are quite significant because she describes herself as part of a group of writers who tackled the issue of passing at that time together with Larsen and White.[8] Moreover, she distances herself from the primitivist fashion of the time, probably one of the

---

[7] Lewis explains the relationship between Stribling's text and Fauset's first novel: "*There is Confusion* was Stribling's *Birthright* rewritten to the approved literary canons of the Talented Tenth" (*When Harlem* 124). Also Sato 69; Johnson, "Literary Midwife" 151.

[8] Apart from his activism in anti-lynching campaigns previously mentioned in chapter three, Walter White published *Flight* in 1926 on the topic of passing

main reasons for the censure she has so frequently received. Even the author herself acknowledges this fact as she recounts the difficulties she encountered when trying to publish her first novel: "White readers just don't expect Negroes to be like this" (qtd. in Starkey 219). Her choice of the genre of passing, then, highlights her intention to use it as the most effective means to unmask the prevailing ideology.

From the outset, the protagonist of the novel, Angela, seems to embody the stereotype of the mulatta discontented with her racial identity. Her sole desire is to pass into the white race which, she believes, has all the positive values she aspires to: "the great rewards of life—riches, glamour, pleasure—are for white-skinned people only" (17). This reflection leads her to meditate on the existing racial system, concluding that "colour or rather the lack of it seemed . . . the one absolute prerequisite to the life of which she was dreaming" (13). Therefore, from the very beginning of the story, the dream world appears in constant association with the other life Angela so desires. In this sense, Angela's idealized viewpoint is similar to Clare's in *Passing*, as both locate all their expectations about material possessions, luxury and comfort in the white race, and thus reject their blackness. Such a rejection is transformed in Angela's case into "pity for her unfortunate relatives" (18). Later it is transmuted into downright repulsion when she focuses her dreams and aspirations on the passing game she shares with her mother, "dreaming excitedly of Saturdays spent in turning her small olive face firmly away from peering black countenances" (19), which would in time lead her to the decision to pass permanently.

As in Clare's case, Angela's lack of acceptance of her racial status also incites her rebellion against a value system that denies her the right to what she regards as her deserved share. Contrary to Clare, Angela inherits the sense of rebellion from her own mother, Mattie, who justifies her excursions into the exclusive white world with "a mischievous determination to flout a silly and unjust law" (15). Obviously, her mother's example is determinant in the protagonist's life since "it was from her mother that Angela learned the possibilities for joy and freedom which seemed to her inherent in mere whiteness" (14). So the supposedly "innocent" Saturday excursions that are for Mattie some sort of pastime or entertainment,[9] leave an indelible imprint on Angela's character and her perception of the world which will affect her well into adulthood (Sollors, *Neither White* 275).

---

[9] Indeed, Mattie and Angela personify two diametrically opposed types of passing: whereas the mother stands for the so-called "convenience or temporary" passing, that is, she passes only in certain appropriate circumstances; Angela becomes the ideal of the "permanent" passer whose

Angela's reflections on her racial provenance and its implications in the first stage of her life mark for her the path to passing; she considers "being coloured in America" as "nothing short of a curse" (53). Her decision to pass echoes the Ex-Colored Man in Johnson's novel: "[A]fter all I am both white and Negro and look white. Why shouldn't I declare for the one that will bring me the greatest happiness, prosperity and respect?" (80). It can be affirmed so far that Fauset almost literally dramatizes the stereotypical story of the mulatto/a, who wants to integrate into the white world leaving behind his/her black identity. But it is precisely at the moment in which Angela "becomes white" that Fauset deliberately subverts the convention of passing by showing the other side of white reality as a corrupt world, where poverty and loneliness abound and where there is no sense of morality. Moreover, together with a negative vision of the white world, Fauset presents Harlem as the ideal site for life, culture, proper morality, and disinterested solidarity.[10]

To articulate the critique of white society, the first image Fauset offers of this world is the contrast between Angela's idealization and the crude reality of Fourteenth Street: "'I am seeing life . . . this is the way people live' and never realized that some of these people looking curiously, speculative at her wondered what had been her portion to bring her thus early to this unsavoury company" (89). The ironic sense that is derived from this disparity is illuminated later when Angela herself discovers the double character of the white world as represented by New York:

New York . . . had two visages. It could offer an aspect radiant with promise or a countenance lowering and forbidding. With its flattering possibilities it could elevate to the seventh heaven, or lower to the depths of hell with its crushing negations. And loneliness! (239)

In the description the dream has turned into a nightmare when reality, so far from idealizations, has given way to the most profound disenchantment. Angela's

---

desire to erase any relationship with her previous African American existence attempts to assimilate completely into the white race. Lewis names both types in his classification of mulatta women who appear in Fauset's and Larsen's works ("Mulatto Woman" 55).

[10] Some critics have suggested the existence of this subversive critique of white society (Sato 71; Bell, *Afro-American Novel* 108; Allen 48), but it is Wilbert Jenkins who, following Lewis' "The Mulatto Woman," demonstrates Fauset's conscious formulation of such a critique and of the superiority of African Americans with respect to whites in his article "Jessie Fauset: A Modern Apostle of Black Racial Pride" (1986).

disillusion is intimately related to her diverse negative experiences in the white world, especially connected to its lack of morality.

Such a lack is ever present in the relationship that Angela maintains with her lover Roger, allowing her to perceive the ignoble character of certain human relations. This dimension is first hinted at by the stories Roger tells her during their courtship, which Angela misinterprets as a sort of definitive rupture with her previous life: "[A]ll her little world, judging it by the standards by which she was used to measuring people, was tumbling in ruins at her feet," and an initiation to a new one which she sees as "made to take pleasure in; one gained nothing by exercising simple virtue" (193). This unexplored perspective of reality is for her "an extension of the old formula which she had thought out for herself many years ago" (193). Evidently, the problem resides in the fact that such a formulation lacks validity, since Angela is applying rules from her previous life to a new one whose norms she practically ignores. The result is inevitably the failure of her relationship and her subsequent disillusion. Although Angela convinces herself that her choice has been just, idealizing the relationship as "the finest flower of chivalry and devotion" (225), she finally acknowledges her real situation with Roger, who "had no thought, had never had any thought, of marrying her" (226-7). Only then is Angela compelled to return to reality and come to terms with the true nature of her affair with Roger and the implications derived from it, as will be examined below.

The fact that Angela allows herself to be compromised in this relationship following the guidelines set by two white women—her friends Paulette and Martha—constitutes a conscious attack on the lack of morality in the white world, inverting the primitivist stereotype of amorality usually ascribed to African Americans. In fact, there are several occasions on which such a subversion is suggested throughout the novel. First, her mother sets the example in the description of her life with a white actress, who holds the racist opinion that "all colored people are thickly streaked with immorality. They were naturally loose" (29). Yet when Mattie asks her for help in safeguarding her honor, the actress exclaims: "If I don't care, why should you?" (29). Angela finds an equivalent attitude in her friend Paulette, who is very outspoken about sexual issues and premarital affairs. The opposition between such white liberalism and African American moralism is evident: "Beyond question some of the colored people of her acquaintance must have lived in a manner which would not bear inspection, but she could not think of one who would thus have discussed it calmly with either friend or stranger" (107). Angela's disapproval of Paulette symbolizes up to a certain point her rejection of Paulette's life-style.

In addition, Fauset resorts to another strategy to completely subvert the pattern of mulatto literature: the inversion of the so-called "blood theory."[11] Fauset effectuates this inversion by means of the presentation of white blood, not black, as the factor that triggers the negative actions of the protagonist. Virginia—Angela's sister—provides a first clue of this inversion when she tells her, "I'm beginning to think that you *have* more white blood in your veins than I, and that it was that extra amount which made it possible for you to make that remark" (81; author's emphasis), adding later: "[P]erhaps there is an extra infusion of white blood which lets you see life at another angle" (168). Angela herself also accepts this point of view when she thinks: "Perhaps this selfishness was what the possession of white blood meant: the ultimate definition of Nordic supremacy" (275), where there is a clear parodic revision of the concept of white supremacy identified with the lowest human instincts, including selfishness.

In opposition to the fundamentally negative image of the white world, Harlem is presented as a sort of paradise on earth, a place filled with "fullness, richness, even thickness of life" (216). Angela is dazzled by this aspect of Harlem on her first visit, when the novelty of passing is still very intense. Her only objection is that "Harlem was a great city, but after all it was a city within a city" (98) and she prefers to live outside it. As the novel progresses, her admiration for African Americans in Harlem increases through the glimpses she catches from her sister Virginia's life, which is clearly representative of the educated upper class: "[S]he was established in New York with friends, occupation, security, leading an utterly open life, no secrets, no subterfuges, no goals to be reached by devious ways" (243). The vast discrepancy between Virginia's way of life and hers helps Angela to an awareness of her true reality and encourages her last decision to return to her former way of life.

But a discussion of the life-style of the African American upper class as depicted in the novel would not be complete without mentioning the symbolic

---

[11] McLendon comments on the existence of this theory connecting it to fairy tales, in which there exists a dichotomy "royal vs. Common" (31), and applies it to racial distinctions and, over all, to the "tragic mulatto" figure (14-16). Also known as "mixed-blood" for the alleged divided inheritance coming from two different races, this figure is usually characterized by lack of satisfaction and restlessness. A further development of this racist theory is the so-called "one drop theory," whereby slave women's children inherited the condition of their mother. For an illustrative summary, see Gossett's introduction (378-406).

significance of the figure of Van Meier,[12] "a man, fearless, dauntless, the captain of his fate" (218). The portrait clearly inverts the stereotype of the weak and subdued African American male, while it simultaneously serves as a useful tool for Fauset's appropriation of the ideology of the "talented tenth":

> Our case is unique . . . those of us who have forged forward, who have gained the front ranks in money and training, will not, are not able as yet to go our separate ways apart from the unwashed, untutored herd. We must still look back and render service to our less fortunate, weaker brethen. (218)

Van Meier's defense of Duboisian racial pride encourages a reappraisal of the African American upper class and facilitates the *dénouement* of the novel, in which Angela abjures passing and reenters the African American community.[13]

Just as Clare felt the need to contact people of color again, Angela "was willing to make sacrifices, let go if need be of her cherished independence, lead a double life, move among two sets of acquaintances" (252). The ambivalence that characterizes her resolution to live two lives echoes Clare's: "I can't placard myself, and I suppose there will be lots of times when in spite of myself I'll be 'passing.' But I want you to know from now on, so far as sides are concerned, I am on the coloured side" (373). Angela declares her allegiance to the African American community openly, but makes reference to the duality of her identity.

Thus, Fauset uses Angela to study the complications implicit in the phenomenon of passing, the roots of its motivation, and the devastating consequences that befall whoever undertakes it.[14] The rejection of passing on the

---

[12] This figure loosely corresponds to W. E. B. Du Bois, with whom Fauset maintained a relationship of friendship and mutual admiration, together with frequent collaborations in *The Crisis* (Rampersad 141). Lewis even considers Du Bois a father for Fauset (*When Harlem* 121-2).

[13] Lewis argues that Van Meier's speech is what mainly instigates Angela to return to her African American community ("The Mulatto Woman" 65).

[14] Recent critics have concurred with my analysis, postulating that Fauset does not deny her African American identity at all, but on the contrary, she makes use of the strategy of passing to defend it. Among them, Branzburg is worth mentioning because she states that Fauset explores passing as "one of the most disruptive forces in the lives of upper-class blacks" (60). McDowell also agrees that "the passing plot affords Fauset a subtle vehicle through which to critique the naive act of passing, but also to analyze the paradoxes of color prejudice in America" ("Regulating Midwives" xxii). Jenkins' article establishes Fauset as actively engaged in the reconstruction of African American history and culture, because she "exhibits a constant condemnation of anyone in her novels of African descent who adopts a white identity" (18). See also Johnson, "Literary

author's part is made explicit in Angela's open condemnation: "All of the complications of these last few years . . . have been based on this business of 'passing'" (354). The joke she had thought to be playing on the dominant system is turned against her literally[15] when it denies her the right to love and happiness with Anthony: "You in your foolishness, I in my carelessness, 'passing, passing' and life sitting back laughing, splitting her sides at the joke of it" (298). It is only when Angela proclaims her African American identity overtly and returns to the African American community, that the two lovers can be reunited. Through passing Fauset both questions the canons established by this convention and condemns the practice of passing itself, thus enabling the consolidation of new parameters to judge both white and black communities. This allows her to insist on the superiority of the latter over the former. Fauset manages, then, to challenge the primacy of the dominant value system, exalting African American virtues over the moral corruption and materialism characteristic of white culture. I would like to further argue that, in a certain sense, the passing convention functions as cover of itself, redefining the category of race as merely a social and cultural construction, and concealing the blunt critique of a racist ideology that promotes the existence of this kind of phenomena to begin with.

⚬⚬⚬

The Sexual Discourse and its Multiple Covers

The passing convention is also instrumental in hiding another critique which truly interests the author, namely the prevailing ideology of gender. As McDowell states in her article "On Face," *Plum Bun* "'passes' for just another novel of passing and for the age-old fairy tale and romance" (76). The novel itself "passes" as a work intended to deal exclusively with Angela's passing and her love life, when actually there exists a highly subversive content that dissects African American

---

Midwife" 146; and the treatment of what Aptheker calls "Afro-American superiority" in Sylvander 16-20.

[15] The references to passing as mockery or game are very frequent in the novel, as the following extract illustrates: "[F]rom the pinnacle of her satisfaction in her studies, in her new friends and in the joke which she was having upon custom and tradition" (108), echoing Johnson's protagonist who also makes the same kind of considerations until he falls in love with his future wife and claims: "[B]ut now I ceased to regard 'being a white man' as a sort of practical joke" (145-6).

female identity and sexuality and redefines them from a female perspective.[16] Fauset uses three other covers, of which McDowell mentions two in the quote above—fairy tales and romance. The third is nursery rhymes, which acquires a great importance as far as the novel's structure is concerned. The deployment of these three traditions reasserts the importance of gender in the novel and its elucidation contributes to a formulation of the concept of "double double consciousness" underlying the representation of African American women Fauset offers in *Plum Bun*.

*   *   *

Fairy Tales: "The Sleeper Wakes" and *Plum Bun*

In *Plum Bun* the fairy tale veneer fundamentally disguises a parody of the romantic conventions of love and marriage in the novel. This parodic content has been ignored up to very recently, despite its pervasive presence in Fauset's work.[17] Nevertheless, fairy tales exert an enormous influence in Fauset's novel, prompting its qualification as "prim and dainty." Indeed, a great number of the events that take place in the novel are informed by Angela's idealized or fanciful conception of the world. Angela's idealization is nurtured by both fairy tales and romance, since both traditions share many of the strategies in the configuration of female subjectivity.[18] Angela seems to be determined to enact the tradition of fairy tales to the last, transforming herself into a beautiful princess who is going to be saved by her white prince charming. However, her illusions are shattered progressively when her

---

[16] Several critics have detected the existence of that subversive substratum following Cary Wintz who calls attention to this feature in her 1974 dissertation:

> In spite of her conservative, almost Victorian literary habits, . . . [Fauset] introduced several subjects into her novels that were hardly typical drawing room conversation topics in the mid-1920s. Promiscuity, exploitative sexual affairs, miscegenation, and even incest appear in her novels. In fact, prim and proper Jessie Fauset included a far greater range of sexual activity than did most of Du Bois' debauched tenth. (72, 78)

Other critics along this line are Sylvander (1981), Feeney (1979 and 1980), Ammons (1987), DuCille (1993), Schockley (1994), McLendon (1995), and especially McDowell (1985, 1990, and 1995).

[17] Only two critics—McDowell and McLendon—have attempted to detail the parodic revision that Fauset elaborates of fairy tales, but even McDowell regards the way in which Fauset undertakes this as "clumsily executed" ("Neglected Dimension" 87). I intend to demonstrate the conscious and intentional use of fairy tales on Fauset's part.

[18] As the second tradition mentioned—the romance or sentimental novel—has been explicated in detail in the previous chapter, I will only cite it in relation to fairy tales when pertinent.

encounters with the real world expose the idealization inherent in the genre. This process of deconstruction stresses the unreality of such tales, and the racist and male chauvinistic biases that hide behind them, used to acculturate women to settle for certain given roles in society and to alienate them from self-expression and self-definition. The novel, thus, provides clues to reconsidering that tradition from an unusual female perspective and proposes constructive alternatives for women's empowerment.

Studying the influence of fairy tales in Angela's vision of life, Eva Rueschmann points out that, from the beginning, Angela as well as her sister Virginia "have both been nurtured on a steady dict of fairy tales in childhood" (123). This diet has been supplied by her mother Mattie, but with a very peculiar ending: "When Angela and Virginia were little children and their mother used to read them fairy tales she would add to the ending, 'And so they lived happily ever after, just like your father and me'" (33). This family scene will mark both the girls' lives, but especially Angela's, since the fantasy presented in those fairy tales constitutes the basis for her future interaction with the outside world.[19] Mattie's addition to the tales also acquires great significance within this framework, because it can be interpreted in strikingly different ways.

To start with, the ending can be explained as Mattie's conscious desire to become a model for her daughters, joining the ranks of all "beautiful princesses saved by the charming prince," in this case, by her husband Junius who was "God" (33) to her. Hence, Mattie would fall into the temptation of idealizing her life and her relationship with her husband, due perhaps to two primary reasons: first, simply because Mattie's perception of her own life is greatly affected by the romantic conceptions embedded in fairy tales; and second, perhaps because of a lack of real happiness and fulfillment. This second possibility would harmonize with her constant need to pass for white in order to compensate somewhat for the routine character of her existence: "[A]ll innocent, childish pleasures pursued without

---

[19] Several critics have analyzed the influence of fairy tales on the psychological development of children. Bruno Bettelheim has been a pioneer applying psychoanalysis in "Reflections. The Use of Enchantment" (1975) and in his book *The Uses of Enchantment* (1975). The main problem Bettelheim's theories pose lies in the fact that he concentrates almost entirely on males, ignoring females. The gender gap is filled by other critics such as Jack Zipes, especially in *Breaking the Magic Spell* (1979) and *Don't Bet on the Prince* (1986), and Jennifer Waelti-Walters' *Fairy Tales and the Female Imagination* (1982), where she accounts for the effect of fairy tales on female acculturation patterns. Other significant contributions in the field are Ruth Bottingheimer's *Fairy Tales and Society* (1986), Kay Stone's "Feminist Approaches to the Interpretation of Fairy Tales" (1986), Maria Tatar's *Off With Their Heads! Fairy Tales and the Culture of Childhood* (1992), and Marina Warner's *From the Beast to the Blonde: On Fairy Tales and Their Tellers* (1995).

malice or envy contrived to cast a glamour over Monday's washing and Tuesday's ironing" (16). Mattie would therefore agree with Angela, who prefers the "delicate niceties of existence" (12) that she enjoys in her excursions to the white world over the dull family life.

Mattie's passing can, therefore, be decoded in two different ways: literally in the sense of racial passing, when Mattie sometimes passes for white while shopping with Angela. But also culturally, since Mattie seems to be absorbing ideals from the dominant white culture. The insistence on the patterns of the rescued princess, the saving prince, and the never-ending happiness after marriage places great pressure on any woman's life. McDowell comments on the powerful role of fairy tales "in conditioning women to idealize marriage and romantic love as the source of their completeness as well as their material well-being" ("On Face" 66). The dichotomy between the world depicted in fairy tales and daily life is quite obvious for any woman, but it is more for women like Mattie or Angela, who as African Americans are compelled to come to terms with their exclusion from this communal fantasy.

On the other hand, the appropriation of fairy tales on Mattie's part could also be read in a positive light, as she adapts them to an African American reality for her daughters' benefit. For her it is completely legitimate to counteract the racist innuendo of fairy tales that employ the same elements used to exclude African American women from the collective fantasy. She does so by starting from the conventional protagonism of white female characters and the connotations associated with different colors in those tales.[20] Mattie's intentional reworking of fairy tales to accommodate unconventional heroines like her daughters aims at revising this racist heritage by introducing significant changes in her version. Mattie's motives would harmonize with Fauset's own attack on the unjust treatment that African Americans are dispensed with in both history and literature:

> I am constantly amazed as I grow older at the network of misunderstanding—to speak mildly—at the misrepresentation of things as they really are which is so persistently cast around us. Sometimes by implication, sometimes by open statement. Thus, we grow up thinking that there are no colored heroes . . . There are no pictures of colored

---

[20] Jack Zipes recognizes the racist component of fairy tales when he states: "[F]airy tales are implicitly racist because they often equate beauty and virtue with the colour white and ugliness with the colour black" ("Introduction" 6).

fairies in the story books or even of colored boys and girls. "Sweetness and light" are of the white world. (qtd. in Jenkins 15)

It is, therefore, completely legitimate to counteract such racist practices by appropriating the same cultural media conventionally employed to ostracize African American women, in this case fairy tales traditionally associated with white women. Indeed, this seems to be the most plausible interpretation of Mattie's forceful revision of the tales she recounts to her daughters.

The changes are not only limited to racial aspects, but extend to another significant area: gender constructions. In this case, too, Mattie deliberately transforms fairy tales to suit her needs, as she very often introduces changes that turn the model upside down. For example, she insists on the importance of a job or a profession in her daughters' future: "'My girls shall never come through my experiences' . . . They were both to be school-teachers and independent" (33). This alteration denotes a distinct departure from convention, since both eventually become economically independent. All these changes affect the girls' development quite deeply, so to a certain extent, Mattie's stories could be defined as fairy tales "with a twist." The twist or metamorphosis that Mattie effects corresponds, then, to a larger strategy employed in the rest of the novel, which then becomes an extended metaphor of fairy tales. This opinion coincides with McLendon's view of *Plum Bun* as "a fairy tale's ironic inversion" (29), hinting at the subversive and deconstructive character of the text.

Following this line, there is an intimate bond that unites the novel and "The Sleeper Wakes," the short story Fauset published in 1920.[21] The main link that connects both works is precisely the conscious and parodic inversion of fairy tale conventions, such that this story can be regarded as a precedent to the novel. Its protagonist, Amy, is also a mulatto girl who grows up fascinated by the "fairy tales read to her" (3), which she later translates to the movies whose plots faithfully reflect the type of fanciful reverie encouraged by fairy tales:

[I]t was the most wonderful picture—a girl—such a pretty one—and she was poor, awfully. And somehow she met the most wonderful people and they were so kind to her. And she married a man who was just

---

[21] McDowell notices such a correspondence between this short story and Fauset's first novel *There is Confusion* in "The Neglected Dimension of Jessie Redmon Fauset."

tremendously rich and he gave her everything. (3)

Similarly to Angela, Amy's true ambition resides in becoming "like the girl in the picture," because "she had nothing but her beautiful face—and she did want to be happy" (4). The three central premises that dominate Angela's and Amy's lives are enclosed here: importance of appearances, longing for riches, and the wish for happiness above all else.

These three features are an integral part of fairy tales and romance legacy as they control the two protagonists' actions in their respective works. First, the emphasis on appearances is evident in Amy's physical description which corresponds to standards of ideal beauty. As Marcia Liebermann observes: "The beautiful girl does not have to do anything to merit being chosen . . . she is chosen because she is beautiful" (188). According to Liebermann, beauty is exalted as "a girl's most valuable asset, perhaps her only valuable asset" (188). Both protagonists adapt perfectly to the proposed pattern: Amy's beauty is repeatedly praised in the narration, culminating in her characterization as "the mere reflex of youth and beauty and content" (4), whereas there are many references in the novel to Angela's magnificent appearance.

The difference between these two women is, however, marked by the divergent use each of them makes of her beauty: in Amy's case her beauty is central only for its racial content, that is, the important trait of her skin is her whiteness—"the pearl and pink whiteness of Amy's skin" (1); whereas Angela's is interesting because of its twofold character of race and gender. Such a discrepancy is indicative of the shifted focus Fauset employs in the novel with respect to the short story: while "The Sleeper Wakes" constitutes a first approach to the negative influence of fairy tales on the formative development of an African American woman and to the frustrated relationships with the opposite sex because of racial considerations, *Plum Bun* offers a wider spectrum in which there is a deeper analysis of both race and gender factors and their interaction.

On the racial plane, Angela's beauty is presented as white, and thus as the key to access her dream-world. Angela possesses a much clearer view than Amy concerning the instrumentalization of her white skin. For Angela her whiteness represents the most direct way to make her dreams come true: "I've thought and thought . . . why should I shut myself off from all the things I want most . . . which are in the world for everybody but which only white people, as far as I can see, get their hands on" (78). On the contrary, Amy voices a complete lack of knowledge about a possible path to fulfill her desires, and she is only able to resort to "an incantation," a method clearly springing from fairy tales: "'I want wonderful clothes, and people around me, men adoring me, and the world before me. I want—everything! It will come, it will all come because I so want it'" (4). Although both of them are clearly influenced by fairy tales, the disparate terms in which the two protagonists phrase the same desire denote a greater or lesser degree of implication in the fantasy world these tales impose: Amy idealizes much more, while Angela seems to be slightly more open to the external reality. The result, nonetheless, is exactly the same, as both characters end up passing in order to fulfill their ambitions. However, Angela assumes this action consciously while Amy does not, because her passing is taken for granted in the narration when the character stays at a "white Y.W.C.A." (5) on her arrival in New York.

Second, questions of gender are much more noticeable in Angela's physical description, which is reiteratively associated to accepted parameters of femininity,[22] as Anthony's words corroborate: "'[Y]our lips, your eyes, your curly lashes are so deliciously feminine'" (280). Her femininity stems naturally from her mother, whom Anthony also describes as "all woman I should say" (280), insisting on the categorization that Angela's father Junius always uses when referring to his wife as "a perfect woman, sweet, industrious, affectionate and illogical" (33). Despite the apparent affinity, there is a disturbing element in Angela that Anthony senses and that will be influential later on in her future: "[B]ut that straight nose of yours betokens strength" (280). That physical trait anticipates an important contrast between her weak and feminine appearance and her strong character which rewrites the stereotypical portrait of Angela as the successful passer. In this sense, the distance between this ideal and Angela's determined attitude reinforces a subversive reading of the novel. It calls for a revision of such female characterization, and at the same time intensifies Angela's quality as a modern and independent woman thanks to her mother's teachings. The fact that she fits the model physically does not necessarily mean that she surrenders to the pressure of

---

[22] Waelti-Walters describes the image of women in fairy tales as "a beautiful doll" (4), whose main features are outlined by Liebermann as "passive, submissive, and helpless" (190). A woman who does not comply with these requirements is quickly transmuted into the exact opposite of the heroine, the witch or stepmother who is recognizable by "extra-human race or extreme ugliness," usually connected to "female wickedness" (Liebermann 196). The latter stereotype is applied to any female character who does not conform to the heroine type. This is especially so if that woman displays power of any kind, which is considered a male prerogative in fairy tales.

the prototype. On the contrary, it emphasizes Angela's deviation from the sanctioned standard.

The gap between appearance and personality also marks Amy, but Angela's case is much more obvious. Although both are characterized with the same adjectives—"cold," "fastidious," "childish," "untouched," and "spoiled," the emphasis is placed on a different aspect in each of the cases. Amy's disparity between appearance and personality is due to her lack of emotions: "[S]he was a little stolid, a little unfeeling under her lovely exterior" (7). For Angela such a divergence falls upon her sense of "practicality." Her common sense determines her actions both as regards race, leading her to pass, and gender, in her relationship with Roger. This feature of her character distances her more than Amy from the ideal proposed by fairy tales, which Waelti-Walters explains as a paradigm for submission and passivity:

> To be acceptable a woman has always had to try and fit the tale. What is demanded of a princess? That she be good, beautiful and long-suffering; that she put up with every misery those around impose upon her. And why? Because then, one day a prince will come and marry her. (11)

The gap that exists between the idealized image above and Amy and Angela's lives once again highlights Fauset's intentional revision of the stereotype, while simultaneously intensifying the character of independent women that both characters claim in their narratives.

The second rule of any fairy tale—yearning for riches, for higher status—is verified in both texts: both women want to climb the social ladder by marrying white partners. Apart from the imposition of a certain kind of female representation, fairy tales also require an acceptance of social roles. As Liebermann phrases it, they serve "to acculturate women to traditional social roles" (185), where "marriage and maternity seem commendable, indeed predestined" (Rowe 211). Both marriage and maternity are suggested as the only possibilities of real fulfillment for women, and any deviation from the established norm results in lack of happiness and in lack of personal and social satisfaction. Women who do not conform to these demands become anomalies, so most tend to internalize the roles of wives and mothers, thus contributing to the perpetuation of the patriarchal order. All women's aspirations are then centered on achieving a suitable marriage and subsequent maternity, completing what could be called the "triangle of perfection"—love, marriage and money.[23] However, the conception of marriage that fairy tales foster, when analyzed in detail, seems to be intimately connected not necessarily to the first category, love, but to money. As Liebermann asserts, "marriage is associated with getting rich" (189), and marriage, social status, and material possessions seem to go hand in hand.[24] The longing for the possesion of material things, for a comfortable and luxurious life, is behind Amy and Angela's idealization of their future. The implicit materialism in their attitude is slightly discerned in Amy's case when her friend Zora advises her: "'[Y]ou must marry wealth'" (6). This provokes Amy's faint reaction to reject "such wholesale exploitation of people to suit one's own convenience" (7). However, her fiancé Wynne seems to intuitively understand Amy's desire for wealth when he proposes marriage to her in the following terms: "'[B]ut anything you wanted in this world could be yours. I could give it to you,—clothes, houses and jewels'" (9). Amy's comment at this point is quite meaningful when she regards marriage as if she were "driving a bargain" (9). To appease her conscience, Amy resorts to fairy tales once more as the suitable justification for accepting Wynne's proposal: "'And after all . . . it really is my dream coming true'" (9). In spite of Amy's realization of a crucial disparity between the romantic vision of marriage provided by fairy tales and the reality she encounters, she chooses in the end to cling to the well-known pattern seeking to adapt reality to its fanciful parameters.

Angela also lets herself be captivated by that ideal, although her materialistic aims are less concealed in the novel. For Angela, the meaning of marriage is summed up in one word, "power," which at the beginning of the novel she defines as follows:

> [A]ll the things she most wanted were wrapped up with white people. All the good things were theirs. Not, some cold reasoning instinct within was saying, because they were white. But because for the present they

---

[23] Therefore love, marriage, and material well-being form an inseparable triangle in fairy tales. The internalization of such an idealization definitely contributes to the perpetuation of the patriarchal order: see Rowe's "Feminism and Fairy Tales" (1986), Waelti-Walters (1982), Zipes in his 1986 introduction, Stone (1986), McDowell's "Regulating Midwives" (1990), and Warner (1995).

[24] Karen Rowe also attests to the materialistic nature of marriage in fairy tales which, she argues, "reduce women to marketable commodities" (216). This view has urged interpretations of marriage as a sort of "exchange" (Waelti-Walters 80) or, even worse, as "a form of prostitution, a vulgar financial arrangement" (McDowell, "Neglected Dimension" 91). All these critics coincide in a direct attack on the institution of marriage through dismantling the idealized vision presented in fairy tales, and acknowledging its commercial character.

> had *power* and the badge of that *power* was whiteness . . . She possessed
> the badge, and unless there was someone to tell, she could possess the
> *power* for which it stood. (73-4; my emphasis)

The passage eloquently discloses its remarkably subversive nature from a racial
point of view: the repetition of the word "power" attached only "for the present" to
the possession of a white skin indicates her purpose of destabilizing the current
racial hierarchy, even insinuating a possible inversion of it. Moreover, it
demonstrates once again Angela's materialistic nature in its reference to "some cold
reasoning instinct" that she has already exhibited previously.

   Although in the paragraph above the notion of power is linked to the racial
context, very soon her reflection on the nature of power leads her to the conclusion
that there is a "limitation" imposed by her female condition. As she recognizes that
the notion of power is also heavily charged with connotations of gender, she revises
it later: "Power, greatness, authority, these were fitting and proper for men; but
there were sweeter, more beautiful things for women, and power of a certain kind
too" (88). This idea, together with her "cold reasoning instinct," leads her to
comprehend that the only way to achieve her share of power is through marriage to
a white man, which will ensure her material well-being as well as, from her point of
view, the protection a woman needs.[25] Her resolution concerning marriage clearly
points to a subversive reading of fairy tales in which marriage is idealized as the
source of security and fulfillment for women apparently on the basis of love, but
actually of money. As she expresses it, "marriage is the easiest way for a woman to
get those things" (112), stressing her material interest over romantic illusions. From
this point on, Angela will try to achieve her goal of marrying Roger. In fact, Angela
demonstrates her instinct for cold reasoning on multiple occasions in her
relationship with Roger, admitting that she is not actually in love with him, but
rather playing a sort of game, or waging a battle whose objective is marriage: "she
saw her life rounding out like a fairy tale" (131). Despite her materialism, Angela
still tries to apply fantasy to her real life.

   The third point in common in the two texts is the protagonists' desire to
attain happiness, which is very related to their notions of marriage and material

---

[25] Zipes investigates power as an essential mechanism in the discursive universe of fairy tales
which is condensed in "Might makes right" (*Breaking* 29) and explained in the following way:
"[H]e who has the power can exercise his will, right wrongs, become ennobled, amass money and

security. Angela's words about her search for happiness are quite telling: "I don't see any sense in living unless you're going to be happy" (70). In Amy's case that desire to be happy corresponds to the quest for the ideal promoted by fairy tales, fulfilled at the beginning of Amy's matrimonial life: "What she wanted she had, ease, wealth, adoration, love, too, passionate and imperious" (11). Her idyllic existence transforms her into "a well-cared for, sleek, house-pet, delicately nurtured, velvety, content to let her days pass by" (11), an existence which stands for the best possible adaptation to fairy tales. According to their pattern, the period of courtship is understood, as Liebermann puts it, as "the most important and exciting part of a girl's life" (199) and which should be the customary end of the story. Indeed, the trouble starts with the fact that the story continues, and the rest of "The Sleeper Wakes" can be interpreted as the most incisive critique of the fairy tale model, especially from a racial point of view. The only problem which disturbs Amy's paradise is the inexplicable "race-pride" of her husband Wynne, which destroys their peace and, consequently, their marriage.

In *Plum Bun*, the main difficulty Angela faces is the fact that the expected marriage never takes place. The protagonist never makes her dream come true, but in time she acknowledges the way in which Roger has taken advantage of her ignorance and innocence. Following her friend Martha's advice, she resorts to all the means at her disposal to ensnare Roger, but in the end she is the only one trapped. Angela's efforts to get herself married are foiled because Roger is looking for quite a different arrangement. Several critics have detected this contentious aspect of the novel as, for instance, Sylvander, who views it as "images of gamesmanship, verging on war, centering appropriately on men's and women's roles" (179). However, it is Ann DuCille who seems to hit the target most closely, when she suggests that "Angela gambles her most valuable stock—her virginity" (436). Angela actually believes she has almost achieved her purpose of persuading Roger to marry her: "[S]he had conquered, she had been the stronger. She had secured not only him but an assured future, wealth, protection, influence, even power" (151), using imagery of warfare to describe her triumph.

Very soon, however, she discovers that Roger's aim is not marriage, but "a passing fancy" (131), an expression that emphasizes the ironic tone of the novel. Another indication of the kind of relationship Roger is looking for is his insistence

---

land, win women as prizes" (29). This description clearly shows power in fairy tales as a male qualification, one which women can only gain access to through marriage to a powerful man.

on wealth and comfort as crucial to Angela. He achieves his purpose when Angela admits her enjoyment of "comfort, beauty and dainty surroundings" (149). Roger will profit from this statement to propose to Angela "to keep a love nest" (182). Her reaction is to turn to fairy tales for guidance, as did Amy before: "Oh if only she could be a girl in a book and when he finally did ask her for her hand, she would be able to tell him that she was going to marry someone else, someone twice as eligible, twice as handsome, twice as wealthy" (183). The problem lies in the fact that reality does not necessarily coincide with the dreams or illusions fostered by fairy tales.

Thus, the analysis of the three fundamental parameters on which fairy tales are usually based demonstrates the parodic intention that destabilizes and subverts them, denying any valid application to the protagonists' lives. In spite of their beautiful and feminine physical appearances, neither Amy nor Angela fit the ideal paradigm: both are mulatta, and both possess personalities which do not suit the idealized female model of fairy tales. Moreover, as far as the longing for riches is concerned, both go beyond the limitations imposed in the traditional fairy tale, exhibiting a materialistic attitude that is placed before their emotions and feelings of love. Finally, their desire for happiness is overshadowed by the manifold difficulties they find in their path, problems of race in Amy's case, and problems of both race and gender in Angela's.

Regarding the obstacles on their way to happiness, both narratives completely invert the norms found in fairy tales: while Amy divorces Wynne and undertakes an independent life, Angela gives in to an extramarital affair with Roger. Furthermore, the discovery of Amy's racial origins brings along unthinkable consequences for her idyllic existence: "[S]he had thought he might not want his friends . . . to know that she was colored, but she had not dreamed it could make any real difference to him" (14-5). As Amy has continued to nurture her romantic ideals, she is taken by surprise by Wynne's unexpected rejection: "she was just the same woman she told herself, she had not changed, she was still beautiful, still charming, still 'different'" (15). Amy's last reflection resonates deeply because it is an indictment of fairy tale precepts, revealing the false values that are hidden behind the cult of physical appearance. Despite her beauty, the "princess" is dethroned because of her racial origins and is compelled to divorce. It is as if this story were the literal inversion of a conventional fairy tale, and the "princess" Amy turned into a frog.

The crucial moment in the narrative is the encounter between Amy and her ex-husband after the divorce. It exemplifies the new kind of relationship Wynne wants to establish with her, closely resembling Roger's proposal to Angela. Amy also believes they are talking about marriage until Wynne declares his intention openly: "A white man like me simply doesn't marry a colored woman" (19). Amy's reaction reveals her horror as she visualizes herself "like the women in those awful novels" (19), referring to the books that Wynne enjoys reading but that to her represent "sheer badness" (11). The opposition between the ideals transmitted to Amy by fairy tales and the unpleasant reality she faces with Wynne is reflected in Wynne's conception of Amy. Reiterating paradigms already analyzed, Wynne accuses Amy of having prostituted herself when they got married: "[Y]ou forget you told me you didn't love me when you married me. You sold yourself to me then" (20). Wynne's accusation leads Amy to comprehend his true feelings towards her: "'He despised me absolutely . . . because I was colored. And yet he wanted me'" (20). With this thought Amy condenses the long history of interracial relationships in which white men have harbored contradictory feelings of hatred and desire. Wynne tries to reenact the historical relationship of concubinage and exploitation between white men and African American women (McDowell, "On Face" 67). Amy's refusal of his proposal constitutes a decisive moment in the inversion of the preceding tradition and a first step towards the attainment of freedom for African American women. In this sense, Fauset is deconstructing that racist history, granting voice and agency to a new kind of African American woman who is able to actively fight against racial and gender oppression.

In Angela's case, the gap between the outcome of her relationship with Roger and the happy ending of fairy tales is even wider thanks to the presence of another crucial component: her sexual desire. Until this crisis, Angela, guided by idealized convictions similar to Amy's, has respected the limitations imposed by social conventions. However, her development from this moment onwards breaks with those conditions, incorporating the sexuality of African American women. This is probably the most meaningful twist of Fauset's novel, as the possibility of an independent sexual life in women is completely inadmissible in conventional fairy tales. Female sexuality is only conceived as part of the general submission of women to their husbands, and its domain is reduced to satisfying the husband's urges and to the conception of offspring. As Rowe states, "[T]he tales implicitly yoke sexual awakening and surrender to the prince" (217). The innovative and, indeed, subversive inclusion of female sexuality leads Fauset to conceal it behind a useful veil of conventionalism.

Despite the use of this cover, the text is filled with sexual connotations. It is, in fact, possible to explore the novel, as Ann DuCille's provocative reading suggests, as "an extended sexual metaphor" (434) and Angela as one of "Fauset's sexually embodied beings" (435). This view completely destabilizes the parameters of fairy tales and calls into question traditional assumptions of female sexuality and identity. When Angela understands Roger's real intention, she does not escape or resist as would be expected. On the contrary, she suffers a crisis "which so frightened and attracted her. She was the more frightened because she felt that attraction" (169). That sense of attraction is phrased as "desires and longings," which recalls Larsen's description of African American female sexuality (see above). The fact is that the sexual character of that attraction is made manifest in the novel and achieves its peak when the growing intimacy with Roger drives Angela to respond to his caresses. At a crucial moment Angela stops resisting as "some treacherous barrier gave way within her" (189). She justifies her attitude with the significant statement "stolen waters were the sweetest" (189). This affirmation is heavily endowed with meaning since it shows a double intentionality: on first sight, it serves as a pretext to pass for white and to enjoy the "joke" on the dominant racial order; but it significantly acquires a new meaning when Angela applies it to her growing sexual desire and to her subsequent relationship with Roger.

From this moment, what the text calls "a curious period of duelling" (190) between Angela and Roger ensues, in which each of them tries to make her/his dreams come true: marriage for her and sex for him. However, Angela quickly loses ground, not so much because of Roger's persistence and his arguments in favor of free love, but because of her own sexual impulses. Indeed, Angela starts to "accept and even inwardly . . . welcome his caresses" (194), admitting her sexual desire later as "one enemy with whom she had never thought to reckon" (198). The realization of that possibility makes her experience "a great fear" (200), which springs not from Roger but from herself and is similar to Helga's depiction of her sexual uneasiness. All this ambiguity and lack of definition bring "a terrible lassitude" (202) which overpowers Angela when, instead of fighting Roger off, she gives in to him. Although this sense of languor could imply a certain degree of passivity on Angela's part, in fact, it is her own sexual longing which acts as the engine for sexual intercourse with Roger. Fauset tries to hide this unconventional episode under the conventional protective cover of Angela's loving surrender to Roger, but Angela's independent and hedonist attitude clearly hints at the subversive quality of the text. Contrary to the protagonists of traditional fairy tales, who are described as passive sexual objects, from the very beginning Angela plays a very active role in her affair with Roger.

As soon as Angela gives herself up to Roger, she begins to look for allegations to exonerate her actions by means of repeating socially accepted patterns of female submission: "[T]his was the explanation of being, of her being; that men had other aims, other uses but that the sole excuse for being a woman was to be just that,—a woman" (203-4). But even in these first moments the ironic substratum pervading the text can be glimpsed when Angela reflects on her unconditional surrender to Roger "with a slight tendency toward self-mockery" (204), revealing her lack of conviction. This tendency to self-ridicule will mean that Angela's subordination is only temporary, because "something outside herself, something watchful, proud, remote, from the passion and rapture which flamed within her, kept her free and independent" (204). Angela not only fractures the traditional idealizations of fairy tales and romance, but also manages to retain a certain degree of autonomy in her relationship with Roger in spite of its sexual and passionate nature. This is corroborated later when the text alludes to her feeling about the relationship: "hers was a curious mixture of materialism and hedonism, and at this moment the latter quality was uppermost in her life" (207). Her attitude is presented in open contradiction to the sentimental idea of love by incorporating two new elements—materialism and pleasure—to the spectrum of the novel. Angela herself voices that attack on convention when she says: "[L]ife . . . came before creed or convention" (224), using it as an excuse for her unconventional behavior.

The employment of the fairy tale convention is a very suitable cover to redefine both Angela's and Amy's lives with an obviously revisionist and subversive intention. From this viewpoint the third strategy used by Fauset—nursery rhymes—also performs the same function. Together with fairy tales and romance, it manages to destabilize the defining parameters conventionally applied to African American women, especially with reference to the expression of their sexuality and to the formation of an alternative sense of identity.

* * *

The Nursery Rhyme or The True Meaning of "Plum Bun"

Up to a certain point the nursery rhymes, romance, and fairy tales share certain characteristics. As in the case of the latter, Fauset's employment of nursery rhymes as a structuring device has also been disqualified as frivolous and irrelevant.[26] However, as several critics have indicated,[27] the choice of a nursery rhyme to give shape to the structure of the novel points to the subversive and parodic component which Fauset conceals behind its apparent "innocence." The transcendence of this song is also noticeable in the title of the novel—*Plum Bun*, and in the fact that it appears on the opening page:

> "To Market, to Market,
> To buy a Plum Bun;
> Home again, Home again,
> Market is done"

The rhyme also provides titles to each of the five sections or chapters the novel is composed of, namely "Home," "Market," "Plum Bun," "Home Again," and "Market is Done." Just as fairy tales are used strategically in the narration, the inclusion of this nursery rhyme also acquires an essential role.

The reasons behind Fauset's use of this strategic cover are as varied as in the case of fairy tales: for the most conventional line of criticism, the nursery rhyme belongs to the set of practices that constitute a sort of "cultural" passing on Fauset's part. That is, Fauset uses an eminently white tradition because of her own assimilation of dominant values, or what Bone calls "a kind of psychological 'passing' at the fantasy level" (4). Nonetheless, Fauset's employment of this tradition can be also read as a conscious appropriation for her literary conception of

---

[26] Most critics ignore nursery rhymes or mention them just in passing, and never consider them an important structuring device. Sato, for example, chooses another paradigm to account for the structure of the novel relating each of the parts with five stages in Angela's passing. This suggests that Fauset "intends to create the effect of universality using this style of writing" (72), obviously disapproving of a universalist approach.

[27] Among them, McDowell, DuCille, and especially Joseph Feeney, whose contribution proves crucial to the elucidation of nursery rhyme patterns in "Black Childhood as Ironic: A Nursery Rhyme Transformed in Jessie Fauset's Novel *Plum Bun*." McLendon argues that the fairy tale is opposed to the nursery rhyme, because "the nursery rhyme situates the story within a socioeconomic setting that conflicts with the fairy-tale setting Angela creates for herself" (30). Although acknowledging the differences between both motifs, I still contend that their use is basically complementary.

African American life in order to emphasize the gap between the vision provided by the rhyme and Angela's reality. In this light, McInnes regards the rhyme as conforming to both "the white male narrative of hope and fulfillment" and "the white male narrative of political and economical opportunism," so "the verse is thus sexually as well as racially ironic" (qtd. in McDowell, "Regulating Midwives" xvii). The parodic intention in the deployment of this convention is, therefore, twofold. As in the case of fairy tales, such a double objective constantly modifies the rhyme itself until it finally becomes "a nursery rhyme with a twist." Its twist mainly lies in Angela's failure to obtain her chosen "plum bun": the expected happy ending never takes place, or at least not in a conventional way. The lack of satisfaction or adaptation to the model is endowed with ironic connotations that affect both the whole novel and the rhyme itself, thus transforming its original meaning.

As Feeney postulates, the main message of the rhyme "emphasizes childhood pleasures and hopes" (66), which is the main basis for Angela's aspirations at the beginning of the novel. However, Feeney continues, "against this background of jollity and hope, Fauset, with stark irony, uses the Mother Goose rhyme to suggest that such childhood hopes are futile for Black Americans" (67). In exactly the same way as the fairy tales called attention to the discrepancy between their idealized content and the real world, the employment of this nursery rhyme also targets this dichotomy and, consequently, the exclusion of African American girls from the collective fantasy. The lack of correspondence between dream and reality incorporates important resonances in the novel: from the racial standpoint, it highlights the fact that only the white race can participate in the possible gratification suggested by the rhyme. From the gender perspective, it hints that Angela is probably more conditioned by her gender than her race when she is unable to make her dream come true and attain her longed-for "plum bun." It is precisely the meaning assigned to these two words that harbors most of the parodic component of the text. This is especially apparent in the sexual connotations which add new nuances to Fauset's critique of gender.

The significance of "plum bun" can be explicated exclusively from a racial stance. According to Feeney, the "plum bun" for which Angela yearns is passing for white, which she identifies with everything she desires so fervently: luxury, wealth, and power (68). Again, the enormous distance between the idealization of what being white means and the crude reality Angela faces while passing as white is foregrounded. She basically encounters a corrupt and materialistic world, of which her affair with Roger is just one more illustration. Feeney analyzes the novel by literally applying the rhyme to each section, and locates the "plum bun" in two specific aspects of each chapter bearing that title: the relationship with Roger and the art school Angela attends (68). These two events are comprised by Angela's idealized vision of what a white identity should entail for her, an idealization that is systematically destroyed through the development of the narration and replaced in due time with an alternative African American concept of life.

However, another, sexual dimension can be added to the possible spectrum of signification of the term "plum bun." This dimension strikingly modifies Feeney's interpretation while simultaneously widening the horizons of Fauset's parodic use of the rhyme. Thus far the sexual content of the book has been read as one of the decisive factors contributing to the destabilization and inversion of the romantic conventions inherent in fairy tales and romance. But this is also true in the case of nursery rhymes, in which the mere notion of sexuality undermines the very foundations on which this children's tradition rests. Indeed, the sexual implications of "plum bun" are quite obvious, as McDowell states when she relates it to the classic blues of the nineteen-twenties ("Regulating Midwives" xxvii), a study that is the basis for DuCille's "Blues Notes on Black Sexuality: Sex and the Texts of Jessie Fauset and Nella Larsen" (1993). In this article DuCille details the erotic iconography attached to African American women as they are represented in the blues. She also signals the way in which both writers—Fauset and Larsen—censure and deconstruct the typical myth promoted by the primitivist fashion of the time, while criticizing the exaggerated pretensions of the African American bourgeoise (422). DuCille furnishes a very illustrative depiction of Larsen's protagonists as "sexually empowered to attract and seduce—to do business in and around the marriage market. But the empowerment . . . is for the most part illusory" (432). This statement could be easily applied to Fauset's *Plum Bun*, since Angela seems to accept and make conscious use of her sexuality, but ends up trapped by it.[28]

Reinforcing the latter interpretation of Fauset's text is Angela's attitude toward her extramarital affair with Roger, which clearly indicates a subversion of the apparent innocence of the nursery rhyme. This subversion is stronger if the

---

[28] Many writers such as Larsen, discussed in the previous chapter, have articulated female sexuality as a trap that secludes women. This characterization is even clearer in fairy tales in which the protagonists are literally imprisoned, eg., "Sleeping Beauty" or "Rapunzel."

"plum bun" is identified with Angela's sexual desire and its implications.[29] The fact that Angela feels happy and satisfied as Roger's lover constitutes enough proof: "If anyone had asked her if she were satisfied with her own life, her reply would have been an instant affirmative" (208). Such an affirmation leads her to adopt a life on the margins of social acceptability, quickly translated into a certain cynicism that allows her to state that "'rules are for ordinary people but not for me'" (207). The main consequence of her rebellion is a sense of aloofness with regard to the society that surrounds her and a rejection of its rules, especially concerning sanctioned sexual behavior. The open defense of her sexual freedom, despite all the covers Fauset used to disguise it distinguishes her from all the female protagonists analyzed thus far.

Even more, Angela claims her sexual freedom not only when she has renounced marriage as the ultimate design of her relationship with Roger, but even when that relationship loses significance for her. Indeed, there is a very telling inversion at this point of the narration: "[F]or some reason he had lost his charm for her, much, she suspected, in the same way in which girls in the position which was hers, often lost their charm to their lovers" (223). Here Angela exchanges roles with Roger, applying to him the condition of lover traditionally assigned to women and reserving an active role for herself. Her role evinces her fundamentally sexual interest in Roger and her need to continue taking the initiative. A clear illustration of how active Angela is in her relation is her decision to go on with her affair despite her disillusion: "[S]he must resolve it [the relationship] by patience, steadfastness and affection into a very apotheosis of 'free love'" (225). However, her active role is undermined by the very same conventions she has rejected, in realizing that "she did not care enough about Roger to play a game for him" (240). Reproposing the idea of game with which she started, Angela seems to have come full circle.

What is even more interesting is Angela's motivation in ending that "game" with him, as it indicates the parodic character concealed in the subversion of the nursery rhyme. According to the rhyme that structures the novel, she should be able to obtain her dreamed "plum bun" in the end, that is, marriage. At this point, according to convention, only two possible endings are acceptable: either she

---

[29] In this sense, I disagree with McDowell when she argues that "for her, the plum is power and influence attainable only through marriage to a wealthy white man. For him, the plum is sex, to be bought and consumed" ("Regulating Midwives" xix). Although the "plum" can be equated to

finally marries and is restored to a virtuous life, or she is definitively condemned for her illicit behavior. Neither of these, however, actually occur in the novel. On the contrary, Fauset offers a third alternative which is a complete deviation from these two models: the figure of the independent woman.

With regard to the first of the three possibilities, Roger excuses himself from the expected marriage proposal by projecting the blame on Angela and recalling the image of the prostitute: "'You knew perfectly well what you were letting yourself in for. Any woman would know it'" (231). The fact that Roger places the blame on Angela discloses his fundamental hypocrisy. But the racial and sexual connotations emerging from their story resonate more loudly. On a racial level, the novel again recaptures the topic of interracial relationships and the way in which throughout history white men have instrumentalized African American women to satisfy their sexual needs. On a sexual level, it goes back to the problematic differentiation of genders and the way in which, in Angela's words, gender conditions "the apparently unbridgeable difference between the sexes; everything was for men, but even the slightest privilege was to be denied to a woman unless the man chose to grant it" (229). Angela denounces this "double standard" and desists in her efforts to save what is left of their relationship.

As Angela herself later confirms, it is the lack of equality between the two of them which cools the relationship because "her dignity was hurt" (230). She is angered by the unjust sexism that relegates women to an inferior position and restricts their personal and sexual freedom. Angela's resentment flares when she exclaims: "'God, isn't there any place where man's responsibility to woman begins?'" (233). This sexist system institutionalizes marriage as the only secure bulwark for women, thereby limiting their self-expression, especially as regards sexuality. Angela's imprecation constitutes a challenge to this convention while affirming women's freedom and inverting the established canons.

The second possibility—punishment of the rebellious woman—never takes place either, so the subversive component of the novel is further strengthened. The lack of punishment for the deviant woman stresses the narration's departure from the sanctioned fairy tales and romance, as Angela does not fit into any of the standard roles: she is neither the princess nor the witch, neither the virgin nor the

---

power on many occasions, Fauset also uses it as a metaphor to investigate Angela's attitude towards her own sexuality.

sinner.[30] Indeed, Angela never voices any kind of remorse. The only feeling she experiences as a result of her failed relationship is shame (actually recalling the Ex-Colored Man's justification for passing), not for having maintained an unconventional affair with Roger, but for the relationship's deterioration and her involvement in "an inexcusably vulgar predicament" (224):

> If she had held in her hand the golden key,—love! But to throw aside the fundamental laws of civilization for passion, for the hot-headed wilfulness of youth and to have it end like this, drably, vulgarly, almost in a brawl! (232-3)

Again Angela acknowledges the enormous importance of her sexual desire as the main origin of her relationship with Roger, but she frees herself from any fault by directing her wrath toward the sexist system. Perhaps the only guilt she acknowledges is to have allowed the affair blow over to the extent that she feels ashamed of it.

The fact that Angela excuses herself from any responsibility is a clear indication of the way in which Fauset exchanges the roles conventionally ascribed to each gender. Angela is represented as the one who attempts to save what is left of the affair and is never accused of being a deceitful or sinful woman. Indeed, the only consequence that their relationship bears for Angela's future is of a strictly personal nature, for she loses her innocence. She also becomes more aware of the effect that her decisions may have on her life, because, as she says, "Roger had taught her an unforgettable lesson" (260). Angela's only conclusion about that "lesson" is tellingly summarized: it "had left no trace on her moral nature; she was ashamed now of the affair with a healthy shame at its unworthiness; but beyond that she suffered from no morbidness" (245). Fauset is clearly parodying and rejecting here the approved ending of the so-called "fallen woman," whose only options were prostitution or suicide. On the contrary, Fauset "revises those narratives in which Eros and celibacy are punished with literal or figurative deaths" (McLendon 45). Angela continues her life even better than before, because "her sum total of knowledge of life had been increased" (245). Now much more realistic in life, she

---

[30] Waelti-Walters articulates this dichotomy between "witch and princess, hag and virgin" as the only female images that the patriarchal tradition has popularized, and she declares that "both roles must be exorcized before a woman can take her place in the world and describe herself in an authoritative discourse" (9-10). I propose a similar interpretation for Fauset's work.

turns to her work as an important source for security and satisfaction and eventually to a relationship based on mutual trust and understanding.

As a result, Angela embraces an alternative way of defining womanhood represented by the independent woman, which obviously becomes a means of self-empowerment. She is neither the loving wife and happy princess of the usual fairy tale ending nor the fallen woman who is punished for challenging the established rules. Opposing these standard resolutions, Fauset presents a secure woman who affirms that "her talent which she had once used as a blind to shield her real motives for breaking loose and coming to New York had now become the greatest, most real force in her life" (332). This third option also serves to reformulate the expectations fostered by the nursery rhyme's title. Now the "plum bun" is no longer understood as marriage, but as her artistic work and her personal freedom. Both ideas are crucial in the text as they produce other changes in Angela's value system, in which love becomes only complementary.[31] The emphasis on her artistic talent is an essential element for comprehending Angela's personal development and her decision to continue her studies in Paris. This decision underlines her choice to lead an independent life, whose only objective and ambition is focused on becoming "an acknowledged, a significant painter of portraits" (375). Finally, the protagonist is able to acknowledge her artistry as her only real dream, ridding herself of previous idealized notions. Thus, Fauset presents a realistic and ambitious woman with precisely defined aspirations.

This new woman is also capable of confronting the true nature of her relationship with Roger: "'What I can't understand is—why shouldn't I, if I wanted to, either try to marry you or to make an ideal thing of our relationship? Why is it that men like you resent an effort on our part to make our commerce decent?'" (320). The reference to "commerce" reflects a new attitude in Angela, who has dropped any romantic convictions about their relationship and explicitly expresses her own feelings. In addition, Angela echoes the rage of other women who, having lived through a similar situation, realize the profound injustice implicit in the dominant hierarchy of gender that denies them the right to act in their relationships and relegates them to the roles of passive victims. The new Angela also perceives the clear-cut dichotomy that exists between the conventional return of the repentant lover and Roger: "[I]n books the man who had treated his sweetheart unkindly often

---

[31] McDowell endorses this interpretation when she affirms: "[I]t becomes clear that she must first be self-sufficient before entering a relationship with a man" ("Regulating Midwives" xx). Allen also stresses this point (63).

returned beaten, dejected, even poverty-stricken, but Roger, except for a slight hesitation in his manner, seemed as jaunty, as fortunate, as handsome as ever" (318). The marked contrast between idealization and reality allows Angela to definitively break out of the mold of female submission and plunge herself into a more fulfilling life-style.

Within this altered framework, there is also a reshaping of the concept of marriage. Up to this point Angela has exhibited an ambivalent attitude towards the institution of marriage: on the one hand, she has idealized it as the desirable outcome of any canonized love relationship; on the other, she has despised it as too restrictive, an attempt to imprison women within the conventional parameters assigned to females. The realistic woman Angela has become does away with idealized pictures of marriage and considers it "a means of avoiding loneliness" (262). Her need for company makes her think about marriage as "the foundation, the substratum" (274), and this thought leads her back to Anthony and his proposal of marriage. Angela's change has been interpreted as a retreat, a backward movement encouraged by Fauset's alleged conservative character. However, Angela's new understanding of marriage would harmonize with her desire to "devote herself to the establishing of permanencies" (251). Although the context of this last sentence is related to her need for authentic friends, it also has to do with her yearning to overcome her loneliness. But before this dream can come true, Angela has to grow up and accept herself. The fact that Fauset delays Angela's final encounter with Anthony, her true love, until the very last page of the novel underlines her deconstructive aim. This love, therefore, is obviously depicted as secondary to Angela's real passion, her art, and her need to work out a valid concept of identity on her own before going back to him.

At the same time, Fauset redefines the concept of personality itself, intimately related to the conceptualization of the notion of race. At the outset of the novel, skin color had outranked any other trait or quality. After her transformation Angela proclaims: "[T]he matter of blood seems nothing compared with individuality, character, living" (354). This statement achieves key significance in the text, as Angela finally manages to free herself from the useless racial load and understands her mother's most important message: "[L]ife is more important than color" (333). The return to the true essence of her mother's advice emancipates her from her mental slavery to the systems of race and gender and encourages her to find herself anew.

The reencounter with her self takes place on her arrival in Philadelphia, where Angela clearly comprehends her mother's perspective and, through it, is able to make sense of her own life: "All I've seen and experienced has been the common fate of most people, a little sharpened, perhaps, a little vivified . . . I've known suffering and love and pain" (366-7). Angela finally understands the reality of her life without idealizing it and without depending on any one person to make it meaningful. Now much more mature, Angela is presented as an adult person responsible for her own actions, quite different from the innocent and insecure adolescent of the beginning of the narration. This maturity allows her to proclaim her racial origin openly and come to terms with its implications. Moreover, this experience encourages her to continue exploring her artistic talent as the main source for her personal and emotional stability. Anthony's appearance with "a tag . . . somewhere" (379) accentuates the final subversion of established canons, as a man is sent as a kind of gift to a woman. With this last "turn of the screw" Fauset rounds off her critique of the dominant racial and sexual model, even suggesting an exchange of roles between the two sexes.

Plum Bum systematically attacks an order in which white values prevail over those of African Americans. Fauset has inverted this racist paradigm, celebrating the way of life of the African American community by means of a consistent critique of white society and a straightforward rejection of passing. Moreover, Fauset has managed to at least destabilize, if not completely invert, the conventional gender apparatus by redefining both love relationships and African American female identity and sexuality, and by proposing an alternative model in which women can achieve full autonomy and voice.

Contrary to widespread readings of Fauset's novel as a mere romance based on fairy tales, a thorough analysis of the text's four cover strategies—passing, fairy tales, romance, and nursery rhymes—unveils a rich and significantly subversive substratum. Through Angela's failed attempts to adapt her life to idealized conventions, Fauset uncovers the destructive, unsettling experience of women who become aware of the conflict between ideals and reality, and of the imposition of certain restrictive roles disguised as the only means for their achieving fulfillment and happiness. The alternative heroine of Fauset's story clearly points at the inadequacy of such codes to regulate women's behavior and to dictate women's sense of identity and femininity. Angela's story serves to disclose the true nature of the racial and gender conditions of the nineteen-twenties, which *Plum Bun* rewrites in consonance with more adequate parameters. Hence, this novel deconstructs all these idealized literary traditions and opens the way for a new, self-empowering interpretation of African American women's identity and sexuality, one that faithfully reflects their own perspective.

CONCLUSION

Ashamed of my race?
And of what race am I?
I am many in one.
Through my veins there flows the blood
Of Red Man, Black Man, Briton. Celt and Scot.
In warring clash and tumultuous riot
I welcome all,
But love the blood of the kindly race
That swarthes my skin, crinkles my hair
And puts sweet music into my soul.

Joseph Cotter
"The Mulatto to His Critics"

The detailed analysis of Johnson's. Schuyler's, Larsen's, and Fauset's texts clearly destabilizes the conventional interpretations that have dominated the reading and reception of these works for too long. The presence of a subversive and parodic substratum common to all these novels speaks to an alternative critical model capable of unearthing the rich. underlying bedrock in which they are grounded. The authors of these works are clearly intent on making use of parody as a suitable means to disclose the subtle but insidious presence of the racist ideology that prevailed in the nineteen-twenties and compelled African Americans to adopt a "double consciousness" to deal with their difficult reality. The parodic component in these novels aligns itself mainly with a direct critique of the established racist *status quo* by showing its most sinister and destructive aspects.

Obviously, the parodic paradigm disavows any assimilationist interpretation of the texts, since it consciously and skillfully deconstructs the parameters that uphold racist ideology and its negative effects on the African American value system. Indeed, the image of the white world transcribed in these novels is everything but ideal, as their critique becomes progressively overt. The image also implies a direct attack on African American institutions that allow for the perpetuation of the dominant order, and on the internalization of this racist code on the part of the African American community of the time. This has been the main reason why many conventional commentators have identified assimilation and betrayal as characteristic of these novels of passing. I contend, however, that the critique of the African American value system reveals two crucial ideas: first, the authors' profound and accurate knowlege of its defective and imitative status with respect to the dominant model, and second, their great awareness of the need to replace it with another one which sets the bases for the configuration of an authentic African American identity. This new notion of self should be supported by an alternative African American ideological framework able to generate a fulfilling sense of identity that liberates itself from prevailing racial stereotypes and constraints.

The authors' well-informed analysis of their contemporary society and, especially, of the African American community proves beyond any reasonable doubt their high degree of social involvement. Far from any traditional depiction of these novelists as traitors to their race, their critical stance shows them deeply concerned with the problems of their society. Difficulties in interpretation seem to have emerged from the critical instruments employed to build up their scathing critique, namely parody, double consciousness, double narratives, and multiple generic covers. The duplicity inherent in all these methods encouraged radically derogatory readings of their works. Nevertheless, I have repeatedly argued here that these critical instruments were intended to work in quite the opposite way, that is, to become useful tools for exploring the dark side of both white and African American communities and to offer new and hopeful directions for the future.

Again we are faced with the inevitable question: but why? Why did they want to protect their critiques with multiple covers that concealed their fundamentally subversive message? Although I could invoke socio-economic motives for their controversial choice related to the background of the nineteen-twenties—the difficult racial situation of the time, the authors' economic dependence on the patronage system that dominated their production, the difficulty of finding an outlet for publication unless works followed primitivist fashions, etc., I still believe that in the end it is the risky nature of the issues which makes such a multilayered disguise absolutely imperative. Hence, they use a series of generic covers in order to convey their unconventional critique of Eurocentric ideology and worldview. They include such problematic aspects as the deconstruction of racist and sexist stereotypes and myths, together with the debunking of dominant representations of key ideas such as racial hierarchy, racial purity, masculinity and femininity, motherhood, standards of beauty, and sexuality.

Because of their hybrid nature and their highly subversive content, all these passing novels can be regarded as double or multiple narratives. I have tried to demonstrate that the narratives themselves "pass" in that they take on a sort of cover, drawing from other genres or modes such as autobiography, satire, romance, fairy tale, science fiction, the sentimental novel, etc., in order to "pass" as mere stories of racial passing when, in fact, they become ideal instruments to reflect upon all kinds of "passing." Thus the deployment of a protective and conventional disguise helps the authors not only to portray racial passing in the literal sense, but also and very importantly, to widen the concept of passing to include cultural, social, class, and even sexual passing. By making use of a multiple "generic passing," the selected narratives ultimately turn into metaphors of themselves: they pass in order to fulfill their mission, proclaiming their unconventional message where notions of race, identity, and gender are constantly deconstructed and reconstructed. The result of a widened concept of "passing" signals, then, the existence of a "passing discourse" embedded within these novels. This passing discourse functions by both sustaining a radical critique of Eurocentric ideology and providing the necessary basis for the reconfiguration of an alternative concept of the African American self, whose importance pervades even contemporary rewritings of the topic.

This conscious effort on the authors' part to reelaborate and redefine the conventions of passing indicates their need to make room for a more useful notion of the passing motif that can accomodate a multiplicity of voices, perspectives, and approaches. Thus, the various forms of concealment and disguise are definite strategies intentionally employed by the writers to account for the multiplicity and hybridity inherent in any attempt to define an African American identity. I have therefore intended this study to contribute to a revision of the parameters usually employed to analyze novels of passing by drawing attention to their enormous influence and their important racial, social, cultural, and personal message, fomenting a new understanding of the difficulties of discovering and consolidating an alternative African American literary canon.

In this chaotic era of rapid and constant evolution, movement, and technology, the four authors we have read—James W. Johnson, George Schuyler, Nella Larsen, and Jessie Fauset—demonstrate their belief in the possibility of effecting change in society by focusing their novels on the plight of passing characters who feel trapped in a suffocating racial and sexual quandary. That is, they need to face a wide variety of oppressions everyday in order to survive and to find a satisfactory sense of self. Ultimately, these novels of passing are serious works of art which make a significant contribution to the ongoing debate over race and identity that dominated the Harlem Renaissance. Moreover, they are also instrumental in delineating a more coherent and inclusive African American canon, where meanings and concepts are constantly revised and updated in the attempt to open up new venues for the shaping of more adequate concepts of self and community.

I do not wish to conclude without mentioning a renewed contemporary interest in passing novels. After the decline of their popularity following the publication of Schuyler's *Black No More,* which seemed to serve as their epitaph, many commentators noted a complete lack of interest in the topic. The result was that no critical treatises mentioned these novels or their authors as representative figures for decades. If they did at all, the critical consensus assigned them almost no relevance and related them with the critique against genteel literature, led by Richard Wright in his well-known 1937 "Blueprint for Negro Writing," in which he claims:

> Under these conditions Negro writing assumed two general aspects: (1) It became a sort of conspicuous ornamentation, the hallmark of "achievement." (2) It became the voice of the educated Negro pleading with white America for justice. Rarely was the best of this writing addressed to the Negro himself, his needs, his sufferings, his aspirations . . . And the mere recognition of this places the whole question of Negro writing in a new light and raises a doubt as to the validity of its present direction. (97-98)

Wright's indictment repeats most of the accusations already outlined throughout this book, fundamentally the authors' assimilationist attitude and their reverence for the prevailing ideology. Even other critics that tried to encourage the investigation of these texts associated them only with the mulatto figure but not with the singular phenomenon of passing.[1]

---

[1] An illustrative example is provided by Catherine Starke, who qualifies the mulatto images from the thirties and fifties as a "greater advancement" (102) with respect to the twenties paradigm, because those mulattoes did not desire to pass into the white race.

Despite this neglect, the interest in passing novels has been revived in recent years, especially thanks to the reprintings of most of the works (all of them having been reedited at the end of the eighties or beginning of the nineties), but also because of the publication of new works that focus on the passing motif. The impact of Shirlee Taylor Haizlip's *The Sweeter the Juice,* published in 1994, is worth noticing. As the author herself asserts in an article significantly entitled "Passing" written a year later, she was overwhelmed by the immediate and massive reaction: "[L]etters began to arrive in a stream that grew to a torrent. By now I have received thousands" (47). This singular reaction discloses the relevance of the passing motif at the end of the twentieth century and the need to continue the line of multiple questioning—racial, social, cultural, and gender—undertaken by the narratives of passing over eighty years ago. The fact that books like Haizlip's awaken such enthusiastic response in our contemporary multiethnic society paves the way for more serious studies of this fascinating topic. Further studies would allow us to understand the complex yet delightful message of the passing motif, one to which I hope to have contributed some new insights. I would like to end on an optimistic note for a multicultural future with Haizlip's inviting reflection:

> It is a consoling idea that everyone on this earth is a shade of the protein called melanin; that black and white alike, we are all a gradation of a color called brown. I know in the blueprint for every human being, there are some billion units of DNA, arranged over twenty-three pairs of chromosomes. Spread throughout that mix are about a hundred thousand genes. No one has counted the human couplings that resulted in genetic mixings and crossovers. And Lucy, that ancient group of fossil bones found in Africa, is the mother of us all. (267-8)

WORKS CITED

ADELL, Sandra. "A Function at the Junction." *Diacritics* 20.4 (Winter 1990): 43-56.

ALDISS, Brian W. *Trillion Year Spree. The History of Science Fiction.* London: Victor Gollacz Ltd, 1986.

ALLEN, Carol. "Migration Through Mirrors and Memories." *Black Women Intellectuals.* New York: Garland, 1998. 47-76.

AMMONS, Elisabeth. "New Literary History: Edith Wharton and Jessie Redmon Fauset." *College Literature* 14.3 (Fall 1987): 207-18.

ANDERSON, Jervis. *This Was Harlem. 1900-1950.* New York: The Noonday Press, 1981.

ANDREWS, William L. *African American Autobiography.* New Jersey: Prentice Hall, 1993.

———. "The Representation of Slavery and the Rise of Afro-American Literary Realism, 1865-1920." *African American Autobiography* 77-89.

———. Introduction. *The Autobiography of an Ex-Colored Man.* By James Weldon Johnson. Harmondsworth: Penguin, 1990. vii-xxvii.

———. *To Tell a Free Story: The First Century of Afro-American Autobiography, 1760-1865.* Urbana: University of Illinois Press, 1986.

———. *Classic Fiction of the Harlem Renaissance.* New York: Oxford University Press, 1994.

———. "The First Century of Afro-American Autobiography: Theory and Explication." *Studies in Black American Literature. v. 1. Black American Prose Theory.* Eds. Joe Weixlmann and Chester J. Fontenot. Greenwood, Florida: Penkevill Publishing Company, 1984. 4-42.

ANGYAL, Andrew J. "The 'Complex Fate' of Being an American: The African-American Essayist and the Quest for Identity." *CLA Journal* 37.1 (September 1993): 64-80.

APPIAH, Anthony Kwame. "Race." *Critical Terms for Literary Study.* Eds. Frank Lentricchia and Thomas McLaughlin. 2nd ed. Chicago: University of Chicago Press, 1995. 274-87.

——. "The Uncompleted Argument: DuBois and the Illusion of Race." *Critical Inquiry* 12 (Autumn 1985): 21-37.

AULLÓN DE ARO, Pedro. *Introducción a la Crítica Literaria Actual.* Madrid: Playfor, 1983.

AWKWARD, Michael. Introduction. *Inspiriting Influences: Tradition, Revision and Afro-American Women's Novels.* New York: Columbia University Press, 1989. 1-14.

BAKER, Houston A., Jr. "In Dubious Battle." *New Literary History* 18.2 (Winter 1987): 363-370.

——. *Blues, Ideology, and Afro-American Literature. A Vernacular Theory.* Chicago: University of Chicago Press, 1984.

——. *Singers of Daybreak.* Washington D. C: Howard University Press, 1974. 17-31.

BAKHTIN, M. M. "Discourse Typology in Prose." *Twentieth-Century Literary Theory.* Eds. Vassilis Lambropoulos and David Neal Miller. Albany: State University of New York Press, 1987. 285-303.

——. *Problems of Dostoevsky's Poetics.* Ed. and Trans. Caryl Emerson. Minneapolis: University of Minneapolis Press, 1984.

——. "Discourse in the Novel." Holquist, *The Dialogic Imagination* 259-422.

BAYM, Nina. *Woman's Fiction: A Guide to Novels By and About Women in America.* Ithaca, New York: Cornell University Press, 1978.

BEALE, Frances. "Double Jeopardy: To Be Black and Female." 1970. *The Black Woman. An Anthology.* Ed. Toni Cade Bambara. New York: New American Library, 1979. 90-100.

BELL, Bernard W. *On Race & Culture.* Eds. Bernard Bell et al. New York: Routledge, 1996.

——. "Genealogical Shifts in DuBois's Discourse on Double Consciousness as the Sign of African American Difference." *On Race & Culture* 87-108.

——. *The Afro-American Novel and Its Tradition.* Amherst: The University of Massachusetts Press, 1987.

BELLOW, Saul. *The Adventures of Augie March.* 1953. London: Weidenfeld & Nicholson, 1954.

BERZON, Judith R. *Neither White Nor Black. The Mulatto Character in American Fiction.* New York: New York University Press, 1978.

BETTELHEIM, Bruno. "Reflections. The Uses of Enchantment." *New Yorker* 8 (December 1975): 50-113.

———. *The Uses of Enchantment. The Meaning and Importance of Fairy Tales.* London: Thames and Hudson, 1975.

BHABBHA, Homi. "The Other Question." *Contemporary Postcolonial Theory. A Reader.* Ed. Pamini Mongia. London: Arnold, 1996. 37-54.

"Black Radiance Cosmetics." *Upscale* (February/March 92): 108.

BLACKMER, Corinne E. "The Veils of the Law: Race and Sexuality in Nella Larsen's *Passing.*" *College Literature* 22 (October 1995): 50-67.

BLACKMORE, David L. "'That Unreasonable Restless Feeling': The Homosexual Subtexts of Nella Larsen's *Passing.*" *African American Review* 26.3 (1992): 475-484.

BLOOM, Harold. *Black American Prose Writers of the Harlem Renaissance.* New York: Chelsea House Publishers, 1994.

BONE, Robert. *The Negro Novel in America.* New Haven: Yale University Press, 1958.

BOTTINGHEIMER, Ruth, ed. *Fairy Tales and Society: Illusion, Allusion, and Paradigm.* Philadelphia: University of Pennsylvania Press, 1986.

BRAITHWAITE, William S. "The Novels of Jessie Fauset." *Opportunity* 12.1 (January 1934): 24-8.

BRANZBURG, Judith. "Women Novelists of the Harlem Renaissance: A Study in Marginality." PHD diss. University of Masachussetts, 1983.

BROOKS, Neil. "On Becoming an Ex-Man: Postmodern Irony and the Extinguishing of Certainties in *The Autobiography of an Ex-Colored Man.*" *College Literature* 22 (October 95): 17-29.

BROTHERS, Barbara and Bege K. Bowers. *Reading and Writing Women's Lives. A Study of the Novel of Manners.* Ann Arbor: U. M. I. Research Press, 1990.

———. "What Is a Novel of Manners?" *Reading and Writing Women's Lives* 1-17.

BROWN, Sterling. *The Negro in American Fiction.* Washington D. C.: Associates in Negro Folk Education, 1937.

———. "A Century of Negro Portraiture in American Literature." *Black Voices.* Ed. Abraham Chapman. New York: New American Library, 1986. 564-89.

BROWN, William Hill. *The Power of Sympathy; or the Triumph of Nature.* 1789. New York: Facsimile Text Society by Columbia University Press, 1937.

BROWN, Williams Wells. *Clotel or the President's Daughter.* 1853. New York: Arno Press and the New York Times, 1969.

BRUCE, Dickson D., Jr. "W. E. B. DuBois and the Idea of the Double Consciousness." *American Literature* 64.2 (June 1992): 21-31.

BURKE, Virginia. "The Veil and the Vision." *Black American Literature Forum* 11.3 (Fall 1977): 91-94.

BUTLER, Judith. "Passing, Queering: Nella Larsen's Psychoanalytic Challenge." *Bodies that Matter.* New York: Routledge, 1994. 167-85.

BUTTERFIELD, Stephen. *Black Autobiography in America.* Amherst: University of Massachusetts Press, 1974.

CAIN, William E. "New Directions in Afro-American Literary Criticism: *The Signifying Monkey.*" *American Quarterly* 42 (1990): 657-63.

CARBY, Hazel V. *Reconstructing Womanhood: The Emergence of the Afro-American Woman Novelist.* New York: Oxford University Press, 1987.

CARROLL, Richard A. "Black Racial Spirit: An Analysis of James Weldon Johnson's Critical Perspective." *Phylon* 32 (Winter 1971): 344-64.

CHESNUTT, Charles. *The Marrow of Tradition.* 1901. Ann Arbor: Ann Arbor Paperbacks, 1969.

——. *The House Behind the Cedars.* Cambridge: The Riverside Press, 1900.

CHRISTIAN, Barbara. *Black Women Novelists: The Development of a Tradition 1892-1976.* Westport, Conn.: Greenwood Press, 1980.

——. "But What do We Think We're Doing Anyway: The State of Black Feminist Criticism(s) or My Version of A Little Bit of History." Wall, *Changing Our Own Words* 58-97.

——. "Trajectories of Self-Definition: Placing Contemporary Afro-American Women's Fiction." Pryse 233-48.

——. *Black Feminist Criticism: Perspectives on Black Women Writers. Perspectives on Black Women Writers.* New York: Pergamon Press, 1985.

COLLIER, Eugenia. "The Endless Journey of an Ex-Coloured Man." *Phylon* 32 (Winter 1971): 365-73.

COLLINS, Patricia Hill. "The Social Construction of Black Feminist Thought." 1989. Guy-Shefthall, *Words of Fire* 338-57.

COOKE, Michael G. *Afro-American Literature in the Twentieth Century. The Achievement of Intimacy.* New Haven: Yale University Press, 1984.

COOPER, Anna Julia. *A Voice from the South: By a Black Woman of the South.* Ohio: Aldine Publishing House, 1892.

CRANNY-FRANCIS, Anne. *Feminist Fiction. Feminist Uses of Generic Fiction.* Cambridge: Polity Press, 1990.

CROUCH, Stanley. "Who Are We? Where Did We Come From? Where Are We Going?" Early, *Lure and Loathing* 80-94.

DALY, Peter et al., eds. *The English Emblem Tradition.* Toronto: University of Toronto Press, 1988.

DAVIS, Angela Y. *Women, Race & Class.* New York: Vintage, 1981.

DAVIS, Arthur P. *From the Dark Tower. Afro-American Writers 1900-1960.* Washington D. C.: Howard University Press, 1981.

DEAN, Sharon and Erlene Stetson. "Flower Dust and Springtime: Harlem Renaissance Women." *Radical Teacher* 18 (1980): 1-8.

DENTITH, Simon. *Bakhtinian Thought. An Introductory Reader.* New York: Routledge, 1995.

DIXON, Thomas. *The Clansman.* New York: Doubleday, 1905.

——. *The Leopard's Sports: A Romance of the White Man's Burden.* New York: Doubleday, 1903.

DOUGLASS, Frederick. "Narrative of the Life of Frederick Douglass." 1845. Gates, *Classic Slave Narratives* 243-331.

DUBOIS, W. E. B. *Dusk of Dawn. An Essay Toward an Autobiography of a Race Concept.* 1940. New York: Schocken, 1968.

——. *The Souls of Black Folk.* 1903. New York: Bantam, 1989.

——. "Awake America." Sundquist, *The Oxford W. E. B. DuBois Reader* 379-81.

——. "Black No More: Being an Account of the Strange and Wonderful Workings of Science in the Land of the Free, A. D. 1933-40." 1931. Lewis, *W. E. B. DuBois. A Reader* 523-4.

——. "Passing by Nella Larsen." Lewis, *W. E. B. DuBois. A Reader* 521-2.

——. "The Concept of Race." Sundquist, *The Oxford W. E. B. DuBois Reader* 76-96.

——. "The Conservation of Races." *The American Negro Academy. Occasional Papers* 1-22. New York: Arno Press, 1969. 5-15.

——. "The Damnation of Women." Sundquist, *The Oxford W. E. B. DuBois Reader* 564-80.

——. "The Younger Literary Movement." *Crisis* 27 (February 1924): 161-2.

——. "Woman Suffrage." Sundquist, *The Oxford W. E. B. DuBois Reader* 377-9.

DUCILLE, Ann. "Blues Notes on Black Sexuality: Sex and the Texts of Jessie Fauset and Nella Larsen." *History of Sexuality* 3.3 (January 1993): 418-44.

DUNBAR, Paul L. *The Sport of Gods.* 1902. Miami: Mnemosyne Publishing Company, 1969.

EARLY, Gerald, ed. *Lure and Loathing. Essays on Race, Identity and the Ambivalence of Assimilation.* Harmondsworth: Penguin, 1994.

EDWARDS, Jay. "Structural Analysis of the Afro-American Trickster Tale." Gates, *Black Literature & Literary Theory* 81-103.

ELKINS, Marilyn. "Expatriate Afro-American Women as Exotics." *International Women's Writing: New Landscapes of Identity.* Eds. Anne Brown and Marjanne Gooze. Westport, Conn.: Greenwood Press, 1995. 264-73.

ELLISON, Ralph. *The Invisible Man.* 1947. New York: Vintage, 1952.

EMERSON, Ralph Waldo. "The Transcendentalist." *Selections from Ralph Waldo Emerson.* Ed. Stephen E. Whicher. Cambridge: The Riverside Press, 1957. 192-207.

EQUIANO, Olaudah. "The Interesting Narrative of the Life of Olaudah Equiano or Gustavus Vassa, the African." 1789. Gates, *The Classic Slave Narratives* 1-182.

ESTEVE, Mary. "Nella Larsen's 'Moving Mosaic': Harlem, Crowds, and Anonymity." *American Literary History* 9.2 (Summer 1997): 268-86.

FABI, Giulia. *Passing and the Rise of the African American Novel.* Urbana: Universiy of Illinois Press, 2001.

FAULKNER, Howard J. "A Vanishing Race." *CLA Journal* 37.3 (March 1994): 274-292.

———. "James Weldon Johnson's Portrait of the Artist as Invisible Man." *Black American Literature Forum* 19 (1985): 147-151.

FAUSET, Jessie Redmon. *The Chinaberry Tree: A Novel of American Life.* 1931. College Park, Md: McGrath Publishing Company, 1969.

———. *Plum Bun.* 1928. Boston: Beacon Press, 1990.

———. *There is Confusion.* 1924. Boston: Northeastern University Press, 1989.

———. "The Sleeper Wakes." 1920. *The Sleeper Wakes. Harlem Renaissance Stories by Women.* Ed. Mary Knopf. New Brunswick, New Jersey: Rutgers University Press, 1993. 1-25.

FEENEY, Joseph J. "Black Childhood as Ironic: A Nursery Rhyme Transformed in Jessie Fauset's Novel *Plum Bun.*" *Minority Voices* 4.2 (Fall 1980): 65-9.

———. "A Sardonic Unconventional Jessie Fauset: The Double Structure and Double Vision of her Novels." *CLA Journal* 22.2 (June 1979): 365-82.

FLEMING, Robert E. "Irony as a Key to Johnson's *The Autobiography of an Ex-Colored Man.*" *American Literature* 43.1 (March 1971): 83-96.

——. "Contemporary Themes in Johnson's *The Autobiography of an Ex-Colored Man.*" *Negro American Literature Forum* 4.4 (Winter 1970): 120-124, 141.

FLITTERMAN-LEWIS, Sandy. *"Imitation(s) of Life*: The Black Woman's Double Determination As Troubling 'Other.'" *Literature and Psychology* 34.4 (1988): 44-57.

FORD, Nick. *The Contemporary Negro Novel: A Study in Race Relations.* 1936. College Park, Md.: McGrath, 1968.

FOSTER, Hannah. *The Coquette.* 1797. New York: Oxford University Press, 1986.

FRYE, Northrop. *Anatomy of Criticism.* 1957. Harmondsworth: Penguin, 1990.

FULLER, Hoyt. Introduction. *Passing.* By Nella Larsen. New York: Collier Books, 1971. 11-24.

GARRETT, Marvin P. "Early Recollections and Structural Irony in *The Autobiography of an Ex-Colored Man.*" *Critique* 13.2 (1971): 5-14.

GATES, Henry Louis, Jr. and Nellie Y. McKay, eds. *The Norton Anthology of African American Literature.* New York: W. W. Norton & Company, 1997.

GATES, Henry Louis, Jr., ed. *Reading Black, Reading Feminist. A Critical Anthology.* Harmondsworth: Penguin, 1990.

——. Introduction. *The Souls of Black Folk.* By W. E. B. Du Bois. New York: Bantam, 1989. vii-xxix.

——. *The Signifying Monkey. A Theory of African-American Literary Criticism.* New York: Oxford University Press, 1988.

——. "'What's Love Got to Do With It?': Critical Theory, Integrity, and the Black Idiom." *New Literary History* 18.2 (Winter 1987): 345-362.

——. *Figures In Black. Words, Signs, and the 'Racial' Self.* New York: Oxford University Press, 1987.

——. *The Classic Slave Narratives.* New York: Mentor, 1987.

——. "Writing 'Race' and the Difference It Makes." *Critical Inquiry* 12 (Autumn 1985): 1-20.

——, ed. *'Race,' Writing and Difference.* Chicago: University of Chicago Press, 1985.

——. "Talkin' that Talk." *'Race,' Writing and Difference* 402-9.

——, ed. *Black Literature & Literary Theory.* New York: Routledge, 1984.

——. "The Blackness of Blackness: A Critique of the Sign and The Signifying Monkey." *Black Literature & Literary Theory* 285-321.

——. "Criticism in de Jungle." *Black American Literature Forum* 15.4 (Winter 1981): 123-127.

GAYLE, Addison Jr. *The Way of the New World: The Black Novel in America.* Garden City, N. Y.: Anchor Press, 1975.

GILBERT, Sandra and Susan Gubar. *The Madwoman in the Attic: The Woman Writer and the Nineteenth-Century Literary Imagination.* New Haven: Yale University Press, 1979.

GILKES, Cheryl Towsend. "The Margin as the Center of a Theory of History." Bell, *On Race & Culture* 111-39.

GILMAN, Sander. "Black Bodies, White Bodies: Toward an Iconography of Female Sexuality in Late Nineteenth-Century Art, Medicine, and Literature." Gates, *'Race,' Writing and Difference* 223-61.

GINSBERG, Elaine, ed. *Passing and the Fictions of Identity.* Durham: Duke University Press, 1996.

GLOSTER, Hugh. *Negro Voices in American Fiction.* 1939. Chapel Hill: University of North Carolina Press, 1948.

GOELLNICHT, Donald C. "Passing as Autobiography: James Weldon Johnson's *The Autobiography of an Ex-Colored Man.*" *African American Review* 30.1 (Spring 1996): 17-33.

GOSSETT, Thomas F. *Race: The History of an Idea in America.* New York: Schocken, 1963.

GRANT, Madison. *The Passing of the Great Race.* New York: Charles Scribner Sons, 1916.

GRAY, Jeffrey. "Essence and the Mulatto Traveler: Europe as Embodiment in Nella Larsen's *Quicksand.*" *Novel* 27 (Spring 1994): 257-70.

GRIFFIN, Dustin. *Satire. A Critical Reintroduction.* Lexington: University Press of Kentucky, 1994.

GUILHAMET, Leon. *Satire and the Transformation of Genre.* Philadelphia: University of Pennsylvania Press, 1987.

GUY-SHEFTALL, Beverly. *Words of Fire. An Anthology of African American Feminist Thought.* New York: The New Press, 1995.

HAIZLIP, Shirlee Taylor. "Passing." *American Heritage* 46.1 (February-March 1995): 46-54.

———. *The Sweeter the Juice. A Family Memoir in Black and White.* New York: Touchstone, 1994.

HALE, Dorothy. "Bakhtin in African American Literary Theory." *ELH* 61 (1994): 445-471.

HARPER, Frances E. W. *Iola Leroy; or Shadows Uplifted.* 1892. Boston: Beacon Press, 1987.

HARRIS, Joel Chandler. *Uncle Remus: His Songs and His Sayings.* 1880. Harmondsworth: Penguin, 1982.

HENDERSON, Mae Gwendolyn. "Speaking in Tongues: Dialogics, Dialectics, and the Black Woman Writer's Literary Tradition." Gates, *Reading Black, Reading Feminist* 116-42.

HILL, Patricia Liggins. *Call & Response. The Riverside Anthology of the African American Literary Tradition.* Boston: Houghton Mifflin Company, 1998.

HINDLE, Maurice. Introduction. *Frankestein.* By Mary Shelley. Harmondsworth: Penguin, 1992. vii-vlii.

HINE, Darlene C. "'In the Kingdom of Culture?': Black Women and the Intersection of Race, Gender, and Class." Early, *Lure and Loathing* 337-51.

HODGART, Matthew. *La Sátira.* Trans. Angel Guillén. Madrid: Ediciones Guadarrama, 1969.

HOLQUIST, Michael. *Dialogism. Bakhtin and his World.* New York: Routledge, 1990.

——, ed.. *The Dialogic Imagination. Four Essays.* Trans. Caryl Emerson and Michael Holquist. Austin: University of Texas Press, 1981.

hooks, bell. *Ain't I a Woman: Black Women and Feminism.* Boston: South End Press, 1981.

HOSTETLER, Ann E. "The Aesthetics of Race and Gender in Nella Larsen's *Quicksand.*" *PMLA* 105.1 (January 1990): 35-46

HUGGINS, Nathan, ed. *Voices from the Harlem Renaissance.* New York: Oxford University Press, 1995.

——. *Harlem Renaissance.* New York: Oxford University Press, 1971.

HUGHES, Langston. "The Negro Artist and the Racial Mountain." *Nation* June 23, 1926: 692-4.

HUME, Kathryn. *Fantasy and Mimesis. Responses to Reality in Western Literature.* New York: Methuen, 1984.

HURD, Myles R. "Rhetoric versus Eloquence in the Afro-American Double Narrative: Perspectives on Audience, Ambivalence and Ambiguity." PHD diss. University of New York, 1985.

HUTCHEON, Linda. *A Theory of Parody. The Teachings of Twentieth-Century Art Forms.* New York: Methuen, 1985.

HUXLEY, Aldous. *Brave New World.* 1932. London: Grafton, 1989.

JACOBS, George W. "Negro Authors Must Eat." *Nation* 12 June 1929: 710-1

JAMES, Joy. "The Profeminist Politics of W. E. B. DuBois with Respect to Anna Julia Cooper and Ida B. Wells Barnett." Bell, *On Race & Culture* 141-60.

JAMES, William. *Principles of Psychology.* 1890. New York: James Pott, 1930.

JAPTOK, Martin. "Between 'Race' as Construct and 'Race' as Essence: *The Autobiography of an Ex-Colored Man.*" *The Southern Literary Journal* 28 (Spring 1996): 32-47.

JENKINS, Wilbert. "Jessie Fauset: A Modern Apostle of Black Racial Pride." *The Zora Neale Hurston Forum* 1 (Fall 1986): 14-24.

JOHNSON, Abby A. "Literary Midwife: Jessie Redmon Fauset and the Harlem Renaissance." *Phylon* 39.2 (June 1978): 143-53.

JOHNSON, James Weldon. 1933. *Along This Way. The Autobiography of James Weldon Johnson.* Harmondsworth: Penguin, 1990.

——. *Black Manhattan.* 1930. New York: Da Capo Press, 1958.

——. *The Autobiography of an Ex-Colored Man.* 1912. Harmondsworth: Penguin, 1990.

——. "Harlem: The Culture Capital." Locke 301-11.

JOYCE, Joyce A. "The Black Canon: Reconstructing Black American Literary Criticism" and "'Who the Cap Fit': Unconsciousness and Unconscionableness in the Criticism of Houston A. Baker, Jr., and Henry Louis Gates, Jr." *New Literary History* 18.2 (Winter 1987): 335-344, 371-384.

JUDY, Ronald A. T. "The New Black Aesthetic and W. E. B. DuBois, or Hephaestus, Limping." *The Massachusetts Review* 35.2 (Summer 1994): 249-282.

KAWASH, Samira. "*The Autobiography of an ExColoured Man*: (Passing for) Black Passing for White." Ginsberg 59-74.

KELLNER, Bruce, ed. *The Harlem Renaissance. A Historical Dictionary for the Era.* New York: Methuen, 1984.

KING, Deborah. "Multiple Jeopardy, Multiple Consciousness: The Context of a Black Feminist Ideology." Guy-Sheftall, *Words of Fire* 294-317.

KOSTELANETZ, Richard. "James Weldon Johnson." *Politics in the Afro-American Novel.* New York: Greenwood Press, 1991. 19-25.

KRAMER, Victor, ed. *The Harlem Renaissance Re-examined.* New York: AMS Press, 1987.

KUBITSCHEK, MissyDehn. "Jumping Out the Window: Nella Larsen's Passing and the End of an Era." *Claiming the Heritage. African-American Women*

Novelists and History. Jackson: University Press of Mississippi, 1991. 183-200.

KUENZ, Jane. "American Racial Discourse, 1900-1930: Schuyler's *Black No More.*" *Novel* 30.2 (Winter 1997): 170-91.

LARSEN, Nella. *Quicksand and Passing.* 1928 and 1929. New Brunswick: Rutgers University Press, 1986.

LARSON, Charles. Introduction. *Black No More.* By George Schuyler. New York: Collier Books, 1971. ix-xx.

LATTANY, Kristin H. "Off-Timing: Stepping to the Different Drummer." Early, *Lure and Loathing* 163-174.

LEMERT, Charles. "A Classic from the Other Side of the Veil: DuBois's *Souls of Black Folk.*" *The Sociological Quarterly* 35.3 (August 1994): 383-396.

LEVY, Eugene. *James Weldon Johnson. Black Leader, Black Voice.* Chicago: University of Chicago Press, 1973.

LEWIS, David Levering, ed. *W. E. B. DuBois. A Reader.* New York: Henry Holt, 1995.

——. *W. E. B. DuBois: Biography of a Race.* New York: Henry Holt, 1993.

——. *When Harlem Was In Vogue.* New York: Oxford University Press, 1981.

LEWIS, Vashti C. "Nella Larsen's Use of the Near-White Female in *Quicksand* and *Passing.*" *Perspectives of Black Popular Culture.* Ed. Harry B. Shaw. Bowling Green, Ohio: Bowling Green University Popular Press, 1990. 36-45.

——. "The Mulatto Woman as Major Female Character in Novels by Black Women, 1892-1937." PHD diss. University of Iowa, 1981.

LIEBERMANN, Marcia. "'Some Day My Prince Will Come': Female Acculturation through the Fairy Tale." Zipes, *Don't Bet on the Prince* 185-200.

LINCOLN, C. Eric. "The DuBoisian Dubiety and the American Dilemma: Two Levels of Lure and Loathing." Early, *Lure and Loathing* 194-206.

LITTLE, John. "Nella Larsen's *Passing*: Irony and the Critics." *African American Literature Review* 26.1 (Spring 1992): 173-82.

LITTLEJOHN, David. *Black on White: A Critical Survey of Writing by American Negroes.* New York: Viking, 1969.

LOCKE, Alan, ed. *The New Negro. Voices of the Harlem Renaissance.* 1925. New York: Atheneum, 1992.

LYNE, William. "The Signifying Modernist: Ralph Ellison and the Limits of Double Consciouness." *PMLA* 107 (March 1992): 319-30.

MACKETHAN, Lucinda H. "*Black Boy* and *Ex-Colored Man*: Version and Inversion of the Slave Narrator's Quest for Voice." *CLA Journal* 32.2 (December 1988): 123-47.

MAKALANI, Jabulani Kamau. "Toward a Psychological Analysis of the Renaissance: Why Harlem?" *Black World* 25.4 (February 1976): 4-13, 93-97.

MCDADE, Georgia Lee. "From Hopeful to Hopeless: A Study of the Novels of Jessie Redmon Fauset." PHD diss. University of Washington, 1987.

MCDOUGALD, Elise. "The Task of Negro Womanhood." Locke 369-82.

MCDOWELL, Deborah. *'The Changing Same.' Black Women's Literature, Criticism, and Theory*. Bloomington: Indiana University Press, 1995.

——. "Transferences. Black Feminist Thinking: The 'Practice' of 'Theory.'" *'The Changing Same'* 56-75.

——. "On Face. The Marks of Identity in Jessie Fauset's *Plum Bun* or Getting Read in the Harlem Renaissance." *'The Changing Same'* 61-77.

——. "In the First Place: Making Frederick Douglass and the Afro-American Narrative Tradition." Andrews, *African American Autobiography* 36-58.

——. "Regulating Midwives." *Plum Bun. A Novel Without a Moral*. By Jessie Redmon Fauset. Boston: Beacon Press, 1990. ix-xxiii.

——. "Boundaries: Or Distant Relations and Close Kin." *Afro-American Literary Studies in the 1990s*. Eds. Houston A. Baker and Patricia Redmon. Chicago: University of Chicago Press, 1989. 51-77.

——. Introduction. *Quicksand and Passing*. By Nella Larsen. New Brunswick: Rutgers University Press, 1986. ix-xxxv.

——. "Reading Family Matters." Wall, *Changing Our Own Words* 75-97.

——. "New Directions for Black Feminist Criticism." *The New Feminist Criticism. Essays on Women, Literature, and Theory*. London: Virago Press, 1985. 186-199.

——. "The Neglected Dimension of Jessie Redmon Fauset." Pryse 86-104.

MCKAY, Nellie Y. "The Souls of Black Women Folk in the Writings of W. E. B. DuBois." Gates, *Reading Black, Reading Feminist* 227-243.

MCLAUGHIN, Andreé. "Black Women, Identity, and the Quest for Humanhood and Wholeness: Wild Women in the Whirlwind." *Wild Women in the Whirlwind*. Eds. Joanne Braxton and Andreé McLaughin. New Brunswick: Rutgers University Press, 1990. 147-80.

MCLENDON, Jacquelyn Y. *The Politics of Color in the Fiction of Jessie Fauset and Nella Larsen*. Charlottesville: University Press of Virginia, 1995.

MCMANUS, Mary Hairston. "African-American Modernism in the Novels of Jessie Fauset and Nella Larsen." PHD diss. University of Maryland College Park, 1992.

MCMILLAN, T. S. "Passing Beyond: The Novels of Nella Larsen." *West Virginia University Philological Papers* 38 (1992): 134-46.

MILLER, James. Foreword. *Black No More.* By George Schuyler. Boston: Northeastern University Press, 1989. 1-12.

MITCHELL, Angelyn, ed. *Within the Circle. An Anthology of African American Literary Criticism from the Harlem Renaissance to the Present.* Durham: Duke University Press, 1994.

MONDA, Kimberly. "Self-Delusion and Self-Sacrifice in Nella Larsen's *Quicksand.*" *African American Literature Forum* 31.1 (Spring 1997): 23-39.

MONTAGU, Ashley. "Appendix A." *Man's Most Dangerous Myth. The Fallacy of Race.* 4th ed. Cleveland: World Publishing Company, 1964. 361-71.

MORRISON, Toni. *The Bluest Eye.* New York: Washington Square Press, 1970.

MOYLAN, Tom. *Demand the Impossible. Science Fiction and the Utopian Imagination.* New York: Methuen, 1986.

NASHE, Thomas. *The Unfortunate Traveller and Other Works.* 1594. Ed. J. B. Steane. Harmondsworth: Penguin, 1972.

NIELSEN, Aldon. "James Weldon Johnson's Impossible Text." *Writing Between the Lines. Race and Intertextuality.* Athens, Georgia: University of Georgia Press, 1994. 172-84.

O'DANIEL, THERMAN B. Introduction. *The Blacker The Berry . . . A Novel of Negro Life.* By Wallace Thurman. 1929. New York: Collier Books, 1970. ix-xix.

O'SULLIVAN, Maurice J. "Of Souls and Pottage: James Weldon Johnson's *The Autobiography of an Ex-Colored Man.*" *CLA Journal* 23.1 (September 1979): 60-70.

ORWELL, George. *Nineteen Eighty-Four.* 1949. Harmondsworth: Penguin, 1984.

OSOFSKY, Gilbert. *Harlem: The Making of a Ghetto. Negro New York, 1890-1930.* New York: Harper and Row, 1963.

PELTON, Robert. *The Trickster in West Africa: A Study of Mythic Irony and Sacred Delight.* Berkeley: University of California Press, 1980.

PEPLOW, Michael W. *George Schuyler.* Boston: Twayne, 1980.

——. "George Schuyler, Satirist: Rhetorical Devices in *Black No More.*" *CLA Journal* 18.2 (December 1974): 242-257.

PERRY, Regenia. *What It Is: Black American Folk Art.* Richmond: Virginia Commonwealth University, 1982.

PETERSON, Dale E. "Notes from the Underworld: Dostoevsky, DuBois, and the Discovery of Ethnic Soul." *The Massachusetts Review* 35: 2 (Summer 1994): 225-248.

——. "Response and Call: The African American Dialogue with Bakhtin." *American Literature* 65.4 (December 1993): 761-775.

PETESCH, Donald. *A Spy in the Enemy's Country. The Emergence of Modern Black Literature.* Iowa City: University of Iowa Press, 1989.

PETRO, Peter. *Modern Satire. Four Studies.* Berlin: Morton Publishers, 1992.

PFEIFFER, Kathleen. "Individualism, Success, and American Identity in *The Autobiography of an Ex-Colored Man.*" *African American Review* 30.3 (Fall 1996): 403-419.

PIETERSE, Jan Nederveen. *White on Black. Images of Africa and Blacks in Western Popular Culture.* New Haven: Yale University Press, 1992.

PISIAK, Roxanna. "Irony and Subversion in James Weldon Johnson's *The Autobiography of an Ex-Colored Man.*" *Studies in American Fiction* 21 (1993): 83-96.

POLLARD, Arthur. *Satire.* London: Methuen & Company, 1970.

PRATT, Annis. "The New Feminist Criticisms." *Beyond Intellectual Sexism: A New Woman, A New Reality.* Ed. Joan Roberts. New York: McKay, 1972. 175-95.

PRYSE, Marjorie and Hortense J. Spillers, eds. *Conjuring. Black Women, Fiction, and Literary Tradition.* Bloomington: Indiana University Press, 1985.

RAMPERSAD, Arnold. *The Art and Imagination of W. E. B. DuBois.* 1976. New York: Schocken, 1990.

RAMSEY, Priscilla. "Freeze the Day: A Feminist Reading of Nella Larsen's *Quicksand* and *Passing.*" *Afro-Americans in New York Life and History* 9 (January 1985): 27-41.

RAYSON, Ann. "George Schuyler: Paradox Among 'Assimilationist' Writers." *Black American Literature Forum* 12.3 (Fall 1978): 102-109.

REILLY, John M. "The Black Anti-Utopia." *Black American Literature Forum* 12 (1978): 107-9.

REX, John. *Race and Ethnicity.* Milton Keynes: Open University Press, 1986.

RICHARDSON, Samuel. *Pamela or Virtue Rewarded.* 1740. Harmondsworth: Penguin, 1980.

ROSE, Peter I. *The Subject is Race. Traditional Ideologies and the Teaching of Race Relations*. New York: Oxford University Press, 1968.

——. *They & We. Racial and Ethnic Relations in the United States*. New York: Random House, 1964.

ROSS, Stephen M. "Audience and Irony in Johnson's *The Autobiography of an Ex-Colored Man*." *CLA Journal* 18.2 (December 1974): 198-210.

ROWE, Karen. "Feminism and Fairy Tales." Zipes, *Don't Bet on the Prince* 209-26.

ROWSON, Susana. *Charlotte Temple*. 1791. Harmondsworth: Penguin, 1991.

RUESCHMANN, Eva. "Sister Bonds: Intersections of Family and Race in Jessie Redmon Fauset's *Plum Bun* and Dorothy West's *The Living is Easy*." *The Significance of Sibling Relationships in Literature*. Eds. Joanna Stephens Mink et al. Bowling Green, Ohio: Popular Press, 1992. 120-32.

RULAND, Richard and Malcolm Bradbury. *From Puritanism to Postmodernism A History of American Literature*. Harmondsworth: Penguin, 1991.

SANTAYANA, George. *La Tradición Gentil en la Filosofía Americana*. Trans. Pedro García Martín. Taller de Estudios Norteamericanos. Universidad de León, 1993.

SATO, Hiroko. "Under the Harlem Shadow: A Study of Jessie Fauset and Nella Larsen." *The Harlem Renaissance Remembered*. Ed. Arna Bontemps. New York: Dodd, Mead and Company, 1972. 63-89.

SCHEUB, Harold. *The African Storyteller. Stories from African Oral Traditions*. Dubuque, Iowa: Kendall/Hunt Publishing Company, 1990.

SCHOCKLEY, Ann A. "Afro-American Women Writers. *The New Negro Movement* 1924-1933." *Rereading Modernism. New Directions in Feminist Criticism*. New York: Garland, 1994. 123-35.

SCHUYLER, George. *Black No More. Being an Account of the Strange and Wonderful Workings of Science in the Land of the Free, A. D. 1933-1940*. 1931. Boston: Northeastern University Press, 1989.

——. "Our Greatest Gift to America." 1927. Huggins, *Voices* 361-65.

——. "Our White Folks." *American Mercury* 12.48 (December 1927): 385-92.

——. "The Negro Art-Hokum." *Nation* 16 June 1926: 662-663.

SCRUGGS, Charles. "H.L. Mencken and James Weldon Johnson: Two Men Who Helped Shape a Renaissance." *Critical Essays on H.L. Mencken*. Ed. Douglas C. Steuerson. Boston: Hall, 1987. 186-203.

——. *The Sage in Harlem*. Baltimore: Johns Hopkins University Press, 1984.

SELDEN, Raman. *La Teoría Literaria Contemporánea.* 1985. Trans. Juan Gabriel López Guix. Barcelona: Ariel, 1993.

SHEESHY, John. "The Mirror and the Veil: The Passing Novel and the Quest for American Racial Identity." *African American Review* 33.3 (Fall 1999): 401-15.

SHELLEY, Mary. *Frankestein.* 1818. Harmondsworth: Penguin, 1992.

SHLOVSKY, Victor. "Art as Technique." 1917. *Twentieth-Century Literary Theory. A Reader.* Ed. K. M. Newton. London: Macmillan, 1988. 23-5.

SHOWALTER, Elaine. "A Criticism of Our Own: Autonomy and Assimilation in Afro-American and Feminist Literary Theory." *The Future of Literary Theory.* Ed. Ralph Cohen. New York: Routledge, 1989. 347-69.

——. "Feminist Criticism in the Wilderness." *The New Feminist Criticism. Essays on Women, Literature, and Theory.* London: Virago Press, 1985. 243-270.

SINGH, Amritjit et al, eds. *The Harlem Renaissance: Revaluations.* New York: Garland, 1989.

——. *The Novels of the Harlem Renaissance. Twelve Black Writers 1923-1933.* University Park: Pennsylvania State University Press, 1976.

SISNEY, Mary F. "The View from the Outside: Black Novels of Manners." Brothers 171-185.

SKERRETT, Joseph T., Jr. "Irony and Symbolic Action in James Weldon Johnson's *The Autobiography of an Ex-Colored Man.*" *American Quarterly* 32 (Winter 1980): 540-58.

SMITH, Barbara, ed. *Home Girls: A Black Feminist Anthology.* New York: Kitchen Table-Women of Color Press, 1983.

——. "Toward a Black Feminist Criticism." *In the Memory and Spirit of Frances, Lora and Lorraine. Essays and Interviews on Black Women and Writing.* Ed. Juliette Bowles. Howard University: Institute for the Arts and Humanities, 1979. 32-40.

SMITH, Valerie, ed. "James Weldon Johnson." *African American Writers.* New York: Scribners, 1991. 219-23.

——. "Black Feminist Theory and the Representation of the 'Other.'" Wall, *Changing Our Own Words* 38-57.

SOLLORS, Werner. *Neither Black Nor White Yet Both. Thematic Explorations of Interracial Literature.* Cambridge: Harvard University Press, 1997.

——. *Beyond Ethnicity. Consent and Descent in American Culture.* New York: Oxford University Press, 1986.

——. "'Never Was Born': The Mulatto, An American Tragedy." *The Masachussetts Review* 27.3 (Summer 1986): 293-316.

SPARK, Muriel. *Mary Shelley.* London: Constable, 1988.

SPILLERS, Hortense J. "Cross-Currents, Discontinuities: Black Women's Fiction." Pryse 249-261.

——. "Interstices: A Small Drama of Words." *Pleasure and Danger: Exploring Female Sexuality.* Ed. Carole Vance. Boston: Routledge and Kegan Paul, 1984. 73-100.

STADLER, Quandra Prettyman. "Visibility and Difference: Black Women in History and Literature—Pieces of a Paper and Some Ruminations." *The Future of Difference.* Eds. Hester Eisenstein and Alice Jardine. Boston: G. K. Hall and Company, 1980. 239-46.

STARKE, Catherine. *Black Portraiture in American Fiction.* New York: Basic Books, 1971.

STARKEY, Marion L. "Jessie Fauset." *The Southern Workman* 61.5 (May 1932): 217-20.

STEPTO, Robert. *From Behind the Veil. A Study of Afro-American Narrative.* 1979. Urbana: University of Illinois Press, 1991.

STEWART, James B. "Psychic Duality of Afro-Americans in the Novels of W. E. B. DuBois." *Phylon* 44 (1983): 93-107.

STODDARD, Lohrop. *The Rising Tide of Color against White World's Supremacy.* London: Chapman, 1920.

STONE, Kay. "Feminist Approaches to the Interpretation of Fairy Tales." Bottingheimer 229-36.

STOWE, Harriet B. *Uncle Tom's Cabin or, Life Among the Lowly.* 1852. Harmondsworth: Penguin, 1981.

STRIBLING, T. S. *Birthright: A Novel.* 1922. London: W. Collins, 1925.

SUNDQUIST, Eric J, ed. *The Oxford W. E. B. DuBois Reader.* New York: Oxford University Press, 1996.

——. *To Wake the Nation. Race in the Making of American Literature.* Cambridge: Belknap Press of Harvard, 1993.

SYLVANDER, Carolyn. *Jessie Redmon Fauset, Black American Writer.* Troy, N.Y.: Whitston Publishing Company, 1981.

TAKAKI, Ronald T. *Iron Cages. Race and Culture in Nineteenth-Century America.* London: The Athlone Press, 1979.

TALLY, Justine. "Powerlessness into Power: Intersecting Gender, Race and Region." *Revista Canaria de Estudios Ingleses* 21 (Noviembre 1990): 19-34.

TARVER, Australia and Paula Barnes, eds. *New Voices from the Harlem Renaissance.* Forthcoming, 2002.

TATAR, Maria. *Off With Their Heads! Fairy Tales and the Culture of Childhood.* Princetown, NJ: Princeton University Press, 1992.

TATE, Claudia. "Desire and Death in *Quicksand,* by Nella Larsen." *American Literary History* 7 (Summer 1995): 234-60.

——. "Allegories of Black Female Desire; or, Rereading Nineteenth-Century Sentimental Narratives of Black Female Authority." Wall, *Changing Our Own Words* 98-126.

——. "Nella Larsen's *Passing*: A Problem of Interpretation." *Black American Literature Forum* 14.4 (Winter 1980): 142-6.

THORNTON, Hortense E. "Sexism as Quagmire: Nella Larsen's *Passing.*" *CLA Journal* 16.3 (March 1973): 285-301.

THURMAN, Wallace. *The Blacker The Berry . . . A Novel of Negro Life.* 1929. New York: Collier Books, 1970.

TUCKER, Jeffrey. "'Can Science Succeed where the Civil War Failed?' George S. Schuyler and Race." *Race Consciousness. African American Studies for the New Century.* New York: New York University Press, 1997. 136-52.

TUSMITH, Bonie. *All My Relatives.* Ann Arbor: University of Michigan Press, 1993.

VAN VECHTEN, Carl. "Introduction to Mr. Knopf's New Edition." *The Autobiography of an Ex-Colored Man.* By James Weldon Johnson. New York: Knopf, 1927. v-x.

WAELTI-WALTERS, Jennifer. *Fairy Tales and the Female Imagination.* Montreal: Eden Press, 1982.

WALKER, Alice. *In Search of Our Mothers' Gardens: Womanist Prose.* San Diego: Harcourt Brace Jovanovich, 1983.

WALL, Cheryl A, ed. *Changing Our Own Words.* New Brunswick: Rutgers University Press, 1989.

——. "Passing for What? Aspects of Identity in Nella Larsen's Novels." *Black American Literature Forum* 20.1-2 (Spring-Summer 1986): 97-111.

——. "Poets and Versifiers, Singers and Signifiers: Women of the Harlem Renaissance." *Women, The Arts and the 1920s in Paris and New York.* Ed. Keneth Wheeler et al. New Brunswick: Transaction Books, 1982. 74-98.

WALLACE, Michele. *Black Macho and the Myth of the Superwoman.* 1978. London: Verso, 1990.

——. "Variations on Negation and the Heresy of Black Feminist Creativity." Gates, *Reading Black, Reading Feminist* 52-67.

WALLINGER, Hanna. "'The Five Million Women of My Race': Negotiations of Gender in W. E. B. DuBois and Anna Julia Cooper." *Soft Canons. American Women Writers and Masculine Tradition.* Ed. Karen L. Kilcup. Iowa City: University of Iowa Press, 1999. 262-80.

WARNER, Marina. *From the Beast to the Blonde: Fairy Tales and Their Tellers.* London: Vintage, 1995.

WARREN, Kenneth. "Troubled Black Humanity in *The Souls of Black Folk* and *The Autobiography of an Ex-Colored Man.*" *The Cambridge Companion to American Realism and Naturalism.* Cambridge: Cambridge University Press, 1995. 263-77.

WASHINGTON, Booker T. *Up From Slavery.* 1901. New York: Airmont, 1967.

WASHINGTON, Mary Helen. *Midnight Birds: Stories of Contemporary Black Women Writers.* New York: Anchor Books, 1980.

——. *Invented Lives. Narratives of Black Women 1860-1960.* New York: Anchor Books, 1987.

——. "The Mulatta Trap: Nella Larsen's Women of the 1920s." *Invented Lives* 159-67.

——. *Black-Eyed Susans.* New York: Anchor Books, 1975.

WHITE, Deborah G. *Ar'n't I a Woman? Female Slaves in the Plantation South.* New York: W. W. Norton & Company, 1985.

WHITE, Walter. *A Man Called White.* 1948. Athens, Georgia: University of Georgia Press, 1995.

——. *Rope and Faggot: A Biography of Judge Lynch.* 1929. New York: Arno Press and the New York Times, 1969.

——. *Flight.* 1926. New York: Negro Universities Press, 1969.

WILLIAMS, Bettye J. "Nella Larsen: Early Twentieth-Century Novelist of Afrocentric Feminist Thought." *CLA Journal* 39 (December 1995): 165-78.

WINTZ, Cary D. *Black Culture and the Harlem Renaissance.* Houston: Rice University Press, 1988.

——. "Black Writers in 'Nigger Heaven': The Harlem Renaissance." PHD diss. Kansas State University , 1974.

WRIGHT, Richard. "Blueprint for Negro Writing." 1937. Mitchell 97-106.

YARBOROUGH, Richard. "The First-Person in Afro-American Fiction." *Afro-American Literary Study in the 1990s*. Eds. Houston A. Baker and Patricia Redmon. Chicago: University of Chicago Press, 1989. 105-34.

YOUMAN, Mary Mabel. "Nella Larsen's *Passing*: A Study in Irony." *CLA Journal* 18.2 (December 1974): 235-41.

ZIPES, Jack. *Don't Bet on the Prince. Contemporary Feminist Fairy Tales in North America and England*. Hauts: Scolar Press, 1986.

———. Introduction. *Don't Bet on the Prince* 1-36.

———. *Breaking the Magic Spell. Radical Theories of Folk and Fairy Tales*. London: Heinemann, 1979.

FORECAAST
(Forum for European Contributions
to African American Studies)

Maria Diedrich; Carl Pedersen;
Justine Tally (eds.)
Mapping African America
History, Narrative Formation, and the Production of Knowledge
The world of African America extends throughout
the northern, central, southern and insular parts
of the American continent. The essays included
in this volume take the creation of that world
as a single object of study, tracing significant
routes and contacts, building comparisons and
contrasts. They thus participate in the reworking
of traditional approaches to the study of history,
the critique of literature and culture, and the
production of knowledge. All are engaged in an
effort to locate the African American experience
within a wider pan-African vision that links the
colonial with the postcolonial, the past with the
present, the African with the Western.
Mapping African America sketches lines that,
far from limiting our geography, extend our
knowledge of the Africanist influence on and
their participation in what is generally called
"Western" culture. This creative challenge to
traditional disciplines will not only enhance
the reader's understanding of African American
Studies but will also help forge links with other
academic fields of inquiry.
Bd. 1, 1999, 256 S., 30,90 €, br., ISBN 3-8258-3328-3

Stefanie Sievers
Liberating Narratives
The Authorization of Black Female Voices in
African American Women Writers' Novels of
Slavery
Three contemporary novels of slavery – Margaret
Walker's *Jubilee* (1966), Sherley Anne Williams's
Dessa Rose (1986) and Toni Morrison's *Beloved*
(1987) – are the central focus of *Liberating
Narratives*. In significantly different ways that
reflect their individual and socio-political contexts
of origin, these three novels can all be read
as critiques of historical representation and as
alternative spaces for remembrance – 'sites of
memory' – that attempt to shift the conceptual
ground on which our knowledge of the past is
based.
Bd. 2, 1999, 232 S., 25,90 €, br., ISBN 3-8258-3919-2

Justine Tally
Paradise Reconsidered
Toni Morrison's (Hi)stories and Truths
Toni Morison's *Paradise* (1998) arrived on
the scene amid vociferous acclaim and much
consternation. Third in the trilogy begun with
Beloved and *Jazz*, this fascinating yet complicated
the novel has sown as much confusion as
admiration. How does it work? How does
the novel close the trilogy? Indeed, a major
complaint among reviewers, why does Morrison
overload us with so many characters and stories?
In this first book-length study of *Paradise*, Justin
Tally securely links the work to Morrison's entire
oeuvre and effectively argues that while all of
the novels of the trilogy are deeply analytical of
the relationship of memory, story and history,
the historical narrative: memory is fickle, story is
unreliable, and history is subject to manipulation.
A master narrative of the past is again dictated
by the dominant discourse, but this time the
control exerted is black und male, not white
and male. Though this stranglehold threatens
to deaden life and put the future on hold,
Morrison's narrative disruptions challenge the
very nature of this "paradise" on earth.
Bd. 3, 1999, 112 S., 17,90 €, br., ISBN 3-8258-4204-5

Dorothea Fischer-Hornung; Alison
D. Goeller (eds.)
EmBODYing Liberation
The Black Body in American Dance
A collection of essays concerning the black body
in American dance, *EmBODYing Liberation*
serves as an important contribution to the
growing field of scholarship in African American
dance, in particular the strategies used by
individual artists to contest and liberate racialized
stagings of the black body. The collection
features special essays by Thomas DeFrantz
and Brenda Dixon Gottschild, as well as an
interview with Isaac Julien.
Bd. 4, 2001, 152 S., 20,90 €, br., ISBN 3-8258-4473-0

Patrick B. Miller; Therese Frey Steffen;
Elisabeth Schäfer-Wünsche (eds.)
The Civil Rights Movement Revisited
Critical Perspectives on the Struggle for Racial Equality in the United States
The crusade for civil rights was a defining
episode of 20th century U.S. history, reshaping
the constitutional, political, social, and economic
life of the nation. This collection of original
essays by both European and American scholars
includes close analyses of literature and film,
historical studies of significant themes and events
from the turn-of-the century to the movement
years, and assessments of the movement's
legacies. Ultimately, the articles help examine
the ways civil rights activism, often grounded
in the political work of women, has shaped
American consciousness and culture until the

LIT Verlag Münster – Hamburg – Berlin – London
Grevener Str./Fresnostr. 2 48159 Münster
Tel.: 0251 – 23 50 91 – Fax: 0251 – 23 19 72
e-Mail: vertrieb@lit-verlag.de – http://www.lit-verlag.de

outset of the 21st century.
Bd. 5, 2001, 224 S., 24,90 €, br., ISBN 3-8258-4486-2

Fritz Gysin; Christopher Mulvey (Eds.)
Black Liberation in the Americas
The recognition that Africans in the Americas have also been subjects of their destiny rather than merely passive objects of European oppression represents one of the major shifts in twentieth-century mainstream historiography. Yet even in the eighteenth and nineteenth centuries, slave narratives and abolitionist tracts offered testimony to various ways in which Africans struggled against slavery, from outright revolt to day-to-day resistance. In the first decades of the twentieth century, African American historians like Carter G. Woodson and W. E. B. Du Bois started to articulate a vision of African American history that emphasized survival and resistance rather than victimization and oppression. This volume seeks to address these and other issues in black liberation from interdisciplinary and comparative perspectives, focusing on such issues as slave revolts, day-to-day resistance, abolitionist movements, maroon societies, the historiography of resistance, the literature of resistance, black liberation movements in the twentieth century, and black liberation and post colonial theory. The chapters span the disciplines of history, literature, anthropology, folklore, film, music, architecture, and art, drawing on the black experience of liberation in the United States, the Caribbean, and Latin America.
Bd. 6, 2001, 280 S., 24,90 €, br., ISBN 3-8258-5137-0

Justine Tally
The Story of *Jazz*
Toni Morrison's Dialogic Imagination
Ever since its publication in 1992, *Jazz*, probably Toni Morrison's most difficult novel to date, has elicited a wide array of critical response. Many of these analyses, while both thoughtful and thought-provoking, have provided only partial or inherently inconclusive interpretations. The title, and certain of the author's own pronouncements, have led other critics to focus on the music itself, both as medium and aesthetic support for the narration.
Bd. 7, 2001, 168 S., 20,90 €, br., ISBN 3-8258-5364-0

Mar Gallego
Passing Novels in the Harlem Renaissance
An Alternative Concept of African American Identity
This book offers an analysis of the unique and significant contribution of "passing" novels to the literary and intellectual debate of the Harlem Renaissance, especially to the search for a definition of a concept of African American identity. The analysis reveals the presence of a subversive component in these novels, turning them into useful tools to explore the "passing" phenomenon in all its richness and complexity. The present study intends to contribute to the ongoing revision of the parameters conventionally employed to analyze "passing" novels by drawing attention to the enormous significance this subgenre entails for the establishment of a coherent and more inclusive African American literary canon.
Bd. 8, Herbst 2002, ca. 224 S., ca. 24,90 €, br., ISBN 3-8258-5842-1

Contributions to Asian American Literary Studies
edited by Rocío G. Davis (University of Navarre) and Sämi Ludwig (University of Bern)

Rocío G. Davis; Sämi Ludwig (Eds.)
Asian American Literature in the International Context
Readings on Fiction, Poetry, and Performance
In their different and yet complementary perspectives, all of the essays in *Asian American Literature in the International Context: Readings on Fiction, Poetry, and Performance* reiterate the universal lesson of pluralism. They are divided into sections that deal with biraciality and biculturality, interethnic negotiations, poetic creations, narrative experiments, and (re)constructing self. The wide variety of approaches reflects the contributors' training in different cultures and across cultures. It showcases refreshing new perspectives in reading that combine the views of literary scholars from three different continents. This collection creates a space for discussion and commentary, of heightened appreciation and increased creativity, a forum that turns the discipline of Asian American Studies into a truly intercultural debate.
Bd. 1, 2002, 272 S., 25,90 €, br., ISBN 3-8258-5710-7

Anglistik / Amerikanistik

Jörg Rademacher
James Joyce's Other Image
Essays in Joyce Criticism
James Joyce's Other Image is the author's multi-faceted response to four years of almost exclusive concentration on *James Joyce's Own Image*, a study on the terms 'image' and 'imagination' in *A Portrait* and *Ulysses*.

LIT Verlag Münster – Hamburg – Berlin – London
Grevener Str./Fresnostr. 2 48159 Münster
Tel.: 0251 – 23 50 91 – Fax: 0251 – 23 19 72
e-Mail: vertrieb@lit-verlag.de – http://www.lit-verlag.de

Having convinced himself that Joyce is a canonical writer even from the removed German perspective, he goes on to explore different aspects of Joyce studies before he addresses *Ulysses* in terms of Shakespeare and Sterne as well as Musil, Joyce, and Bachmann in terms of their "fictional memoirs of the Hapsburg Empire".

Since the focus is on textual presence rather than on personal (and possibly absent) influence, a pedagogical case study of how Sterne's and Shakespeare's works may be read through *Ulysses* and an essay on Joyce's "Omnipresence in Contemporary Literature" seem in order.

Finally, a fictional trialogue between George Moore, James Joyce, and Samuel Beckett maps out a move beyond the realm of criticism.

Bd. 2, 1996, 144 S., 20,90 €, br., ISBN 3-8258-2079-3

Wolfgang Munzinger
Das Automobil als heimliche Romanfigur
Das Bild des Autos und der Technik in der nordamerikanischen Literatur von der Jahrhundertwende bis nach dem 2. Weltkrieg
Bd. 3, 1997, 224 S., 24,90 €, br, ISBN 3-8258-2741-0

Jost Hindersmann
MLAIB und ABELL
Periodische Fachbibliographien, CD-ROM- und Online-Datenbanken zur Anglistik
Im vorliegenden Band werden die beiden wichtigsten periodischen Fachbibliographien zur Anglistik, die MLA International Bibliography und die Annual Bibliography of English Language and Literature, untersucht und formal und inhaltlich miteinander verglichen. Neben den Print-Versionen werden auch die CD-ROM- und Online-Versionen detailliert vorgestellt. Diese Studie, verständlich geschrieben und mit vielen Abbildungen anschaulich illustriert, wendet sich an alle Studenten und Dozenten der Anglistik. Sie erklärt die verschiedenen Suchmöglichkeiten in den Bibliographien und Datenbanken und gibt Tips für die erfolgreichsten Suchstrategien.
Bd. 4, 1997, 96 S., 10,90 €, br., ISBN 3-8258-3358-5

Holger Boden
Two World Wars and One World Cup – Krieg, Sport und englischer Humor
Für die meisten Menschen, deren Sozialisation nicht in Großbritannien stattgefunden hat, ist der dort beheimatete "typisch englische" Humor oft schwer verständlich, manchmal sogar unverdaulich. Was haben schließlich Weltkriege mit Fußball zu tun? Warum zieren – im späten 20. Jahrhundert – Stahlhelme die Titelseiten britischer Zeitungen im Vorfeld eines sportlichen Vergleiches mit Deutschland? Und was soll so lustig sein an TV-Serien, die jede Menge Situationskomik in einen Schützengraben projizieren?

In humortheoretischen, historischen und soziologischen Ansätzen sucht der Autor dieser Arbeit nach Faktoren der Genese der englischen "Kriegskomik" und versucht, deren Wirkung und Rezeption einzuordnen. Die hierzulande für heikle Themen prädestinierte Schublade "Satire" stellt sich dabei als viel zu klein heraus.
Bd. 5, 1998, 112 S., 15,90 €, br., ISBN 3-8258-3851-x

Jörg Rademacher (Hrsg./Ed.)
Modernism and the Individual Talent/Moderne und besondere Begabung
Re-Canonizing Ford Madox Ford (Hueffer)/Zur Re-Kanonisierung von Ford Madox Ford (Hüffer). Symposium Münster June/Juni 1999
Following their first gathering in Münster, Westphalia, the city of Ford's ancestors, Fordians present a multi-faceted image of this Anglo-German and Francophile English Modernist. International interest in the Hueffers' German background will be triggered by two articles on Franz Hüffer and the references to Münster and Westphalia in Ford's writings. Excursions in politics and poetry and Ford in context provide a framework for "Aspects of *Parade's End*", the edition and simultaneous translation of which into major European languages forms the most important project for the new Millennium.

Nach ihrer ersten Tagung in Münster, Westfalen, der Stadt der Vorfahren Fords, bieten Ford-Forscher und -Freunde ein vielfältiges Bild des Deutsch-Engländers und frankophilen Autors der englischen Moderne. Ausflüge in Politik und Poesie und Ford im Kontext seiner und unserer Zeit bieten einen Rahmen für die "Aspekte der Tetralogie *Parade's End*", deren Edition und zeitgleiche Übersetzung in wichtige europäische Sprachen das bedeutendste Projekt für das neue Jahrtausend darstellt.
Der Band enthält Zusammenfassungen in deutscher Sprache, eine Bibliographie und ein Register. Geplant sind überdies eine Anthologie ins Deutsche übersetzter Texte Franz Hüffers und Ford Madox Fords sowie ein Bildband mit deutschen und englischen Texten, der drei Generationen der Hüffer in Münster und Westfalen dokumentarisch porträtiert.
Bd. 6, 2002, 224 S., 25,90 €, br., ISBN 3-8258-4311-4

Ulrike Ernst
From Anti-Apartheid to African Renaissance
Interviews with South African Writers and Critics on Cultural Politics Beyond the Cultural Struggle

LIT Verlag Münster – Hamburg – Berlin – London
Grevener Str./Fresnostr. 2 48159 Münster
Tel.: 0251 – 23 50 91 – Fax: 0251 – 23 19 72
e-Mail: vertrieb@lit-verlag.de – http://www.lit-verlag.de

The focus of this collection is the cultural and literary policy of the tripartite alliance (ANC, SACP, COSATU) after its denouncement of 'culture as a weapon'. Three shifts are noted between 1990–2000: the end of apartheid, the alliance's accession to power, and the change of presidency from Nelson Mandela to Thabo Mbeki, including the adoption of a neo-liberal macro-economic policy.
The investigation stresses the importance of the role of writers and intellectuals in political and societal transformation processes that have a tendency to destroy the agency that initially set them in motion. Startling revelations are being made, which highlight the emptiness of much Rainbow Nation sloganeering.
Bd. 7, 2002, 208 S., 20,90 €, br., ISBN 3-8258-5804-9

Andreas Lienkamp; Wolfgang Werth; Christian Berkemeier (Hg.)
"As strange as the world"
Annäherungen an das Werk des Erzählers und Filmemachers Paul Auster
Paul Auster ist nicht nur einer der populärsten, sondern auch der interessantesten Autoren der amerikanischen Gegenwartsliteratur. Seine Bücher und Filme sind der gelungene Beweis, dass man auch im Zeitalter der Postmoderne spannend, unterhaltsam und dabei doch literarisch anspruchsvoll erzählen kann.
Ohne Scheuklappen verbindet Auster Leichtigkeit und Tiefgang, eingängiges Fabulieren und erzähltechnische Finesse. Seine Romane und Kurzgeschichten lassen sich als packende Detektivgeschichten, aber auch als metaphysische Spekulationen über Zufall, Schein und Identität lesen.
Keineswegs erschöpfend angelegt, mag dieser Band Anregungen für die Auseinandersetzung mit dem Werk eines zeitgenössischen Erzählers und Filmemachers bieten.
Bd. 8, 2002, 170 S., 20,90 €, br., ISBN 3-8258-6046-9

Christa Jansohn (Hg.)
„Ein Drama nicht von Shakespeare"
Dokumentationsband zur Teilung der deutschen Shakespeare-Gesellschaft
Bd. 9, Herbst 2002, ca. 304 S., ca. 30,90 €, gb., ISBN 3-8258-6094-9

Victor Grove
Hamlet
Das Drama des modernen Menschen
Hamlet, das Drama ist nicht leicht zu lesen. Dies war Motivation für den Autor, mit der vorliegenden Abhandlung den Weg zu bahnen, damit dieses monumentale Werk zahlreichen Menschen zugänglich wird. Einige hundert Jahre zurückliegend wird Shakespeare's Hamlet unter seiner

Hand zu einem aktuellen Werk.
Das Buch schrieb *Dr. Victor Grove* nach zahlreichen Vorträgen, die er an Universitäten und Hochschulen, für amerikanische und britische Truppen sowie für deutsche Kriegsgefangene gehalten hatte. Heute, 50 Jahre später, in einer zunehmend von Skepsis und Lähmung belasteten Welt - vor allem nach dem „11. September 2001", ist *Das Drama des modernen Menschen* aktueller denn je.
Bd. 10, Herbst 2002, ca. 248 S., ca. 30,90 €, br., ISBN 3-8258-6224-0

Hans Werner Breunig
Verstand und Einbildungskraft in der englischen Romantik
S. T. Coleridge als Kulminationspunkt seiner Zeit
Ausgehend von Rousseau und Hume wird das Vorurteil, die Romantik stehe in ihrer Gefühlsbetonung im Gegensatz zur angeblich rationalen Aufklärung, relativiert, sofern sowohl bei Hume als auch in der Romantik die aktive Realität im Gefühl liegt. Ein zuverlässigeres negatives Kriterium für die Romantik liegt hingegen darin, ob von der emotionalen metaphysischen Erhebung über die Welt, wie sie die Romantiker oft im Hinstarren ('gazing') erlangen, wieder eine Rückkehr in die Verstandeswelt willkommen sei. S. T. Coleridge, der sich eingehend auch mit der deutschen Philosophie befasste, darf in seiner intellektuellen Vielseitigkeit als Kulminationspunkt der englischen Romantik gelten.
Bd. 11, Herbst 2002, ca. 352 S., ca. 25,90 €, br., ISBN 3-8258-6244-5

Zeit und Text
Münstersche Studien zur neueren Literatur
herausgegeben von Prof. Dr. Ernst Ribbat und Prof. Dr. Lothar Köhn (Universität Münster)

Maria Cäcilie Pohl
Paul Fleming
Ich-Darstellung, Übersetzungen, Reisegedichte
Bd. 1, 1993, 421 S., 30,90 €, br., ISBN 3-89473-579-1

Melanie Schütte
Facetten des "Menschen"
Studien zur Biographie und zum Erzählwerk Eugen Roths
Bd. 2, 1993, 248 S., 24,90 €, br., ISBN 3-89473-670-4

Uwe Schadwill
Poeta Judex
Eine Studie zum Leben und Werk des Dichterjuristen E. T. A. Hoffmann

LIT Verlag Münster – Hamburg – Berlin – London
Grevener Str./Fresnostr. 2 48159 Münster
Tel.: 0251 – 23 50 91 – Fax: 0251 – 23 19 72
e-Mail: vertrieb@lit-verlag.de – http://www.lit-verlag.de

Der Autor versucht in seiner Studie "POETA JUDEX" die spannungsreiche Wechselwirkung zwischen E. T. A. Hoffmanns Dichter- und Richterberuf aufzuzeigen. Indem er die literarischen und juristischen Arbeiten des Romantikers vor dem Hintergrund seines Lebens und seiner Zeit miteinander vergleicht, gelangt er zu dem Schluß, daß Hoffmann nicht nur keine 'Doppelexistenz' führte, daß es ihm nicht nur gelang, sein juristisches Denken in sein poetisches Verfahren zu integrieren, sondern daß eben dieses sich in einem hohen Maß gerade aus seinem Denken, seinem Ethos und seiner Erfahrung als Richter speist.

Bd. 3, 1993, 568 S., 35,90 €, br., ISBN 3-89473-717-4

Ulrike Schlieper
Die "andere Landschaft"
Handkes Erzählungen auf den Spuren Cézannes
In einer Zeit der flüchtigen Fernsehbilder lenkt Peter Handke die Aufmerksamkeit bewußt auf die Ruhe der Gemälde Cézannes. Die *Lehre der Sainte-Victoire* von 1980 denkt jene Prophezeiung des Malers vom Beginn dieses Jahrhunderts fort, die gerade heute aktuell wirkt: "Man muß sich beeilen, wenn man noch etwas sehen will. Alles verschwindet."
Das Interesse dieser Arbeit gilt Handkes Versuch, in Auseinandersetzung mit der (Bild-)Landschaft Cézannes und den Erzählprinzipien Adalbert Stifters eine Form des Schreibens zu entfalten, die es möglich macht, die "andere Landschaft" des noch nicht durch die Macht des Sekundären vereinnahmten Seins neu zu entdecken. Dabei soll gezeigt werden, daß Handke bereits seit den Anfängen seines Schreibens zu dieser Landschaft literarisch unterwegs ist.

Bd. 4, 1993, 328 S., 30,90 €, br., ISBN 3-89473-718-2

Thomas Düllo
Zufall und Melancholie
Untersuchungen zur Kontingenzsemantik in Texten von Joseph Roth
Joseph Roth – ein vermeintlich unmoderner Autor, ein kulturpessimistischer Kritiker der Weimarer Republik, ein melancholischer und rückwärtsgewandter Verklärer der österreichisch-ungarischen Doppelmonarchie während seines Exils? Gegenüber diesem geläufigen Urteil wird in der vorliegenden Monographie ein anderer Joseph Roth, ein neuer im bekannten kenntlich. 'Zufall und Melancholie' fragt danach, wie ein sensibler Traditionalist den Kontingenzdruck der Moderne literarisch und ästhetisch meistert. Damit werden Roths neusachliche und kulturkritische Texte, die moderner anmutenden Flaneurs- und Stadttexte, die filmkritischen Schriften und die Darstellungen des melancholischen Klimas

der Doppelmonarchie in neue Horizonte gerückt. Die Schlüsseltexte dieser problemgeschichtlichen Arbeit über die Zufalls- und Melancholiesemantik in Roths Werk bilden der frühe Roman 'Die Rebellion', die neusachliche Erzählung 'April' und die 'Geschichte der 1002. Nacht' sowie einige Denkbilder aus den zwanziger Jahren.

Bd. 5, 1994, 371 S., 30,90 €, br., ISBN 3-89473-819-7

Frank Werner Raepke
Auf Liebe und Tod
Symbolische Mythologie bei Robert Müller – Hermann Broch – Robert Musil
Gegenstand dieser Arbeit ist das durch die mythogene Topik von Liebe und Tod repräsentierte Darstellungsproblem literarischer Mythologie: in Zeiten eines verschärften Bilderverbots das Absolute neu erfinden zu müssen. Die untersuchten Autoren erweisen sich einerseits als Erben klassischer Kulturkritik, die seit Rousseau Eros und Tod in einer zirkulären Denkfigur als Arche und Telos jener, Neue Mythologie genannten triadischen Geschichtsphilosophie konzipiert. Indem sie metapherntheoretische Begriffe ins Zentrum ihrer Werke stellen – Tropen (Müller), Symbol (Broch) und Gleichnis (Musil) –, reflektieren sie jedoch auf neue Weise, daß der Mythos als Erfindung der Moderne gerade von der Unmöglichkeit symbolischer Versöhnung lebt.

Bd. 6, 1994, 288 S., 24,90 €, br., ISBN 3-89473-788-3

Woo-Young Lim
Experimente der Selbst-Darstellung
Dramaturgien des jungen Goethe (1765 – 1786)
Goethe war ein Mann des Theaters und ein leidenschaftlicher Experimentator mit allen in seiner Zeit möglichen Dramaturgien. Die vorliegende Studie beschreibt die Vielfalt der vom jungen Goethe bis zur Italienreise geschriebenen Dramentexte und erläutert ihren Zusammenhang mit den kulturellen Prozessen des 18. Jahrhunderts. In einer Interpretation der "Theatralischen Sendung" werden die Linien zusammengeführt. Noch ein Goethe-Buch? Ja, aber ein notwendiges und interessantes.

Bd. 7, 1994, 312 S., 30,90 €, br., ISBN 3-8258-2246-X

Torsten Hitz; Angela Stock (Hg.)
Am Ende der Literaturtheorie?
Neun Beiträge zur Einführung und Diskussion
In den letzten Jahren war zunehmend die Tendenz der Literaturtheorie zu beobachten, sich immer mehr davon zu entfernen, Theorie der Literatur im engeren Sinne zu sein. Sie entwickelte sich zur Texttheorie, zur Theorie des allgemeinen Diskursgeschehens, schließlich zur Theorie der kulturellen Praktiken, von denen Schreiben, gar

LIT Verlag Münster – Hamburg – Berlin – London
Grevener Str./Fresnostr. 2 48159 Münster
Tel.: 0251 – 23 50 91 – Fax: 0251 – 23 19 72
e-Mail: vertrieb@lit-verlag.de – http://www.lit-verlag.de

literarisches Schreiben, nur noch eine unter unzähligen sein konnte.
Dieser Sammelband läßt die Entwicklung von der Theorie der Literatur zur allgemeinen Theorie (des Diskurses? der Sprache? der Medien? der Kultur?) noch einmal Revue passieren. Er versteht sich aber nicht als ein Abgesang auf die Literaturtheorie, sondern als ein Versuch, die wichtigsten Positionen der letzten Jahre aus heutiger Perspektive zu beleuchten. Neben Hermeneutik, Psychoanalyse und Intertextualität werden auch Diskurstheorie, Dekonstruktion, Feminismus und New Historicism sowie neueste Entwicklungen analysiert. Historisierung und Aktualisierung ergänzen sich, so daß die Aufsätze sowohl als Einführungen als auch als Diskussionsbeiträge gelesen werden können.
Bd. 8, 1995, 184 S., 17,90 €, br., ISBN 3-8258-2487-X

Sabine Fischer-Kania
Geschichte entworfen durch Erzählen
Uwe Johnsons "Jahrestage"
"Geschichte ist ein Entwurf". So heißt es in der letzten Eintragung der Romantetralogie *Jahrestage* von Uwe Johnson (1934–1984). Diese Sentenz wirft, poetologisch gelesen, prinzipielle Fragen des Verhältnisses zwischen Literatur und Historiographie auf, thematisiert deren Analogie und Differenz. "Geschichte" erscheint als offenes Konstrukt. Unter Rückgriff auf rezeptionsästhetische und intertextuelle Kategorien und Verfahren wird in der vorliegenden Monographie untersucht, inwiefern sich diese an exponierter Stelle des Romans postulierte Vorstellung von Geschichte auf mehreren Ebenen der *Jahrestage* entdecken läßt. Es wird gezeigt, wie das epochale Romanwerk Uwe Johnsons als breit angelegter Geschichtsdiskurs, der in eine Pluralisierung *der* Geschichte mündet, gelesen werden kann.
Bd. 9, 1996, 272 S., 24,90 €, br., ISBN 3-8258-2746-1

Volker Zumbrink
Metamorphosen des kranken Königssohns
Die Shakespeare-Rezeption in Goethes Romanen "Wilhelm Meisters Theatralische Sendung" und "Wilhelm Meisters Lehrjahre"
Noch einmal werden hier die "Hamlet"-Passagen in Goethes "Wilhelm Meister" analysiert. So freilich, daß in der intertextuellen Lektüre der "ganze" Goethe und der "ganze" Shakespeare in spannungsreichen Kontakt miteinander und daneben mit zahlreichen zeitgenössischen, aber auch späteren Texten geraten. Zugleich wird auf neue Weise gezeigt, wie das morphologische Denken Goethes sich nicht nur in Details, sondern im narrativen Gesamtprojekt des "Wilhelm Meister" realisiert hat.
Bd. 10, 1997, 520 S., 40,90 €, br., ISBN 3-8258-3205-8

Phillan Joung
Passion der Indifferenz
Essayismus und essayistisches Verfahren in Robert Musils "Der Mann ohne Eigenschaften"
Bd. 11, 1997, 360 S., 35,90 €, br., ISBN 3-8258-3281-3

Ingeborg Nerling-Pietsch
Herders literarische Denkmale
Formen der Charakteristik vor Friedrich Schlegel
Bd. 12, 1997, 236 S., 24,90 €, br., ISBN 3-8258-3287-2

Jörg Ennen
Götter im poetischen Gebrauch
Studien zu Begriff und Praxis der antiken Mythologie um 1800 und im Werk H. v. Kleists
Bd. 13, 1998, 400 S., 25,90 €, br., ISBN 3-8258-3613-4

Lothar Köhn
Literatur – Geschichte
Beiträge zur deutschen Literatur des 19. und 20. Jahrhunderts. Mit einer Einführung von Thomas Düllo
Bd. 14, 2000, 400 S., 25,90 €, br., ISBN 3-8258-4069-7

Sibylle Plassmann
Die humane Gesellschaft und ihre Gegner in den Dramen von J. E. Schlegel
Bd. 15, 2000, 320 S., 30,90 €, br., ISBN 3-8258-4868-x

Markus Kippel
Die Stimme der Vernunft über einer Welt des Wahns
Studien zur literarischen Rezeption der Hexenprozesse (19. – 20. Jahrhundert)
Bd. 16, 2001, 328 S., 25,90 €, br., ISBN 3-8258-5226-1

Brigitte Riemann
Das Kabarett der DDR: "… eine Untergrundorganisation mit hohen staatlichen Auszeichnungen … "?
Gratwanderungen zwischen sozialistischem Ideal und Alltag (1949–1999)
Bd. 17, 2001, 320 S., 25,90 €, br., ISBN 3-8258-5610-0

Hyun-Seung Yuk
Das Prinzip 'Ironie' bei Martin Walser
Zu den Poetik-Vorlesungen und den Erzählwerken der mittleren Phase
Bd. 18, 2002, 208 S., 20,90 €, br., ISBN 3-8258-5920-7

LIT Verlag Münster – Hamburg – Berlin – London
Grevener Str./Fresnostr. 2 48159 Münster
Tel.: 0251 – 23 50 91 – Fax: 0251 – 23 19 72
e-Mail: vertrieb@lit-verlag.de – http://www.lit-verlag.de